*To a better and peaceful future for all countries in the Middle East and North Africa, as well as their citizens.*

# NEW DIRECTIONS
## In The Middle East

Editors

*Mohammed M. Aman, PhD*

*Mary Jo Aman, MLIS*

**Westphalia Press**
An imprint of the Policy Studies Organization

Washington, DC
2014

# New Directions in the Middle East

CIP
Aman, Mohammed M.
Edited by Mohammed M. Aman and Mary Jo Aman.
Washington, DC: Westphalia Press, 2014.

ISBN-13: 978-1941472019
ISBN-10: 194147201X

Middle East & North Africa-Policy and politics
Arab Spring
Arab-Israel Peace
Aman, Mary Jo, Jt. editor

Printed in the United States of America

**Westphalia Press**

An imprint of Policy Studies Organization
1527 New Hampshire Ave., NW
Washington, D.C. 20036
info@ipsonet.org

Updated material and comments on this edition
can be found at the Westphalia Press website:

www.westphaliapress.org

# TABLE OF CONTENTS

# PREFACE

This book, ***New Directions in the Middle East***, is the second volume that contains three parts which include the select and edited papers presented at the Third Annual Middle East Dialogue in 2013 held in Washington, DC as well as from the first AMEPPA Conference held in Ifrane, Morocco in November, 2012. They are:

- **Part Five**: Israel/Palestine Divide;
- **Part Six**: Communication, Media, and the Arab Awakening; and
- **Part Seven**: Management and Conflict Resolution. Each part is preceded by a preface written by the Editors of this volume.

The authors of the papers managed to tackle the major issues that are crucial to helping Middle East and North African countries advance beyond the stalemate of the status quo and moving forward to a better tomorrow. The first issue is the unresolved conflict between the Palestinians and the Israelis which went into deep freeze after the Camp David and the Oslo Accord. The US Secretary of State John Kerry, at the behest of President Obama, is attempting to introduce a new legacy similar to that which President Carter managed to accomplish with Sadat and Begin at Camp David. It remains to be seen if Secretary Kerry would be able to achieve what could be a milestone if the Israelis and Palestinians manage to reach a landmark peace agreement.

The Arab Spring now turned into Arab bitter winter has done little to achieve what many had hoped to be a major step forward in the MENA region. Egypt is mired in a political and bloody conflict after the military ousted the democratically elected president Mohammed Morsi, who is now on trial— just as his predecessor, Hosni Mubarak. In Libya, Bahrain and Yemen, the situation remains unstable and the political disputes are far from being settled. Syria is mired in a civil war that defies any predictions for ending soon; and a dark cloud is hanging over the region with even more economic, social and political conflicts that defy solutions. Will the Arab energy that was evident three years ago on the Internet and social media be directed to rebuilding and reforming the region politically and economically, or will the hands of censors turn off the lever and shut down any constructive dialogue and exchange among the citizens for fear of criticism and exposing various forms of abuse and corruption by the new powers or existing regimes? Unfortunately we have already seen this, not just in the Arab Spring nations, but throughout the region, as more bloggers who are accused of insulting or criticizing their own governments are sentenced to long years in prison, not to mention being tortured or exiled. Recent events demonstrate how the media has been used in favor of or against the systems of government in place. As new leaderships emerge to replace old ones, the former have resorted to the old system of censorship of the Internet, media and shutting down satellite channels that are not considered mouthpiece of the current regime.

Contributors to Part Seven address issues of public administration and leadership. It has been said that the crisis in the MENA countries is a management and leadership crises especially in the public sector which dominates the economy after years of nationalization that began with the Egyptian military revolution in 1952. Public sector leaders in MENA countries, like their countries' political leaderships, are depicted as relying on authoritative approaches and styles of leadership in the application of their duties and absence of transparency. Such and related issues of public administration, management and leadership are treated by experts in public administration, management, and leadership. As the authors point out, a major part of the MENA region's problems rest with political and managerial incompetence, poor productivity and job performance, coupled with ethical and moral issues such as bribery, *wasta*, nepotism, as well as persistent unemployment, especially among Arab youth due to poor schooling and academic preparation, gender inequality and other imbalances in the workforce. The authors tackle problems of a sluggish public sector and a weak private sector which complicate matters further as well as a lack of creativity that fails to compete with the global business and technological advancements and entrepreneurships.

As with Volume One, The views expressed by the authors in this volume are their personal views and do not represent the views of institutions with which they are affiliated, the Policy Studies Organization (PSO), *DOMES*, or its editors. Because of its balanced treatment and the nature of the delicate issues presented about the most sensitive region of the world, this monograph will be a valuable addition to every academic course, office, and library collection where expert and novice readers alike can be introduced to varied points of view.

The editors wish to thank the authors and co-authors who contributed to this volume and responded kindly to our editorial comments and questions. We also wish to express our sincere thanks to the MED2013 Conference planners, organizers, sponsors, panelists, panel chairs, and discussants. They all made this conference and the publication of this book possible. Special thanks to the leadership and staff of the PSO, and in particular, its President and Co-Chair of the MED Conferences, Dr. Paul J. Rich; Executive Director Daniel Gutierrez-Sandoval; Whitney Shepard, Director of Development and Programs; Matthew Brewer, Director of Outreach and Open Source Materials; and Devin Proctor, Director of Media and Publications for their strong support of and dedication to the MED Conferences and their publications. Special thanks to the University of Wisconsin-Milwaukee for its continued support of the MED Conferences and to graduate assistants Tina Jayroe, and Brittany Khateeb for their assistance.

We hope that the authors' writings and observations as presented in this volume will help lift the MENA region from its current position to a much better level of advancement that could bring ever-lasting peace, stability and prosperity to *all* its citizens.

*The Editors*

# NEW DIRECTIONS
## In The Middle East

# PART FIVE

## Israel/Palestine Divide

Among the persistent foreign policy challenges facing the post-Arab Spring rulers as well as the second Obama administration is the Israel/Palestine dispute, including expansion of unlawful settlements, the Bush era proposal for the "Road Map," and a framework for resolving the Israeli/Palestinian conflict based on a "two-state solution." The matter has been further complicated by Israeli electioneering rhetoric to attack Iran's nuclear installations, further expansions of Israeli settlements on Arab lands, and most recently, the internal struggle between Islamists and Arab governments as seen in Egypt, with the removal of President Mohammed Morsi, as well as the Arab-wide hostility toward Hamas and Hizballah. The papers presented in this section of the book underscore the well-known fact that the United States' foreign and domestic policy is influenced more by the unconditional support of Israel, and in preserving its security and demographic concerns, than in the fulfillment of Palestinian national aspirations or Arab states' desire to reach a just and durable peace with Israel.

All politics are local and this is more evident in the case of Israeli politics. Any efforts to reach a comprehensive peace agreement with the Palestinians have to be sold to the Israelis and Palestinians by their respective leaders who are facing local opposition from extremists on both sides. The Arab Spring brought with it a fundamental change in the relations between citizen and state in the Middle East. The authoritarian nature of many regimes in the Arab world is being challenged and transformed, and Arab citizens now demand their fair share in the decision-making processes and in economic improvements. There is less fervor among the Arabs—who are now occupied with more pressing domestic problems—about championing the Palestinian cause through the old tired rhetoric of their autocratic rulers. It is noticeable that the usual chants against Israel and America among Arab street demonstrators were absent from any of the Arab Spring demonstrations. This was unlike what the Arab leaders and their propaganda machines have conditioned their people to think. They have used earlier conflicts with the West as the Arab rallying cry to divert the attention of the masses from domestic economic and social problems, and to legitimize their dictatorial grip on power. The Palestinian issue has seemingly been forgotten and ignored amidst other more immediate economic, political concerns, and police brutality grievances. Yet, while the civil strife is going on in Syria and Egypt—the two strong advocates of the Palestinian cause—the eyes of the world were focused on Washington during the summer of 2013, as representatives of the Palestinians and Israelis met to solve their own political and territorial problems. The Arab Spring has also revealed ramifications for the Palestinian internal political disputes over the division of power and the need for dialogue between the two major power factions, Hamas and the Palestinian Authority (PA) in the West Bank. More recently, Hamas has suffered a major setback when it was declared a terrorist organization by the member states of the Gulf Cooperation Council (GCC). There is no doubt that President Barak Hussein Obama wishes to have his own Camp David moment similar to that of President Jimmy Carter and the late peace-makers, Anwar El-Sadat and Menachem Begin.

Dr. Josef Olmert surveys the major milestones and principal figures involved in negotiating peace between the Arabs and Israelis. While Olmert was a participant in the failed Israeli–Syrian negotiations, his knowledge of and his brother's involvement as the then Israeli prime minister help make the narrative of peace negotiations more personal and familiar to outsiders. The pull and push from diverse Israeli political and religious parties and populace have shaped Israel's negotiations with the Palestinians and the rest of its Arab neighbors.

Following on Dr. Olmert's political analysis, Dr. Ido Zelkovitz uses empirical analysis to examine the geopolitical changes and outcomes of the Arab Spring and the impact they may have on the Palestinian political system and the peace process. Zelkovitz discusses the ramifications of the Arab Spring on the struggle for political hegemony in the Palestinian Authority. In his view, the Palestinian case is unique in that the Palestinians do not hold exclusive sovereignty over the West Bank and the Gaza Strip. Furthermore, since June 2007, these two territories have been controlled by rival political movements, with strikingly different worldviews. These considerations, together with the continued Palestinians' struggle for an independent state, suggest a somewhat different future Arab Spring than befell MENA countries in 2011. In contrast to the former, the "Palestinian Spring" feature calls for the end of the internal political divide among Palestinian factions and not for the toppling of the existing regimes or dictators. Both Fatah and Hamas, who wished to maintain their current strongholds and further accumulate political power in view of the continued struggle for hegemony, are attentive to these public sentiments.

Faced with increasing international isolation due to its opposition to peace negotiations with the Palestinians, Israel has been gaining diplomatic inroads with China, the world's largest economy and historically a strong ally of the Palestinian cause and leadership. News of Israel's active involvement in shaping the Sino-Israel policies is reported widely inside China and Israel. Such involvement was first done clandestinely, beginning in the 1980s, and publicly since the 1990s even without formal recognition of the State of Israel. In the meantime, the Sino-Palestinian relationship has moved from former front position to present back seat priority for the Chinese government that recently hosted an elaborate state visit for Prime Minister Netanyahu. Analysis of the Sino-Israel and Sino-Palestinian relationships is carefully presented from a Chinese perspective by Dr. Yiyi Chen. According to Dr. Chen, China is becoming more proactive in the international sphere, and he further suggests that China may take "a more assertive role in trying to facilitate solving the Israel-Palestinian conflict."

# Israeli Elections and the Middle East Peace Process

## Josef Olmert

## Abstract

It is arguably the case that Israeli parliamentary elections arouse worldwide interest, which distinctly surpasses interests given to elections in countries far bigger than Israel in terms of population and size, as well as economically. There are some possible explanations for this state of affairs. It may be, as Israelis jokingly say, that "Jews are news," or perhaps it has to do with Israel being the Holy Land, or the centrality of the country in Middle East politics, ever a region of the world whose politics are of crucial importance to global political and economic stability. In particular, the implications of the elections on the Israeli–Palestinian peace process, which for many, seems to be the linchpin of the entire Middle East situation, are closely watched and are at the core of the international fascination with the country and its politics.

# Introduction

The most recent elections on January 22, 2013, were no exception in regard to the attention and interest they provoked throughout the world. Nearly four decades of the Middle East peace process—a timespan in which Israelis went to the polls 12 times—provide enough historic and contextual perspective to enable us to try and examine the connection between these elections and the subsequent configuration of elected *Knessets* (the Israeli parliament), and also the major developments in the peace process. It must be emphasized that Israeli politics, policies, and actions, while of great importance, constitute just one element of a complicated situation whose evolution through the years is predicated on the politics, policies, and actions of the Arab sides of the conflict, and also those of the international community—especially the United States. Thus, this paper does not provide an answer to the important question of the Middle East Peace Process: *quo-vadis*? Rather it relates to the Israeli component and input on it, as can be judged from the repercussions of some of the recent Israeli parliamentary elections.

## Voting Patterns in Israel in the Last Four Decades: Demography, Religion, Culture, and the Impact on the Peace Process

The political history of Israel—as measured by its parliamentary elections—can be roughly divided into two distinct periods: the first, from 1948, the year when the state was established, to 1977, a period characterized by the total domination of the Zionist Labor Movement. The second, which started with the historic Likud victory in the elections of 1977, continues to the present day. It is significant to note that Likud's hold on Israeli politics has been far weaker than the absolute domination of the Labor Movement in its heyday (Aronoff, 1993; Yanai, 1981). In fact, the Labor domination was already in place in the pre-state days in what was called the *Yishuv* (the state in the making), starting in the 1920s. Labor domination was based on the following three important foundations:

First, the large majority of the Jewish population were European (Ashkenazi) Jews, many of whom moved to the country with the stated goal of establishing a national, secular, and socialist Jewish state. Second, the Religious Zionist community as well as the non-Zionist ultra-Orthodox Jews were locked in a political alliance with the Labor Movement. Both groups cooperated on the basis of the principle of "live and let live," as the Labor Movement acknowledged. Their particular interests in education and in running religious affairs, and the religious sector in turn, recognized the overall political supremacy of the Labor Movement, and had no objections to their foreign and security policies. Third, the *Sepharadic* (Jews from Muslim and Arab countries) were a very small minority in the Jewish community in the pre-State years.

Being defined by their traditional, observant style of life, they considered themselves—and were considered by the majority—as being outsiders, something which pushed many of them toward the right wing on account of its favoring religion and tradition, as well as its being more conservative in regard to social issues. Many Sepharadic Jews were also drawn to the right wing because of its more hawkish positions concerning the developing conflict with the Arab population of Mandatory Palestine and the Arab States around Israel after its establishment. Many of these Jews harbored ill feelings toward Arabs due to the harsh treatment of Jews in Muslim and Arab countries. After 1948, almost all Jews that were formerly residents of these countries were pushed out and ended up as refugees in Israel.[1] The ill-treatment of Jews in Arab and Muslim countries was always overshadowed by the legacy and impact of the Holocaust of European Jewry in World War II, but for many Sepharadic Jews, the emphasis on their own predicament enabled them to create a narrative similar to that characterizing the history of European Jews, thus making it easier for them to connect with the overall national-Zionist ethos of persecution. Yet, their early history in their new country was, in many cases, painful and characterized by cultural, social, and political friction with the Socialist-dominated European majority.

Menachem Begin (Golan & Nakdimon, 1978) was the historic leader of the Israeli right wing and former commander of the National Military Organization (IZL) fighting the British in Mandatory Palestine—which had a significant Sepharadic membership. Begin realized the depth of these people's inherent nationalist feelings as well as their sense of alienation toward the ruling Ashkenazi-Socialist establishment. From the early days of independent Israel, Begin diligently and patiently cultivated their support. He also realized that the changes taking place in the orthodox communities, especially Religious Zionists (among them the historic alliance with the Labor Movement) came under growing scrutiny in the 1960s and the early 1970s.

Under Begin's charismatic leadership, a new electoral coalition was created in Israel, composed of secular nationalists, Religious Zionists, and a majority of the Sepharadic Community. The common denominator was the shared sense of being outsiders… being rejected by the Labor establishment. But there was also a great deal of ideological affinity, insofar as the attitude toward culture and society. This was understandable considering Israel's policies toward the Arab–Israeli conflict. Begin represented the hawkish end of Israeli politics; his party was the sole bearer of the idea of *Shlemut Hamoledet* (Greater Israel), even after 1948 when the question of the borders of the newly established state seemed to be settled (Shapira, 1991).

The effects of two wars, that of 1967 (Oren, 2002) and the Yom Kippur War of 1973,[2] led to the great political upheaval of 1977 in Israel. The first led to a dramatic transformation in the Religious Zionist community as the result of the war. The reunification of Jerusalem and the occupation, considered by many Israelis as the liberation of the West Bank and known as Judea and Samaria, were taken by the Religious Zionist to be a divine act. This was a step toward the final redemption of the Jewish people in their historic homeland; in other words, a political issue. The fate of the occupied territories and the relationships between Israel and the Palestinians ceased to be a mundane dilemma and became a test of religious belief. This had something to do with "higher powers," and with it came the inevitable political result: the end of the Historic Alliance between the Religious Zionist constituency—numbering about 12%–15% of the Israeli electorate and the Labor Movement. The new alliance between them and the Likud Party has had a crucial impact on Israeli politics, particularly because it makes it virtually impossible for a Likud government to pursue a policy with regard to the Palestinian issue, which is based on what may be the acceptable parameters of foreign policy under normal circumstances—that is, the interplay between interest and capacity, or the application of cost–benefit considerations. When foreign policy is dictated by Rabbinical decrees, which are purported to convey the word of God, it is no more a textbook foreign policy, but rather a reflection of the Holy Book. While Likud is a secular party, the Religious Zionists can be considered a messianic movement, and with the support of religious Likud members, they have developed political influence far outweighing their nominal numerical strength. From Likud's own perspective, the war of 1967 and its results seemed to confirm a historic commitment to "Greater Israel." A doctrine which was considered a political fantasy, an expression of pure extremism, suddenly seemed to be vindicated by reality. Begin finally ceased to be the pariah of Israeli politics.

The war of 1973 destroyed what was left of the claim of the Labor Movement to be the responsible, mature, balanced voice of Israeli politics. The circumstances leading to the war, its initial stages, and the traumatic number of casualties, as well as the sights of Israeli soldiers being taken prisoners, indicated to many that the old establishment failed them in the most dramatic way, and that collective anger added another dimension to Begin's changing image. Now, it was Begin who seemed a realistic, sober politician, one who could fill the vacuum created by the failure of the old guard of the Labor Movement.

The results of the 1977 elections were astounding as they completed the processes started before and described above, cementing the Likud–Sepharadic–Religious coalition, which for most of the last four decades has had a clear demographic and political edge in the Jewish population. This demographic edge was dramatically enlarged and became virtually out of the reach of the old establishment, with the addition of well over a million Jews from the former Soviet Union who moved to Israel in a span of five years in the late 1980s to the early 1990s.

The inclusion of these people in the Likud-led coalition requires an explanation. Many of them came without any religious background, a partnership with religious parties seemed odd and unnatural. Also, Likud is based on a Sepharadic constituency whose cultural background conflicted with that of the mostly-European Russian Jews. Except for one important round of elections in 1992, a coalition was created and has been in place since. What made it possible was a combination of reasons that follow.

The Russian immigrants formed their own party, first Israel *B'Aliyah,* led by the legendary Zionist freedom fighter Nathan Sharanski, and later Israel *Beitenu,* led by Avigdor Lieberman. Being organized in their own sectarian party enabled the vast majority of the Russians to feel that they had maintained their unique communal identities while merging with their new compatriots in a political alliance, thereby playing a meaningful role in the political life of their new country.

In the last elections (January 2013), the Israel Beitenu party merged with Likud into one unified electoral block, and the results were not good, as they lost three to four seats to parties of the center. In particular, *Yesh Atid,* led by Yair Lapid, is largely an Ashkenazi, secular, middle class party and one that could appeal to Russian immigrants because it shied away from any connection with the left wing while espousing a dovish attitude toward a political solution with the Palestinians. It also advocated a strong military response to terrorism originating from Gaza. Most of the Russian immigrants are still terrified by the left wing in Israel, as anything connected with leftism is a painful reminder of life in the "Socialist Heaven"—a life they are happy to have left behind. Surveys conducted among Russian Jewish immigrants in the United States also show strong support for the Republican Party.[3] This places them at variance with the majority of the American Jewish community known to be Liberal-Democratic.

Russian immigrants, while secular by and large, tend to support a moderate if not outright conservative approach to social issues. This has proven to be a strong connection between them and the rest of the Likud-led electoral coalition. But what has proven to be the strongest connection is the Radical Nationalist approach of the vast majority of Russian immigrants in the sense that "we came to our homeland, and no longer hide our identity, and we can be proud Jews." Statements like this are common among Russian immigrants. This kind of political discourse and orientation make them natural, inevitable members of the Likud-led coalition. There is an added regrettable element here, and this is the fact that these people came from a distinctly totalitarian society whose level of tolerance toward minorities was minimal, perhaps non-existent. This kind of attitude, when applied to the Israeli situation means intolerance and even bigotry toward Israeli-Arab citizens and Palestinian-Arabs at large. Thus, it was nationalism, either secular-Israeli, or religious, or Israeli-Russian which connected the dots and cemented the Likud-led electoral coalition. Nationalism in this context means policies with regard to the peace process, which dramatically narrows the ability of a Likud-led coalition to make the historic decisions needed if peace between Israel and the Palestinians is to be attained. Surely, Israeli decisions alone will never be enough to achieve this very elusive peace and Palestinians are required to make their necessary decisions, but this is beyond the scope of this paper. With all of the above in mind we can turn to an analysis of some Israeli elections including the most recent, and their impact on the peace process both when the elected government was Likud-led and when it was not.

# Menachem Begin, the 1977 Elections, Egypt and the Palestinian Question

Menachem Begin was, for many years, described by his political rivals in Israel as well as the world as a "war monger"—a classic right wing Arab-hater, whose election would lead to an inevitable new Arab–Israeli war. In short, the man went through a process of personal and ideological demonization. Then, on November 19, 1977, only six months after the elections, the entire world witnessed with astonishment and admiration the almost unbelievable sight of President Sadat of Egypt, leader of the largest Arab country in the Middle East, greeted by the "monstrous" Menachem Begin at the Ben-Gurion Airport in Tel-Aviv. How could this happen?

Clearly, President Sadat demonstrated an unexpected and brilliant combination of personal courage, political wisdom, and historic vision—all of which gained him a place in the hall of fame of the greatest leaders of the 20th century. The historic and enduring importance of the Egyptian–Israeli peace process cannot be overestimated, and Sadat made it possible (Hurwitz & Medad, 2011). But what about Menachem Begin? Begin established a coalition based on Likud and the religious parties to the right of Likud, and added the Centrist Democratic Movement for change, led by retired General Yigael Yadin. This was a somewhat unnatural coalition as Yadin and his movement were to the left of Likud, surely far to the left of the Religious Right, but Begin included him so that he could position himself and Likud in the center of the coalition and of Israeli politics, thus blurring its party and his own extreme right wing image. Begin needed to do that, not just out of public relations considerations, but mainly because he had a peace initiative in mind, one that could be swallowed by the religious right, and strongly backed by Yadin.

Realizing his domestic political constraints, Begin initiated peace negotiations with Egypt, which included a complete territorial withdrawal from the Sinai Peninsula, occupied in the 1967 war, in return for an Egyptian agreement that did not push for a parallel territorial concession to the Palestinians, one that Begin, as a Likud leader did not want to make, nor could make, due to the inevitable religious resistance from the right, and internal Likud objections. Begin knew that any territorial settlement with the Palestinians was beyond his political reach. Instead, he offered the Self-Rule Interim Plan, which stood no chance of being accepted by the Palestinians in the absence of an Israeli commitment for a complete territorial withdrawal from the West Bank in the future. Neither the Israeli right wing, whether secular Likud, nor the religious parties were ready to make peace with the Palestinians, then or now.

The Begin initiative showed that while realizing the need to make peace arrangements with the neighboring Arab states, Likud made a distinction between what is considered *Eretz Israel*, or the West Bank, and other territories, such as Sinai, or the Golan Heights. Another Likud government, that was headed by Prime Minister Netanyahu, was ready to trade the Golan in return for peace with Syria in the late 1990s

(Olmert, 2011). Ten years later, Ehud Olmert's government was engaged in talks with Syria and according to unconfirmed reports, the Israelis were ready to give up the Golan Heights. While Olmert was at that time the leader of *Kadimah*, it is important to note that he was a Likud member almost all of his political career, and his policy about the Golan reflected an attitude that was not an anathema to Likud thinking, though it was never universally supported by the party.[4]

However, with regard to the Palestinians, any settlement is bound to lead to a near-total, if not total withdrawal from the disputed territories of the West Bank/Judea and Samaria. And the fact is, the Likud-led, right wing coalition had already proved in 1977, as it did later, that it was inherently incapable of doing this. Likud remained the party of Eretz Israel, first under Begin, and then under other leaders. Secular nationalism, the Likud style, and religious nationalism of the Religious Zionists created a strong ideological bond focused on preservation of Eretz Israel under Israeli control. This prevented it from being under Palestinian control, and came with strong, ongoing support for the construction of Jewish settlements in the disputed lands. The same Menachem Begin who gave up on Sinai, including the Jewish settlements there, was the leader who gave a tremendous boost to the project of settlements in Judea and Samaria, and made sure that everybody knew that he did it willingly and not as a result of pressures from the religious right wing.

Begin's Egyptian initiative also made it clear that in order for Israel to make huge concessions, territorial and otherwise, the government should be led by a charismatic, authoritative leader. Begin was charismatic and authoritative so he managed to keep his party behind him, but for the small group which left. However, even he could not maintain its complete unity; more militant elements within Likud left, establishing the *Tehiyya* Party. This was not a significant loss to Likud at the time, but still indicated a political importance that any attempt by a Likud government to make dramatic concessions to the Palestinians would be resisted by Secular Nationalists, and not just by the Religious Right.

## Yitzhak Rabin, the 1992 Elections and the Oslo Accords

The Oslo Accords[5] that were negotiated secretly by representatives of the Israeli government and the Palestine Liberation Organization (PLO) in Oslo in 1993 led to a dramatic breakthrough in the hitherto deadly, incurable Israeli–Palestinian conflict. Accords were signed, a grand ceremony took place on the south lawn of the White House, and Nobel Peace Prizes were granted to Yitzhak Rabin and Shimon Peres of Israel, as well as Yasir Arafat, Chairman of the PLO. As final peace between parties was *not* achieved by the Accords, and much violence and misery continued to dominate the Israeli–Palestinian landscape, the Accords came through vitriolic criticism. The rejection came particularly from Palestinian rejectionists, mainly Hamas and Fatah dissidents, as well as from Israeli right wingers, both religious and Secular

Nationalists. Oslo became a dirty word in the political vocabulary of both ends of the anti-reconciliation camp, among Palestinians and Israelis.

Yet, the Oslo Accords did not deserve the derision and hostility with which they have come to be viewed by so many Palestinians and Israelis. They have led to the normalization of the conflict whereas, before Oslo, this was one-dimensional, characterized by violence without any political dialogue and recognition. Afterwards, it became a conflict more in tune with other similar situations in the world where violence, political dialogue, negotiations, and talks about peace are thrown together creating a different reality on the ground and also in the search for a political solution.

The Israeli elections of June 23, 1992, made it possible for the Israeli side to open a new page and become involved in the peace negotiations with the PLO. This was something that under Likud-led governments seemed a fantasy. After 15 years of a Likud-dominated Israeli political scene, segments of the Israeli electorate became disenchanted with the governing right wing party. The reasons may be: 1) the failure of the Madrid Peace Conference (convened in November, 1991) which initially aroused a sense of optimism;[6] 2) the continuing violence of the first Palestinian *Intifada*; 3) the deteriorating economic situation, and the rift between Prime Minister Shamir and President George H. W. Bush; and 4) the difficult absorption of the first wave of Russian immigrants. All of these factors contributed to the resounding Likud defeat. Still, with the exception of the Russian vote, which defected from the Likud electoral coalition for the first and last time, the other components of this coalition remained loyal, and the popular vote for the right wing was larger than that of the Labor Party and the left wing *Meretz* Party. However, it was divided among many splinter groups as many votes were given to small factions which failed to cross the bar of 1% of the vote—the then minimum for Knesset representation (today it is 2%).

What enabled Rabin to move ahead with the secret Oslo process and led to a successful end was his ability to include the *Shas* Party, a Sepharadic Orthodox party, in his coalition. Shas, which was only established in 1984 (Peled, 2001), derived its voters from Likud, which in fact was, for all intents and purposes, the religious wing of the Likud Party. However, after the 1992 elections, it was lured out of the Likud orbit by a substantial political reward of important portfolios in the Rabin government. There were also some *Halachic* (Religious) rulings by the spiritual head of the party, the charismatic Rabbi Ovadia Josef, indicating a softer, more conciliatory approach to the question of territorial concessions in Eretz Israel. Still, the main incentive for the Shas to join the Labor Movement under Rabin was the prospect of getting lavish state support for their educational system. This was something that seemed to lead to a correction of past discrimination against Sepharadic Jews.

Their support for the Oslo Accords enabled Rabin to have them approved in the Knesset, but then the party started a process of repenting its vote due to the enormous pressure brought to bear on the more moderate leadership by the much more militant right wing rank and file membership. Clearly, this pressure was ever more effective because of the overall failure of the Oslo Accords to stop Palestinian terrorism. In the elections of 1996, the personal contest between the Likud-right wing Netanyahu and the Labor-left wing candidate, Shimon Peres, the party supported the former, thus making his victory inevitable. The victory was hailed by many Israelis as the repudiation of the Oslo Accords, though Prime Minister Netanyahu never formally renounced these Accords.

The Shas proved though that it was and perhaps still is the weaker link in the Likud-led coalition, mainly due to the fact that some of its leaders, particularly the charismatic Arye Der'I, have been distinctly more moderate than their voters. This duplicity has characterized Shas from its early days through to the present. Along with the defection of Shas, it was also Rabin's personal prestige as a war hero that led many Israelis, who were otherwise reluctant to support reconciliation with the Palestinians to do the same in 1993 because they trusted Rabin personally.

Thus, while Rabin could hardly be conceived as a charismatic leader in the mold of Menachem Begin, he mastered enough personal weight and stature to help him navigate the Oslo process and complete it despite the strong right wing opposition. These were the tactical skills of negotiations and political maneuvering of Shimon Peres, the foreign minister who successfully facilitated talks with the PLO. However, it was the leadership of Yitzhak Rabin that made it acceptable to a bewildered Israeli public, much the same as Menachem Begin's personal leadership saw the peace process with Egypt through to a final treaty. Part of the treaty included the uprooting of Jewish settlers from the Sinai against tremendous opposition by the religious right as well as certain elements within his own party.

## Ariel Sharon, the 2003 Elections and the Gaza Disengagement Plan

Ariel Sharon had very little in common with Menachem Begin but for two elements. Both were vilified, slandered, and thrashed for most of their public career for being people of war and anti-peace. The two worked hard to become prime minister of the state. When they finally came to the Promised Land, they seemed to have changed course. Rather than initiating war, they strove hard to achieve peace. There was another similarity, Begin was an admired, even idolized politician in the eyes of his supporters, as was Sharon—who had an aura of heroism attached to his name since the 1950s and even more so after his performance in the 1973 war.[7]

Here is where the resemblance ends and the contrasts surface. On February 6, 2001, Sharon crushed the incumbent Prime Minister from the Labor Movement (the last Labor prime minister in Israel), Ehud Barak in a landslide victory (63% of the vote) in the last-ever elections to be held under the Direct Election Law. On January 28, 2003, the Likud Party under Sharon won a decisive victory in the Knesset elections, and as a matter of fact, established a coalition with the religious right and Avigdor Lieberman, with his Russian constituency. Sharon decided to change the course of the conflict with the Palestinians—perhaps as a reaction to the propaganda campaign depicting him as a war monger, perhaps out of belated political enlightenment, or for other reasons. And in the absence of an agreement with the Palestinian Authority (PA), which succeeded the PLO, Sharon decided to conduct a unilateral Israeli withdrawal from the Gaza Strip, and in the process, uprooted all 8,000 Jews living in Jewish settlements in the vicinity of Gaza.

Sharon believed that getting rid of Gaza with its more than a million Palestinian residents would: 1) improve Israel's demographic balance with the Palestinians; 2) pay Israel political dividends in the international arena; and 3) not be vehemently resented by the Likud—like the religious right. Gaza, in his mind was never considered as sacred to these people as the rest of Eretz Israel.

On this last point, he was proved tragically wrong; in fact, he should have known better. Likud Prime Minister Yitzhak Shamir was under pressure from some of the Likud moderates in the run-up to the Israeli elections of 1992 to show flexibility with regard to the fate of the Gaza Strip. He disdainfully rebuffed these pressures, claiming that Gaza was part of Eretz Israel.[8] Not surprisingly, Sharon's plan aroused a rebellion within Likud, with one half of the parliamentary caucus against the party, including Benjamin Netanyahu. A fierce resistance was also registered among the Likud rank and file membership. Avigdor Lieberman was opposed as well as the National Religious Party and the Shas Party. The plan was still approved in the Knesset on October 26, 2004, by a vote of 67 to 45, with only 21 of the 67 from Likud approving.

Sharon carried the day only with the support of the Labor Party and other smaller parties, but without his own party, let alone all those to the right of Likud. For him, the vote was the last straw in his struggle against the right wing of his party; and he broke away from Likud and established the Kadimah Party. In the moment of truth, Likud was split, and Sharon lost control of his own party over an issue concerning the fate of a part of Eretz Israel. Likud remained the party of Eretz Israel, though for a while, weakened and numerically demoted. Still, the very word "disengagement" has become a dirty word in Likud's vocabulary, and with it, the notion of dismantling Jewish settlements.

The lesson of this disengagement plan regarding internal Israeli politics and the peace process was very obvious; there is no sign that it is different now than what it was a few years ago. The established right wing, whether secular or religious, is not ideologically capable of accepting the need for an almost complete territorial concession in what they consider Eretz Israel. The implication about the peace process is, sadly, all too clear—it is inconceivable that a coalition of Likud and its traditional partners can move the process forward, as did Menachem Begin, Yitzhak Rabin, and Ariel Sharon.

# The Israeli Elections of January 2013 and the Peace Process

The January 22, 2013 election results turned out to be almost precisely as predicted by the repeated polling during the campaign. The combined bloc of Netanyahu's Likud and his Foreign Minister Avigdor Lieberman's Israel Beitenu remains by far the largest single party. Though it lost a significant number of seats, it was larger than anticipated by most polls. There was also no surprise regarding the success of the revamped Religious Zionist Jewish Home Party, led by Naftali Bennett, which gained seven seats—all coming from Likud voters, as was well demonstrated by a careful examination of polling stations in traditional Likud strongholds.[9]

There was also no big surprise concerning the success of Yair Lapid's new *Yesh Atid* (we have a future) Party. He took most of his votes from the near-defunct Kadimah Party, and only very few seats from the right wing—mainly votes of Russian immigrants who were attracted to him by his distinctly secular approach, and some liberal-minded Likud voters who were turned off by the sharp turn to the right of the Likud list of candidates in these elections. Many of the Likud more moderate, liberal-oriented members, such as Benny Begin, Dan Meridor, and Michael Eytan, all ministers and veteran Likud politicians, were pushed off the list of Knesset candidates, as a result of a sustained campaign by more militant Likud radicals. They were replaced by younger, much more nationalist supporters of settlement expansion, and the overall message was clearly a Likud sharp turn to the right.

Altogether, Likud and its partners lost only 3–4 seats. But while the overall number of seats lost was not too significant, the political implications could have been very significant. This is because the traditional Likud–Religious coalition has only 61 seats, a majority of two in the Knesset of 120, and Netanyahu realized that with such a slim majority it would be virtually impossible to govern. Thus, he had to turn to the Yesh Atid Party, who conditioned any coalition on the exclusion of the ultra-Orthodox parties, the historic partners of Likud. Netanyahu had to swallow a bitter pill, and the alliance that was in place for so many years, could possibly have come to its end. The full repercussions of this development are yet to unfold, but the possibility that the ultra-Orthodox will cooperate in the future under different circumstances with more dovish parties is not to be ruled out, though it still seems somewhat of a political fantasy. Thus, Netanyahu has been forced to include Yair Lapid in his government, contrary to his expectations prior to the elections.

Lapid, a TV presenter and son of former Justice Minister Yosef (Tommy), is situated at the very center of Israeli politics. He has shied away, as if from a plague, from the left wing brand. As soon as the elections were over, his surrogates went overboard to affirm the fact that the young politician was deeply rooted in the very center of Israeli politics and society. Lapid is a conservative right wing politician as far as the economy is concerned; liberal on social issues; dovish on the Palestinian issue; proponent of the

Two-States Solution and opponent of expansion of settlements; and very much opposed to a partition of Jerusalem. Yet, all this is always presented with a very strong hawkish emphasis on security matters, including unconditional support of the two Gaza wars of 2009 and 2012. Moreover, the rhetoric he uses to justify both the dovish and hawkish positions is classic Zionist narrative, reflecting a profound belief in the just cause of Israel and the Zionist ideology. Lapid made it clear during the campaign, that domestic, rather than foreign policy issues dominated his agenda. So it was no surprise that he opted to get the treasury portfolio in the new government, rather than the Foreign Ministry. The coalition agreement between him and Netanyahu devoted just 35 words to the question of the peace process with the Palestinians; in other words, only lip service. There was no mention at all of the Two-States Solution.

Another partner of Netanyahu in the new coalition is former Kadimah leader and Foreign Minister Tzipi Livni who ran at the head of the Movement Party, polling only six seats. Much like Lapid, she is known for her dovish positions as well as for an insistence on strong military response to terrorism. She also enthusiastically supported the two Gaza wars.

The Religious Zionist Jewish Home Party, under Naftali Bennett is the only religious party which sits with Netanyahu in his new government. While that may seem a natural match, it is not so. In this case, what meets the eye is just part of the story. Bennett is the rising star of right wing politics in Israel, a potential challenger for Netanyahu as the leader of the Israeli right wing—both its secular and nationalist wings. He clings to the traditional line of opposition to the Two-States Solution and supports the settlements and hawkish security policies. However, he is engaged in a systematic campaign to extricate himself from the total identification with only Religious Zionist voters. He has received many votes of disgruntled Likudniks and has an appeal to more centrist, secular, young professionals by virtue of being a successful businessman and being married to a secular woman.

In many respects, he and Lapid are the new Siamese twins of a new style of politics in Israel. Their opinions converge with regard to the economy and the need for ultra-Orthodox Yeshiva (religious school) students to enlist for proper military service. They differ sharply though on the Palestinian issue, he is much closer to Netanyahu and the ultra-Orthodox parties.

That said, the question is: If and how can the third Netanyahu government move ahead in any meaningful way with regard to the stalemated peace process with the Palestinians? The common denominator of the new government is not the question of a political solution with the Palestinians. On this issue, there is no agreement between the various factions represented in the coalition. The first priority for them is to deal with pressing domestic issues, particularly the question of the enlistment of ultra-Orthodox youngsters in the Israeli Army. The various factions, particularly Lapid and

Bennett will conduct their affairs with a view toward the possibility of early elections. This seems to be a plausible political scenario considering the fact that the coalition is composed of parties which have not had much in common on other issues, particularly regarding the peace process. The raucous nature of Israeli politics is such that things can change dramatically, as one or more of the coalition partners will reassess its interests and decide to opt out for early elections. One of the issues which could trigger such a development is the peace process; that is, an intolerable American pressure on Netanyahu, a significant Palestinian concession which will require an Israeli response, a very significant change in one of the neighboring countries, or a resumption of a full-scale third Palestinian Intifada. All is likely, but not inevitable. What seems less likely is a shift in the Likud Party which will enable Netanyahu to move ahead and conclude a lasting peace deal with the Palestinians.

## Likud-Led Government will not Make a Historic Compromise with the Palestinians

The cumulative experience of the effect of Israeli elections on the peace process leads us to some inescapable conclusions:

First, Likud is a Nationalist Party whose core political–ideological ethos is the preservation of a large part of the West Bank/Judea and Samaria under Israeli control; maintaining the unity of Jerusalem and continuing to expand existing Jewish settlements in the disputed lands. There are Likud politicians who are more flexible and ready for greater compromises—Netanyahu himself may be one of them. However, in the current parliamentary Likud caucus there is no majority for the Two-States Solution because the Lieberman faction, composed mainly of immigrants from the former Soviet Union, is strongly opposed to this solution and, together with the Likud, own more radical right wingers. They will neutralize any move by Netanyahu in this direction. To put it bluntly, Likud will have to split, as happened under Sharon, in order to join forces with the center and left wing parties and advance a historic compromise with the Palestinians. So long as this does not happen, a prime minister from Likud will not be able to do that.

Second, there seems to be no change in the religious right, of either the Jewish Home Party or the ultra-Orthodox, in terms of the support for the settlers and the resistance to make significant territorial concessions in Judea and Samaria, and particularly in Jerusalem. The influential Rabbis who guide these parties politically seem to be as strong as ever in their opposition to any major breakthrough with the Palestinians. The weaker link is the Shas Party, but the leadership will hesitate to go against the well-stated positions of its electorate whose right wing sympathies are well established in every public opinion poll. The fact that the new Netanyahu government does not include the ultra-Orthodox may sour the relations between the leadership, but is not likely to bring about a dramatic change in well-established political positions which are so deeply rooted on religious rulings.

Third, the Likud-led electoral coalition has an automatic support of at least 60 of the 110 seats which are given to Jewish-Zionist parties. Ten seats belong to the Arab, anti-Zionist parties, which are perfectly legitimate players in the political game. However, relying on their support in order to move through a radical, far-reaching territorial concession is a risk, amounting to near political suicide. A move of some seats from the Likud-led coalition to the center is not impossible; it had already happened in 1992, under Rabin, and in 2013, with the rise of Lapid. But a real, fundamental change in the voting patterns of Israelis is contingent on deeper social and cultural changes, which may happen in the future. However, the nature of such changes is such that they take a lot of time to ripen and materialize. The example of what happened after the signing of the Oslo Accords can also provide us a model for what can happen in the future. There should be a decisive majority of Jewish members of the Knesset (MKs) supporting a historic compromise in order to have it approved by the Knesset, and more importantly, by the people at large. This is another reason why voting patterns have to radically change in order to facilitate a crucial political decision for the Two-States Solution.

Fourth, it is also the case that the political landscape in Israel has grown more atomized, and there is not one dominant party which has enough political power to bring about big changes. Begin's Likud had 45 seats in 1977, Rabin's Labor had 44 in 1992, and Netanyahu has only 31 in 2013. Clearly, his dependence on his allies is unavoidable and is bound to considerably restrict his freedom of action.

Fifth, any discussion on Israeli politics cannot take place without referring to the overall reality of the conflict with the Palestinians in particular, and Middle East politics in general—subjects which are out of the scope of this paper, as well as a discussion of the role of the international community, especially that of the United States. Clearly, Israelis do not vote in a vacuum and their voting is greatly influenced by the developments in the environment of which they are a part.

Sixth, Israelis are also clearly influenced by the quality of their political leadership. Israel is having a leadership crisis; gone is the generation of the founding fathers, and no suitable alternative is in the offing. Benjamin Netanyahu finds it difficult to wear the shoes of Ariel Sharon, let alone those of Menachem Begin. The same applies to current prominent figures of the center and the left. The historic experience as described above shows that historic decisions, which reflect a departure from well-entrenched ideologies and concepts, require leaders with historic vision, political courage, and sweeping charisma. Israel is still in search of them.

# Notes

1. Only the second Netanyahu government, with Foreign Minister Lieberman and his deputy, Danny Ayalon, turned the plight of Jewish refugees from Arab countries into a major theme of Israel's foreign policy.

2. There is a vast number of books on the 1973 war, and from the standpoint of this particular article, the most relevant outcome of the war was the fact that in the elections of December 1973, taking place after the war, the Likud, under Begin raised its number of seats in the Knesset from 31 to 39, thus making the victory in the 1977 elections almost inevitable.

3. There are 800,000 Russian Jews in the United States; many of them are concentrated in such areas as Brighton Beach in Brooklyn, NY where the votes are tilted strongly towards the Republicans.

4. Olmert hoped that by offering the Golan to Syria, the Syrian dictator, Bashar al-Assad, might be willing to renounce his alliance with Iran. The Gaza war of 2009 put an end to these negotiations.

5. The Oslo Accords were so secretive that, despite the notorious tendency of Israelis and Palestinians to leak to the press, they were led to their successful end without any damaging premature leak. When they were finally announced, there was a sense of shock in Israel, which, for a while, paralyzed the right wing, as their leadership was completely taken by surprise.

6. The Madrid Conference was convened with high expectations, which reflected a genuine exhaustion in Israel, at least, from the on-going first Palestinian Intifada. Contrary to the public mood, Prime Minister Shamir was skeptical and distinctly unenthusiastic about the entire process.

7. Sharon was in the army reserves during the war, and was called to duty to command a division. His success in the war paved his way to a position of prominence in Israeli politics in general, and in the right wing in particular.

8. Shamir almost fired Minister Roni Milo, one of his close confidants, for raising in public the possibility of leaving Gaza.

9. The move from Likud to the Jewish Home Party took place mainly in towns dominated by a mostly-Sepharadic, traditional population.

# The Palestinian Reconciliation Process and its Impact on the Political System: A Post-Arab Spring View

## Ido Zelkovitz

## Abstract

The Arab Spring brought in its wings a fundamental change in the relations between citizens and state in the Middle East. The authoritarian nature of many regimes in the Arab world is being challenged and transformed, and the Arab public now demands its fair share in the decision-making processes. In contrast, the Palestinian arena was seemingly unmoved. This article discusses the ramifications of the Arab Spring on the struggle for political hegemony in the Palestinian Authority (PA). The Palestinian case is unique in that the Palestinians do not hold exclusive sovereignty over the West Bank and the Gaza Strip. Furthermore, since June 2007, these two territories have been controlled by rival political movements, with strikingly different worldviews. These considerations, together with the continued Palestinian struggle for an independent state, suggest a somewhat different Arab Spring than that experienced by the Arab states. The "Palestinian Spring," so to speak, calls for the end of internal political divide and not for the toppling of the existing regimes. Both Fatah and Hamas, who wish to maintain their stronghold on the Palestinians, and continue to acquire more political power, were attentive to these public voices.

# Introduction

The outbreak of the Arab Spring was met by a weak and fragmented Palestinian society, which was in the process of searching a path out of the political deadlock it had encountered. In the wake of the complex reality that emerged, both the Palestinian Authority (PA) in the West Bank and the Hamas government in Gaza scrambled for ways to secure their utter political dominance—each in its own stretch of land—and discuss internally how to overcome the crisis they were each facing.

Has the Arab Spring, which is changing the face of regimes across the Arab World, passed over the Palestinian society? For many years, in fact since the Nakba of 1948 up until the establishment of the Palestinian Authority (PA), Palestinians enjoyed somewhat of an advantage, compared to their Arab counterparts—their leadership was not granted the opportunity to downright suppress its people. Up until the founding of the PA, the Palestinians had not established a sovereign rule within a territorial continuum, which would probably have developed into a monarchic or republican pattern based on mechanisms of oppression. Furthermore, the effort to build a Palestinian state would depend on the Palestinians succeeding in transforming their internal politics and organizational dynamics (Sayigh, 1997, p. 692).

## The Evolvement of Palestinian Civil Society

Paradoxically, the national oppression of the Palestinians in the Arab states and under Israeli rule in the West Bank and in Gaza has created the infrastructure for the development of a robust civil society. This society has formed an integral part of the mechanism which has been central to the state-building process of the renewed Palestinian national identity (Frisch, 1998, p. 131).

The key role, assumed by society since 1948 in maintaining the Palestinian identity, has created a sphere of discourse characterized by openness and the granting of political leeway (Brand, 1988, p. 5). These preserved the principle of national unity around which all Palestinians could gather, in spite of the difficulties, differences, and divisions that have occurred within the various Palestine Liberation Organization (PLO) factions since the late 1960s (Cobban, 1985, p. 11).

It was precisely the establishment of the PA which suppressed the vibrant civil society, as it subjected the inhabitants of the West Bank and Gaza to a structured regime based on the model of surrounding oppressive Arab states. The civil society organizations and the student movement, which had challenged the Israeli military regime, were either absorbed or persecuted by the Palestinian mechanism. In addition, the financial channels which supplied funds to the civil society came under the supervision and monitoring of the PA (Parsons, 2005, p. 175).

# The West Bank and Abbas' State-Building Woes

Two years after the commencement of the Arab Spring, the political apparatuses in the West Bank and the Gaza Strip are still profound, and the civil society is dormant. Between 2010 and 2011, the voices heard in the West Bank praised the stability of Palestinian President Mahmoud Abbas's regime, and the economic indicators pointed to stability, and even improvement in certain parameters. As it appeared in a report published by the International Monetary Fund (2011), or in the words of Abbas:

> The reports issued recently by the United Nations, the World Bank, the Ad Hoc Liaison Committee (AHLC) and the International Monetary Fund confirm and laud what has been accomplished, considering it a remarkable and unprecedented model. The consensus conclusion by the AHLC a few days ago here described what has been accomplished as a 'remarkable international success story' and confirmed the readiness of the Palestinian people and their institutions for the immediate independence of the State of Palestine. (Abbas, 2011, para 33)

The report, handed by the IMF, was found inaccurate. In 2012, a year after the report was published, demonstrations against the socioeconomic problems took place around the West Bank. The demonstrations spread out to the Gaza Strip, where a man set himself on fire to protest against the poor conditions and standard of living. Abbas, as well as other Fatah members, knew that these demonstrations, without a firm economic base-structure, might get out of hand and turn against them.

Hamas, on the other hand, by virtue of its monopoly over power, had managed to tighten its grip on the Gaza Strip. The fear in the Gaza Strip did not go away, and the violent events of the summer of 2007 were still fresh in the minds of the population.

Yet, one must ask whether such matters could actually affect the current situation, considering the changes in the Arab world and the notion that the younger generation draws encouragement and strength from the increased freedom of expression and their ability to generate change. Comparing the Arab world with the Palestinian Authority, one must bear in mind that the millions can gather. A reality of the division is decisive, not only regarding affairs between Gaza and the West Bank, but also within the West Bank.[1]

The Palestinian experience teaches us that the old guard is willing to enter deliberation and even negotiate a change in the political power distribution, so as to preserve their position of strength. While in the Arab world, the masses flooded the streets and demanded the removal of tyrannous regimes, the Palestinians' city squares, by and large, remained vacant. The only voices heard in the Palestinian public squares were the calls to end the intra-Palestinian divide. The young protesters staged a march of protest on November 15, 2011, backed by a widespread Internet campaign on social networks such as Facebook and YouTube.

Nevertheless, the young Palestinian population, thirsty for change, harbors vast reservoirs of energy. Some of them feel that the reconciliation attempts between Fatah and Hamas will lead them nowhere. Those voices that rose up in the civil society sphere, such as "Palestinians for Dignity," did not anticipate initially that the region's revolutions would cause an immediate stir. That is because of the reality as they saw it:

> We face two layers of oppression: Palestinian self-rule in the West Bank and Gaza, and the Israeli occupation. One glaring obstacle is that it is very easy to criticize young people like us and say, 'What are you doing, you traitors and collaborators with the enemy? You need to focus your attention on the occupation and not on the Palestinian regime.' I think we grasped that in our case, the situation is going to be very different, thus, we decided to concentrate on matters that connect between the two layers—such as security coordination, or political prisoners who are confined in either Israeli prisons or Palestinian Authority and Hamas jails. (Hass, 2012)

In response, the leaderships of Fatah and Hamas were apparently attentive to the young voices. The geopolitical changes in the Arab world and the inability of one side to overshadow the other paved the way for discussions.

The willingness of both parties to enter into deliberations regarding an intra-Palestinian reconciliation is one of the most striking outcomes of the Arab Spring. The futile tactical maneuvers initiated by Mahmud Abbas in his plea to the United Nations managed only limited achievements. These efforts may have reinforced his image as a stubborn leader true to his path, and preserved a certain level of Palestinian hope, but they did not change the political situation on the ground. The flexibility toward Hamas displayed by President Abbas is an indication of the despair which took hold of the PA decision makers—on account of their Israeli counterparts. For instance, the Abbas address at the UN Assembly was meant for Palestinian and international ears. The speech itself was firm and utterly ignored the Israeli partner, with whom Abbas is ultimately supposed to sit down with and negotiate (Abbas, 2011).

The despair which prevailed among Palestinian decision makers in the West Bank was compensatedby the celebrations of the PA officials who managed to secure the Palestinian bid to join UNESCO. This achievement was an indication of Abbas's strategy—continued diplomatic efforts aimed at guaranteeing an official recognition of Palestine as the 194th member of the United Nations.

Abbas attempted to put the diplomatic efforts of the PA back on the Palestinian agenda and sideline the gains of Hamas following the prisoner exchange of Israeli soldier Gila'ad Shalit. In the last round of the battle over public opinion between Fatah and Hamas, Abbas gained the upper hand, after showing his might vis-à-vis the United States. The fact that Abbas continued with his plea to the UN despite objections of the United States infuriated the U.S. State Department. The American threat to withhold their funding to UNESCO only increased the popularity of Abbas in the Palestinian street, which not only perceives the U.S. as Israel's major ally, but also as a symbol of global imperialism. (Cole, 2006)

## Hamas and the Challenges of the Arab Spring

In the Gaza Strip, Hamas failed to leverage the prisoner swap with Israel to present an alternative which would truly challenge Abbas. The Palestinian Authority () managed to contain the spontaneous outbursts of jubilation in the wake of the prisoner exchange between Hamas and Israel, and even held back from preventing the display of Hamas flags in the West Bank, a scene not witnessed in quite some time. The Shalit deal was made possible by the changes brought forward by the Arab Spring. Hamas, which initially found itself in a tight spot following the events, managed to emerge geopolitical conditions are extremely different. Palestinians do not have a "Tahrir Square" in which as a robust movement capable of adapting to changing times.

Yet, the Arab Spring did not initially bode well with the Islamic party. The uprising in Syria severely limited the maneuvering options of the Damascus-based Hamas politburo. Naturally, Hamas had to support the Syrian masses and the Muslim Brotherhood movement in Egypt, as many of those who took to the streets identified with its values. However, the fact that Syria supports Hamas and acts as its patron prevented Khalid Mishal and other group leaders from clearly declaring their opposition to Bashar al-Assad's regime. In response to the turmoil in Syria, Hamas sought to get closer to Egypt. The inking of the internal Hamas-Fatah reconciliation agreement on the 27th of April, 2011 in Cairo, was the first sign that Hamas was willing to make compromises on its way back to the center of the public arena.

The same agreement was refused by Hamas in October 2009, but the geopolitical changes required that Hamas make a sacrifice. As soon as it signed the reconciliation deal with Fatah, a path for dialogue with Egyptian intelligence was created. The fact that Hamas demonstrated flexibility in this matter prompted heads of Egyptian intelligence to exert heavy pressure on the movement in an attempt to push forward other issues.

The heightened tensions along the Egyptian border with Israel after the terror attacks near Eilat in August 2011 actually enhanced the dialogue between Israel and Egypt on a series of security-related matters (Ben-Yishai, 2011). This dialogue was also a factor in promoting the prisoner swap deal, as Egypt wanted to prove that it was still a central player in the post-Mubarak era, and able to fulfill the role of the responsible mediator.

However, it must be remembered that there are also power struggles within Hamas. Once the group forcefully took over the Gaza Strip, becoming the sovereign power there, it began to bear direct responsibility for the lives of Gazans. Hamas in Gaza has received heavy blows since the takeover and Shalit's kidnapping, culminating in operation *Cast Lead*—a three-week armed conflict in the Gaza Strip between Israel and Palestinian militants that occurred between December 27, 2008 and January 18, 2009.

Beyond the heavy price that the movement paid, it also required rehabilitation of the Strip—a poverty-stricken territory that is one of the most crowded places on earth. Gazans raised their eyes to the West Bank, where Abbas has succeeded in establishing state infrastructure, and concluded that Hamas had failed them. Hamas's inability to do the same in Gaza led the Hamas Gaza leadership to apply extra pressure on Hamas's leadership in Damascus. The Arab Spring had elevated the position of Hamas' leadership in Gaza at the expense of the political bureau in Damascus. The economic uncertainty, resulting among others from the financial crisis in Iran, curbed the fundraising capabilities of Hamas "outside," and reduced its influence over the Hamas Gazan leadership (al-Rabi' al-'Arabi, 2012).

Nevertheless, Hamas is attentive to the changes which have occurred in the Arab world following the Arab Spring, and is adjusting itself accordingly. Hamas had concluded that the next confrontation with Israel will de decided not in the battlefield, where Israel is far superior, but in the diplomatic corridors. On the political front, the main rival of Hamas is not Israel but Fatah, which is the backbone of the PLO (Palestinian Liberation Organzation), the sole legitimate representative of the Palestinian people since the resolution of the Arab League Conference at Rabat in 1974.

## Hamas' Quest for International Recognition

Ever since it was established, Hamas has aimed to succeed the PLO as the legitimate representative of the Palestinian people. The path to realizing this goal is by taking over the PLO from within. Hamas' demand that the gates of the PLO be opened to them might transform the intra-Palestinian power balance, to include not only a redistribution of power and Hamas' participation in PLO decision making, but also the allocating of financial resources to the movement, and its eventual legitimization in both the Arab-Muslim world and the international community.

The recent travels of legitimization by the Hamas leadership to Egypt, where Ismail Haniyah met the heads of the Muslim Brotherhood during December 2–26, 2011, and Turkey, in which Khalid Mishal was greeted by Prime Minister Erdoğan on March 16, 2012, are a step in this direction. Yet Hamas' request to open a representative office was declined by the Turkish government on January 30, 2012. Turkish government spokesman and Deputy Prime Minister Bülent Arınç reported that Hamas' office being based in Turkey was out of the question. He added that news reports claiming the Turkish government would give the Palestinian group some millions of dollars in aid were also not true ("Turkey says won't host Hamas office," 2012).

It should be taken into account that Turkey is the only NATO alliance member that recognized Hamas as a legitimate organization, since the latter formed a government in the Palestinian territories following the democratic elections in 2006. The fact that Turkey put the nail in the coffin of a Hamas office in Ankara does not necessarily represent a change in its overall policy regarding the movement. Possibly, Turkey chose not to undermine the position of the PLO as the sole representative of the Palestinians. Abbas' visit to Turkey on the 20th of November 2011, to meet the senior Palestinian detainees who were released in the Shalit deal, and deported to Istanbul, testifies to this case (Levi, 2011). Haniyah's visits to Tunis, and the warm welcome he received there ("Gaza leader promises," 2012), symbolically demonstrate the historic and cultural changes which have occurred in the Middle East following the Arab Spring. The same city which treated Arafat as a mayor, and where Fatah activists flocked to its restaurants and cafés, was now extending its warm welcome to Ismail Haniyah, head of the Hamas government in Gaza.

Hamas is currently in the process of searching for political legitimacy. For this reason, the Hamas leadership is trying to garner support in the Sunni domain by playing down its relations with Iran, one of its major strategic assets. Against this backdrop, the differences between the Hamas "outside" and "inside" leaderships are made all the more clear. The Hamas leadership within the Gaza Strip, traditionally considered more moderate in terms of its ideology, is now pushing to strengthen the ties with Iran—possibly at the expense of Khalid Mishal's initiative to consolidate the Sunni camp by tying the knot with the Muslim Brothers in Egypt. The driving force behind the wooing of Iran is Ismail Haniyah, who is seeking to strengthen his position vis-à-vis Hamas "outside" and secure additional financial channels. Haniyah ignored the requests of the Qatari and Kuwaiti rulers to cancel his stopover in Iran during his visit to the Gulf States in February 2012. ("Masadir lil-al-Quds: Nasa'ih Khalijia li-Haniyah bi-'adm ziarat Iran," 2012)

Furthermore, during Haniyah's visit to Iran, he adopted a hard line approach. He challenged the efforts led by Mishal, and instead emphasized the strategic importance of the alliance with Iran. In his speech to the crowds gathered to celebrate the 33rd anniversary of the Islamic revolution in Teheran, he vowed that Hamas would not abandon the path of armed struggle and would never come to terms with the existence of Israel ("Ismail Haniya says," 2012).

The proclamations of Haniyah presented him as in opposition to Mishal, but they did not upset his initiative. The declared acceptance by Hamas' "outside" leaders of PLO's strategy to establish a Palestinian state within the 1967 borders is not a strategic change, but rather a tactical maneuver. In actual fact, Hamas adopted some of the principles of the PLO's Ten-Point Plan of 1974, those exact same principles Khalid Mishal was required to endorse when he sought to participate in the election for the Kuwaiti office of the General Union of Palestinian Students (GUPS) as head of a Palestinian-Islamic list. Mishal had then refused this demand and the gates of the PLO where closed to him (Rabbani, 2008).

Nowadays, Mishal paradoxically acknowledges Israel's existence, but rejects its right to exist. In addition, Hamas has also declared that it does not denounce the path of violence, and when discussing the changes the movement is undergoing, or in the words of Khalid Mishal: "What is needed today…is to have resistance in all forms, both armed and public" ("Hamas' Meshaal urges," 2011). This proclamation should not be taken lightly. Hamas is an adaptive movement, yet its fundamental worldview is anchored in religious precept it cannot shake off.

To a certain extent, Hamas' demand to become integrated in the PLO establishment as part of the intra-Palestinian reconciliation process might put a spoke in its wheel. Ever since the PLO signed the Oslo Accords, Hamas has attempted to appropriate to itself the ethos of armed struggle with Israel at the expense of Fatah. Since Hamas became the ruling party, *de facto*, in the Gaza Strip, more and more activists have broken away from the movement, on account of their objection to what they perceived as political pragmatism.

Indeed, the more that Hamas tightened its grip on Gaza, the more the friction between Hamas and Israel decreased—especially considering the lesson learned by Hamas from Operation Cast Lead. Today, Hamas is contending with the turbulence of the Arab Spring and attempting to achieve intra-Arab legitimacy as a springboard toward international recognition. The rise of Islamist regimes in Egypt and Tunis has given it a bit of encouragement since those regimes can provide the movement with both the legitimacy it seeks and financial support.

The search for legitimacy is critical for understanding Hamas's conduct. Entry into the PLO would give the movement political status and the ability to take part in the national decision-making processes from which it is presently excluded. After all, the PLO is recognized by the Arab League as the sole legitimate representative of the Palestinian people.

Hamas has made tremendous efforts to shatter the PLO's constitutional status. The visit to the Gaza Strip by the Emir of Qatar, Hamad bin Khalifa al-Thani was a significant diplomatic achievement for the organization. It was a complete breach of the political siege of the Gaza Strip, which had psychological effects too; after all, it was not a visit by a minister or member of the Muslim Brotherhood to see the difficult situation in Gaza, but an official visit by a head of state that is not only legitimate but has strategic influence. It could change the whole attitude toward Hamas in other countries.

Furthermore, the Qatari visit and lifting of the diplomatic siege of Gaza is another stage in widening the rift between Fatah and Hamas. The diplomatic recognition of

Hamas harms the political standing of the PLO and reinforces the belief among Hamas leadership that it can offer a real leadership alternative for the Palestinians.

Paradoxically, political recognition of Hamas increased following the results of Operation Pillar of Defense.[2] Hamas managed to manufacture political gains in this campaign and became the de facto negotiating partner of the Israeli and U.S. leadership through Egyptian mediation. The war helped Hamas finally break the siege on the Gaza Strip, which suddenly turned into a sort of "Mecca," following the pilgrimages made to Gaza by all of the foreign ministers of the Arab League, the Prime Minister of Egypt, and the Turkish Foreign Minister.

For Hamas, the outcome of Operation Pillar of Defense was the closing of a circle from the beginning of the Arab Spring. If the Arab Spring found Hamas with its back against the wall and politically weak, the Islamic spirit carried by the regimes of the Arab countries, along with the results of Operation Pillar of Defense, turned the table.

Hamas succeeded in turning its resistance over the eight days of fighting into a myth, and leveraged the awareness in the Arab world that it had succeeded in upsetting the balance of terror with Israel. At the end of the fighting, Hamas had achieved an internationally guaranteed agreement, while providing itself with the image of the representative of the Palestinian issue and becoming a legitimate and important political player in the regional system.

# Conclusion

The marriage between Fatah and Hamas is not a match made in heaven. This is made evident by the processes set in motion by the Cairo Accord, which was, in actual fact, a declaration of principles in anticipation of future reconciliation. The Doha Declaration which followed, under the auspices of the Qatari Crown Prince, Shaykh Jassim ibn-Hamid the Second, further demonstrated the parties' willingness for reconciliation in spite of their different motivations. The Doha Declaration concluded that Abbas will head the temporary government of "technocrats," which would pave the way for presidential and parliamentary elections to be held in proximity to the re-institution of the Palestinian National Council—the PLO legislative body which elects the Executive Committee. In the press conference that followed, Hamas Leader Mishal elaborated on the nature of the reconciliation:

> We are serious, both Fatah and Hamas, in healing the wounds and ending the chapter of division and reinforcing and accomplishing reconciliation.... We want to inform our people that despite the fear of the many meetings being held which might not be implemented, there is a seriousness in ending the split and strengthening Palestinian unity in order to confront the Israeli occupation. ("Abbas to head unity government" 2012)

It seems that the Doha Declaration is but another bend in the long and winding road toward inter-Palestinian reconciliation. Fatah and Hamas are searching for a new path in order to revive parliamentary life in the Palestinian territories. The fact that each has enabled its rival to celebrate its founding in public rallies, held on December 13, 2012 for Hamas and on January 4, 2013 for Fatah, shows a will for political normality. Along with the great many political power demonstrations, the Fatah rally was accompanied by a visit consisting of Fatah leaders from the West Bank which also included senior Fatah security officers. Thus, Fatah and Hamas need to re-think about ending their split.

Yet, one must remember that significant differences between the parties still remain. Each movement marches to a different tune, and their visions in term of society and culture do not coincide. It is difficult to predict how the long process of reconciliation will unfold, yet one fears it might bear a resemblance to the talk between Israel and the Palestinians—prolonged, strenuously detailed, and strewn with obstacles.

## Notes

1. In the West Bank separations prevail between "A" areas, and checkpoint barriers proliferate.
2. A military struggle between Israel and Hamas which began after the assassination of the head of the Hamas military wing Ahmad Jabari. The operation continued with an eight-day exchange of blows between Israel and Hamas November 15–21, 2012.

# The Basis of China's Pro-Palestine Stance and the Current Status of its Implementation

## Yiyi Chen

## Abstract

This paper is built upon the author's previous attempt to review Sino-Israel relations from the Chinese perspective, where it is argued that the relationship is at a crossroads because China is increasingly more proactively involved in the international arena, which will inevitably lead to a more assertive role in trying to facilitate solving the Israel–Palestinian conflicts. The author also affirmed that China is more supportive of the Palestinians. In this paper, the author will further analyze China's pro-Palestine stance, give empirical evidence of this preference by Chinese intelligentsia, and provide insight into the decision-making mechanisms of the Chinese government in terms of its diplomatic policies. The author also wants to demonstrate that, despite the evident pro-Palestine tendency of Chinese scholars and consequently the government, little has been done to implement this preference. The Israelis still have a sizable time window to achieve a fair and just peace agreement with the Palestinians. In the long run, China's pro-Palestine inclination will work more and more against Israel, in contrast to the strong pro-Israel inclination of the United States.

# Introduction

In my 2012 article, I made the statement that China's first priority in its diplomacy is its relationship with the United States, and China seeks to maintain its relatively friendly relationship with the United States. But at the same time, China will try to balance this priority with some checks, serving as a constant reminder to the United States that without China's cooperation, the United States would be hard pressed to achieve many of its goals in the international arena. By "playing" this type of *Tai chi*, the Chinese government, on the one hand, will demonstrate to its people that it has an independent standpoint on many international issues. With this understanding, it is much easier to understand China's take on the Iranian nuclear issue, the Korean Peninsula issue, etc. On the other hand, the Chinese government is still trying to preserve the Chinese Communist Party (CCP)'s established internal consensus of foreign policy for the past three decades, i.e., *Taoguangyanghui*, or "keeping a low profile." The latter point means that China will probably never take a diametrically opposed position against the United States when the United States core national interest is in jeopardy, for obvious reasons.

Another point I made in the aforementioned article regards the important role the national mentality of being a sufferer of imperialism plays in China's foreign policy choices (Chen, 2012). This is reflected in China's sympathy with the Zionism movement more than one century ago when China was suffering from Western imperialism. It is also reflected in present day China's sympathy for the Palestinians who lost part of their homeland to the Jews during the imperialistic rule of the region.

Until 1945, China had been the sufferer of imperialism. Stemming from that, today, the mentality of a sufferer is instilled in the Chinese mind, with years of patriotic education. To understand China's attitude towards other nations and foreign matters, one has to learn the modern history of China—from the Opium Wars in 1840, through the Boxer Uprising,[1] until the Japanese invasion from 1937 to 1945. Memory of the suffering determines much of that attitude, whether it be towards Japan regarding the Diaoyu/Senkaku Island (an island lost to the imperial Japanese navy in 1895), the United States, Russia, or any European country. For that same reason, China voted against military intervention in Syria. In the Chinese mind, when China was weak, both economically and militarily, any country that had ever sent soldiers to China does not have the right to tell China what to do today, because China never sent a soldier to any of these countries.

With the above background, it becomes easier to understand China's attitude in many international affairs, including that towards the relationship between Israel and Palestine. In the case of the Palestinian–Israeli conflict, if we can say that both China and the United States are motivated to facilitate the Israeli–Palestinian peace process, while the United States tilts more towards the protection of Israel's interests, China tilts more towards helping the Arab side. This is because in the Chinese way of explaining the conflict, the State of Israel was established by allying with the imperial powers of its times, first with the British Kingdom, then with the Soviet Union, and finally with the United States. Meanwhile, the Palestinians have obviously been sufferers of imperialism. Although no public media phrases the matter this way nowadays in China, it is still deeply rooted in the thinking of the Chinese who care about this issue, specifically the scholars who publish in this field. My aforementioned article additionally argues that the Chinese also favor the Palestinians more due to reciprocity, i.e., returning the favor of the Arab countries' support for China in the international arena in the 1960s to 1970s, when China was isolated by the animosity of the West.

In this article, I will take a microscopic view that focuses on the group of scholars and journalists who have published writings on the topic of Israel and Palestine. I have also included in my data set the theses covering this topic by recent Chinese graduate students. By analyzing these papers, I want to show the quantitative evidence for the above mentioned tendency of Chinese scholars.

Later, I will explain how their views will directly influence the leaders of the country. Finally, I will also deduce from the number of publications, the fact that, in the short term, China does not have the will to, nor is it capable of, contributing significantly to the peace process.

## How the Chinese Government Makes Decisions

Many times, I am asked by American and European scholars about how the Chinese government makes decisions. My answer is simple—by listening to the Chinese scholars. The process is much more complicated in practice, however. Although China does not have a Western style democracy, its political system, especially its foreign policy decision process, is not as simple as one would imagine of a monarchical dictatorship. There are no public testimonies organized by a congress or senate committees—the Chinese People's Congress is not a policymaking body, per se. The decisions are made based on extensive consultation with China's scholars and a massive number of policy papers channeled through a multi-hierarchical think-tank system. There is a competitive mechanism for scholars to submit policy papers to different organs of the government. Via different channels, they are evaluated and selected by a quasi-peer review process, the high quality ones submitted to higher levels of government entities, eventually to the desks of the top leaders. I will not delve into the technical details of this system here.

My colleague, Daniel Bell was recently involved in a discussion with Eric Li and Yasheng Huang concerning meritocracy at the top of the Chinese Communist Party's ruling elite (Daniel, 2013).[2] Assuming Bell's meritocracy as the top theory reflects the reality of the CCP governing body, the very top of the party is to be trusted to make the right judgment calls on behalf of the whole country, since these are promoted from the bottom, and are made by very experienced managers and decision makers. However, I am going to argue later that, even though we assume the CCP's meritocracy as the top mechanism works effectively at handling domestic economic issues, it is much less effective at making foreign policy decisions due to the criteria of the diplomat selection process and the inertia of the "keep a low profile" tradition of the past several decades.

With the above mechanism of decision making explained, we can easily understand that however complicated the mechanism itself may be, decisions need to be made based on the wisdom and suggestions by each individual scholar. The "brain power" of the Chinese government depends on the total sum of all the "brains" of the Chinese intelligentsia, i.e., the scholars in various research universities and think-tanks.

## The Scholars and Their Views

What I want to do here is dissect the views of Chinese scholars on the conflict between Israelis and Palestinians. The data I will be working with are the articles published on the topic over the course of six years (1992–1994, and 2010–2012). These include scholarly articles published in peer-reviewed academic journals, travelogues, and opinions published in reputable newspapers and magazines. All articles were written in the Chinese language, published within mainland China.

Most, if not all, policy papers submitted through the system to the Ministry of Foreign Affairs and the central government are authored by these papers' authors. Their opinions reflect, to a very large extent what the government thinks, since the government has no incentive or other reason to play against its expert advisors.

Both the government think-tank and university scholars publish their scholarly works in academic journals. Luckily for us, these works reside in a centralized database system that archives all Chinese scholarly journals, especially those in the arts, humanities, and social sciences. This centralized database is called "Comprehensive online fulltext database for Chinese journals."[3] The database collects all Chinese academic journal articles in an exhaustive manner, which includes all doctoral dissertations, master's degree theses, conference proceedings, yearbooks, and articles in important newspapers published in China. There are several entry points (web portals) into the database,[4] and anyone who has access to the database can conduct exhaustive searches, as well as download full text papers.

For the purposes of this paper, searches are done in the following databases within the larger system:

1.  China Academic Journals Full-text Database

2.  China Doctoral Dissertations Full-text Database

3.  China Master's Theses Full-text Database

4.  China Proceedings of Conferences Full-text Database

5.  China Yearbooks Full-text Database

6.  China Core Newspapers Full-text Database

All searches were done in the Chinese language,[5] the search conditions defined as below: Searching against the full texts of all 1992, 1993, 1994, 2010, 2011, and 2012 data collected in the above databases, with both the term "Israel" and the term "Palestine" used in the subject.[6]

The results of each year are listed below:

1.  There were 41 search results in the year 1992, and among them, 37 relevant results have been counted. The first five results are statistical facts, counted as four (there is one repetition among these five results), and there is one repetition in the search result, thus these two are counted as one.

2.  There were 77 search results in the year 1993, and 76 relevant results counted.

3.  There were 68 search results in the year 1994, one repetition discounted, thus leaving 67 relevant results. It is easy to observe that most of the news pieces and commentaries focused on the prospect of signing a peace treaty in 1993–1994.

4.  There were 75 search results in the year 2010, with one repetition; and 74 counted.

5.  There were 77 search results in the year 2011; and all counted.

6.  There were 83 search results in the year 2012, with one repetition discounted; and altogether, 82 results counted.

This author read through all the resulting articles and gave an assessment to each. Every effort has been made to apply the same standard of assessment while reading every article.[7] Based on their individual assessments, the articles are put into one of the three following categories: (1) neutral report or conclusions (N), (2) pro-Palestinian comments or conclusions (P), and (3) pro-Israeli comments or conclusions (I).

| Percentage of Pro-Palestinian articles and Pro-Israeli articles for each year: | | | | | | | |
|---|---|---|---|---|---|---|---|
| | **Pro-Palestine** | **P%** | **Pro-Israel** | **I%** | **Neutral** | **N%** | **Total** |
| **1992** | 8 | 21.62 | 10 | 27.03 | 19 | 51.35 | 37 |
| **1993** | 7 | 9.21 | 15 | 19.74 | 54 | 71.05 | 76 |
| **1994** | 9 | 13.43 | 15 | 22.39 | 43 | 64.18 | 67 |
| **2010** | 18 | 24.32 | 7 | 9.46 | 49 | 66.22 | 74 |
| **2011** | 32 | 41.56 | 12 | 15.58 | 33 | 42.86 | 77 |
| **2012** | 32 | 39.02 | 11 | 13.41 | 39 | 47.56 | 82 |

The following graph renders the above data visually.[8]

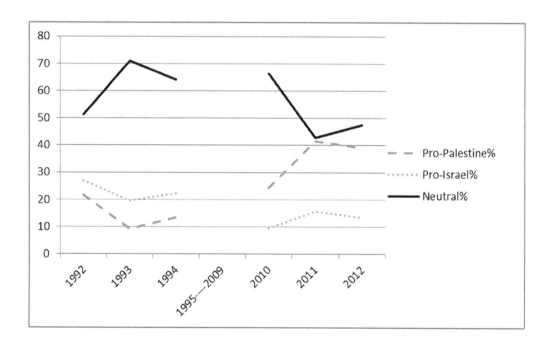

The results are quite clear—the number of articles with a P assessment dramatically increased, while the number of I and N articles have both decreased. The high percentage of I in the 1992–1994 period is understandable, since China and Israel established a formal diplomatic relationship in January of 1992. The Chinese media and scholars showed great interest in the country at the time, and these feelings were mostly positive. Before 1992, most Chinese media reports and research on the region are about the struggle of the Palestine Liberation Organization against Israel's occupation.

Chinese media is not only censored by different levels of the Chinese Communist Party's publicity entities, but is also self-censored by the authors themselves. This was especially true in the early 1990s. Therefore, after the newly established governmental relationship between China and Israel, it was unseemly to write about the negativities of Israel. To glorify the struggle of the PLO was also an obviously inappropriate subject about which to write. The Chinese media and scholars took note of this point, and joined in to celebrate the spirit of the moment. Therefore, for the small number of P articles in the 1992–1994 period that average only eight pieces per year, most of the authors were journalists stationed in the region, having firsthand knowledge of the area and conflicts on the ground. Their articles tend to be of a more narrative nature, expressing sympathy with the Palestinians. We might tentatively call the time between 1992 and 1994 the "honeymoon" period of Sino-Israel relationship.

However, when we advance to the 2010–2012 period, most, if not all of the authors of media articles and research papers have been to the region. All have firsthand knowledge of the region. The fact of actually being in Israel and Palestine did not create more admirers of Israel, but more sympathizers of the Palestinians. This is at least what is reflected by the percentage of I and P articles.

When we compare the articles from the two periods, besides the change in numbers, there is also an easily observable change in the quality and depth of the research conducted. For example, an article by Fan Hongda, "Observations of the Current Conditions of Palestinians in Hebron H2 Sector," (Fan, 2012) is based on his own extensive field trips in the city. The article came to the conclusion that is unquestionably P:

> As the only Palestinian city in which there are Jewish settlements, Hebron, especially its H2 Sector has been an epitome of Israel-Palestine conflict. Palestinians in H2 Sector have suffered too much from the neighbor settlers, Israeli police and the army. During the Second Intifada (Palestinian rising), Palestinians in H2 Sector were under more fierce attack. Even if only for the national image, Israel should change its policy and initiatives in H2 Sector. (Fan, 2012)

Another article deserves special attention here because it relates precisely to the subject I am addressing. In a 2012 article, Xu Jin asserts that Israel's public diplomacy is a failure (Xu, 2012). The article's full English abstract is quoted here:

> Since the new millennium, Israel's national image has decreased to its lowest point in the international community, even in the Western world. One of the causes is the failure of its Public Diplomacy. Israel performed very badly in its three forms of Public Diplomacy: Public Relations, Media Diplomacy and Culture Diplomacy. The main causes of its failure of Public Diplomacy included its misconception of Public Diplomacy, the outdated bureaucracy, the lack of resources and the wrong measures taken by the government. In recent years, Israeli government has increased its attentions on the Public Diplomacy while some scholars have presented a lot of policy advices on the bureaucracy adjustment and Media Diplomacy. However, we must point out

that Israel's bad national image cannot be attributed entirely to the failure of its Public Diplomacy; the more essential cause is its stubborn attitude and policy to the Palestinians. Its Public Diplomacy actually functions as an accelerator or a retarder to the tide of its national image. (Xu, 2012)

It is quite clear that this article belongs to P.[9]

As we noted above, this type of in-depth analysis with very pointed opinions and stances are becoming more and more prominent in articles published during the past three years. Nevertheless, most of the analytical articles take a neutral stance, trying to present both sides and show no favoritism to either side of the conflict.

Before 1992, other than in the army intelligence, Chinese college students could only find one place to learn Modern Hebrew, which was Peking University's Modern Hebrew Program, established in 1985. Today, there are at least a dozen Jewish/Hebrew Studies programs all over Chinese universities, [10] while the number of Islamic/Arabic Studies programs remains virtually unchanged. With this statistical background, intuitively, we would expect to see more I articles showing up. On the contrary, to our surprise, we observe a dramatic increase of the relative number of P articles. And some of the P articles are written by students and scholars who know the Hebrew language and Israeli culture very well, and had spent at least one year in Israel and Palestine.

Another perceptible fact is that there are more and more graduate level students (mostly master's degree level) who are trained in studying the region. Their theses show similar percentages of I, P, and N. This means that this future generation of scholars, most of whom will eventually hold a teaching or think-tank position, will keep the P trend going, if not accelerating it.

It is also evident that for a country the size of China, the number of total articles on this topic produced since 1992 is relatively small when compared with the number published each year in the United States.

## Implications for Chinese Foreign Policies

To be sure, the above-mentioned authors of all the articles do not represent the complete set of scholars who are influencing the Chinese government. However, many of these authors are certainly influencing the decision-making process, and many others who are not now influencing it are moving towards that role in their career path. We can safely assume that the Chinese stance on Israel and Palestine in the future will be as pro-Palestinian as today, if not more so.

Nevertheless, this does not necessarily spell trouble for Israel due to the following reasons:

First, China is becoming more and more pragmatic in terms of its foreign relationships. Economic forces are playing a more prominent role in China's foreign policy decisions. Israel still has plenty of advantages in terms of technological trade and innovations that can benefit China tremendously if cooperation is conducted in the right manner, with negative influence from the United States minimized.

Second, for the same economic reasons, China does not see many benefits to working very closely with either the Hamas, or the Fatah leadership in the political arena; this will definitely irritate Israel and the United States, while bringing no substantial economic benefits. The only value for China in helping the Palestinians is in advocating fairness in the international world, and balancing the United States pro-Israel policy in the region.

China has no intention of providing substantial financial support for the Palestinians in the form of direct foreign aid. Quite the contrary, China thinks Palestine's immediate siblings, the Arab nations, should be the source of foreign aid to them. Furthermore, there is already a plethora of Western European and American aid to the region competing with itself.

This strategy of no direct foreign aid does not prevent China from experimenting with economic involvement to indirectly influence the political balance in the region so that China can be considered a proactive actor in the peace process. For example, this author led a 30 member delegation of business people, investors, and think-tank scholars to visit the city of Ramallah in February of 2012, in search of economic partnership and investment opportunities. The team met members from the Palestine Investment Fund, the Bank of Palestine, the Palestine Monetary Authority, the Palestine Security Exchange, the Arab Palestine Investment Company, the Amaar Real Estate Group, the PALTEL (Palestine Telecommunications Company) Group, Wataniya Mobile, PADICO (Palestine Development and Investment Company) Holding, the Palestine Economic Policy Research Institute, MADAR (the Palestinian Forum for Israeli Studies), Birzeit University, and the Palestinian Authority government officials.

As this was the first time visiting the region for most of the members of the delegation, they did not go back to China impressed by the business and investment opportunities in Palestine. The size of the population and economy are not attractive to Chinese investors and entrepreneurs, especially after experiencing firsthand the hindrance of Israel's security measures put onto Palestine's economic development. The complicated visa application process, the security checks between Ramallah and Jerusalem, the time-consuming security scrutiny in Tel Aviv airport, even with the top-down green light from the Israeli government for expediting the group's movement, as well as the omnipresent complaints by the Palestinians in every meeting against Israel's human-imposed limitations on all aspects of economic development and trades, all collectively influenced the investors to respond most politely to our survey regarding whether that they might consider Palestine as a destination for trade or investment when there is a stable peace agreement between Israel and Palestine. To our surprise, many of the Chinese Muslim members who had extensive business experience in the Middle East expressed the most pragmatic attitude in this regard. This fact further confirms my earlier statement about economic factors weighing more prominently in terms of Chinese (at least business people's) views towards Israel and Palestine.

Economic factors on both the Israeli and Palestinian sides work favorably for Israel. That is, the attractiveness of Israel and the unattractiveness of Palestine in terms of economic cooperation point in the opposite direction of the mental and intellectual preferences of the Chinese scholars and journalists. Now, facing the dichotomy between the economically driven market forces and the conscious driven scholarly forces, we want to weigh which will play a more prominent role and guide the future direction of China's policy towards the Israel–Palestine conflict.

## Future Directions

This author believes for now and the foreseeable future, economic gravity will play a more prominent role in influencing Chinese foreign policy decisions. Factors other than economic considerations will evolve to be more significant over time during China's transition from a just-achieved economic powerhouse to a country more concerned with international rules and fairness, sustainability of international peace, and its own development environment.

I stated that economic factors grab all the attention and weigh heavily in China's foreign policy, including that in the Middle East, because that has been the case in China's domestic development for the past three decades. China has successfully focused all energy and resources on domestic economic development for 30 years because the pivotal leader Deng Xiaoping correctly concluded that most of China's international suffering was due to the country's weakness in economic development. During the period of internal development, Deng put forward the strategy of "Hide our capabilities and bide our time," or a better translation of the Chinese term *Taoguangyanghui*, "Keep a low profile" while handling international affairs. As a consequence, China has successfully trained a plethora of elite governors and strategists specialized in economic growth. In the foreign relations arena, albeit with the efficient meritocracy, no visionaries emerged. Chinese diplomats of all levels are used to handling international matters by passively doing nothing, because there is no need to develop independent strategies. Keep a low profile is *the* strategy; all they need to do is implement it. Consequently, there are few strategists among the elite of the foreign policy team. What China has is a team of diplomats who are reactive responders to events as they unfold. China has no creators of events to begin with. China is too accustomed to seeing the show as a passive audience. China never ran a show before, and does not have the ambition to run one now. In such an environment, it is not hard to understand why economic factors are still the predominant force pushing forward most, if not all, foreign affair decisions.

However, the situation is changing. We have at least two indicators pointing in this direction.

First, the new leadership might break the momentum of the non-interference and non-involvement policy in the Middle East region. Even though non-interference is still the official policy concerning Syria, the fact that Chinese businesses, especially state-owned businesses that have suffered tremendously after Kadhafi's fall in Libya, [11] have already caused multiple entities within the Chinese government and think-tank circles to conduct in-depth discussions to evaluate the potential damage to Chinese interests in the Middle East if al-Assad falls. The new Chinese leadership's high profile confrontation against Japan regarding the East China Sea Diaoyu/Senkaku Islands demonstrates the departure from a low profile stance in international affairs. The control of the island by China will undoubtedly bring economic benefits such as oil and gas resources. But materializing these resources can take quite some time, and is not necessarily an attractive financial investment in the short run. The main purpose of the hawkish show is that it is trying to reclaim the island lost over a century ago. For every Chinese, the government's stance makes a very strong statement: China is no longer a weak country to be bullied by all imperialist powers, as was the case more than a century ago—China is an economic and military power capable of claiming what is rightly China's. This is justice, and China wants to see justice served in the international arena.

This Chinese stance will inevitably spread to all foreign affair concerns, including the Middle East. The following quote from a retired diplomat summarizes the official point of view of the Chinese (note particularly to the statement "China's Middle East policy upholds the principle of supporting the justice side"):

> The complex contemporary situation in the Middle East is created by many factors, most of which are closely around the religious, ethnic and territorial conflicts. The formation of these conflicts has its historical reasons. The historical experiences of Palestinian Arabs and Jews determine their different fundamental positions. Modern Zionism, regarded as the initiator of the Middle East problem, has profound impact on Israeli domestic politics. The United Nations Partition Plan for Palestine and the founding of the state of Israel lead to the contemporary Arab–Israeli conflict. The interests of major powers including the United States are concealed behind the conflicts, and China's strategic interests are closely related to the conflicts in the Middle East. In such context, China's Middle East policy upholds the principle of supporting the justice side, and actively involves in peaceful settlement of the question of Palestine. (Sun 2010)[12]

The ideology of the leadership and the scholarly inclination favoring the Palestinians is one thing, but for this inclination to be implemented in foreign policies and tobe effectively executed is quite another. Between them, there is a huge gap needing to be bridged by nothing less than sincere political reform towards a truly democratic social system. This is something that even the new leadership has not shown the courage to tackle. For now, the government can only test the waters with the Diaoyu Islands, and hopefully will not lose control of its own people's support while stretching its muscle with the Japanese in the process. If this exercise turns out to be successful, China might start to consider places as far away as the Middle East, which has never been an important part of China's foreign strategy after the Zhou Enlai years and the Bandung Conference.

The second indicator is the central government, admitting several years ago that the educational system in China had not trained enough talent to work on issues in the Middle East. Relying on the few scholars trained in the West will not be enough to implement any strategy. The Ministry of Education realized this shortcoming and has since been encouraging "regional studies" among the top universities. One prominent achievement of this effort is that plenty of younger generation Chinese scholars are sent to the region to gain firsthand knowledge. Most of them come back with a more pro-Palestinian stance. Their inclination is already revealed and will be more so in the government's foreign policies. We might be witnessing the turning point at this juncture, though the above two indicators do not spell death for the pro-Israeli elements.

Nevertheless, the efficiency of the initiative of the Ministry of Education is admittedly doubtful. Academic corruption has diverted the large influx of funds to existing interest groups in academe that have nothing to do with regional studies. Lack of transparency is as serious an issue in academia as it is in the Chinese government. No meritocracy system is a substitute for built in checks and balances.

The United States as an influential factor in Chinese foreign policy is also not to be ignored. The children of many of prominent Palestinian politicians, including many of those of diplomats themselves, are studying in United States universities. They tend to adopt moderate thinking during their studies, and are influencing their parents and other compatriots. This is also the case for Chinese children, who bring back to China a more pro-Israeli attitude from United States campuses. Eventually, these two camps will merge, and together, they will also merge with the Israeli moderates. Perhaps for both Israel and Palestine, a faster reconciliation in the short term between the two is best for both, particularly Israel. Since the longer we wait for the final peace deal to be made, the more likely the Middle East will see a more pro-Palestine China wanting to voice its opinions. With the weakening United States influence in the region, and the growing clout of China, whether China turned fully democratic or not, the odds are not favoring Israel.

# Notes

1. The incident refers to the Eight-Nation Alliance intervention in China during the Boxer Uprising in 1900; it was an alliance of Austria–Hungary, France, Germany, Italy, Japan, Russia, the United Kingdom, and the United States military forces.2. Regarding these top leaders qualification and selection process, see Li, E. X. (2013). The life of the party. *Foreign Affairs, 92*(1), 34–46; and the rebuke of Huang, Y. (2013). Democratize or die. *Foreign Affairs, 92*(1), 47–54.

2. The database is published by *China Academic Journals Electronic Publishing House*, technology is powered by Tongfang Knowledge Network Technology Co., Ltd (Beijing). The latter was one of the publicly traded companies fully backed by the famous Tsinghua University, the alma mater of both the Chinese president Hu Jintao, and his son Hu Haifeng, who used to work for this company.

3. The most important Chinese portal is http://www.cnki.net/. There is also an English portal, http://oversea.cnki.net/kns55/, both retrieved January 26, 2013. However, preliminary testing proves that searching with English keywords using the English version does not work properly, with a search term "Israel and Palestine" returning two results for the year 2012, with only one being relevant. Even searching a single term "Palestine" does not work properly, with 69 results; and within these results, more than half are irrelevant. For the search results using Chinese terms, please see below.

4. See note above regarding the ineffectiveness of searching using the English language.

5. The Chinese language uses the same set of characters to represent both the noun and the adjective forms, as well as the nationality designation; thus, whereas in English, one would have to use "Israel," "Israeli," "Palestine," and "Palestinian" etc., possibly with a wildcard to exhaustively search anything related to Israel and Palestine, just one term is needed in Chinese for anything related to Israel, and one term for anything related to Palestine.

6. One has to admit that it is hard to keep an absolutely objective standard during the evaluation process. Nevertheless, as we can see from the overwhelming trend in the result chart, even with some misses to one or two articles here and there, it is still within the tolerable margin of error, and does not affect the result significantly.

7. Due to time constraint, this author has not conducted an exhaustive reading of all the articles published between 1995 and 2009. The following table (2) listed the number of total articles resulting from the same search criteria for these 15 years.

| 1995 | 1996 | 1997 | 1998 | 1999 | 2000 | 2001 | 2002 | 2003 | 2004 | 2005 | 2006 | 2007 | 2008 | 2009 |
|------|------|------|------|------|------|------|------|------|------|------|------|------|------|------|
| 70 | 88 | 66 | 82 | 49 | 82 | 121 | 170 | 115 | 91 | 88 | 162 | 129 | 102 | 109 |

8. For readers who are interested in knowing the basis on which Xu Jin drew his conclusion, here are the English sources he quoted in his article (there are an additional 10 Chinese sources that I will not list here; I did not re-format the search engine output): Shils, E., & Cutler, D. R. (1968). Ritual and crisis. *The Religious Situation*. Boston, MA: Beacon; Entman, R. (2004). Projections of power: Framing news, public opinion, and United States foreign policy. Chicago, IL: University of Chicago Press; Iraq and peace in the world. Retrieved from http://ec.europa.eu/public_opinion/flash/fl151oniraq_en.pdf;

Trevor, A., & Cassie, W. (2010). The BBC and the Middle East: The documentary campaign, 2000–2004. Retrieved from http://www.bbcwatch.co.uk/...; Paulin, T. (2013). In Wikipedia: The free encyclopedia. Retrieved March 24, 2013, from http://en.wikipedia.org/w/index.php?title=Tom_Paulin&oldid=539379561; Joshua, M. (2003) Covering the Intifada: How the media reported the Palestinian uprising; Bret, S. (2002). What's wrong with Israel's Hasbara? *Jerusalem Post*; Shaul, R. S., Tamir, S., & Itay, G. (2010). Incoherent narrator: Israeli Public Diplomacy during the disengagement and the elections in the Palestinian Authority. *Israel Studies*; Ronit, A., Assaf, I., Steven S., & Ayela, Z. (2008). Culture diplomacy: An important but neglected tool in promoting Israel's public image. Retrieved from http://portal.idc.ac.il/SiteCollectionDocuments/Cultural_Diplomacy.pdf; Margalit, T., & David, M. (2007). Social integration and public relations: Global lessons from an Israeli experience. *Public Relations Journal, 33*(4), 387-397; Human Rights Watch Report (2010). Jenin: IDF military operations. Retrieved from http://www.hrw.org; and Phil, R. (2002). Even journalists are wrong sometimes. *The Independent*; Gary R. (2005). Marketing a new image. *New York Jewish Week*.

9. I am aware of the following universities: Peking University, Beijing Foreign Studies University, Beijing University of Communications, Shanghai Foreign Studies University, Fudan University (Biblical Hebrew only), Nanjing University, Nanjing Jinling Theological Seminary (Biblical Hebrew only), Sichuan Foreign Studies University, Sichuan University (Biblical Hebrew only), Shandong University, Henan University, Luoyang Foreign Studies University, and The Central University for Nationalities (Biblical Hebrew only), etc.

10. The amount of losses in investment by China is hard to gauge, the number revealed by different authorities changes along with the development of the event. For an earlier version, see "China counting financial losses in Libya," Retrieved October 2, 2011, from http://english.sina.com/china/p/2011/0303/362644.html; for a different (relatively later) version, see "China's investment in Libya is more than $20 billion and the amount of loss is difficult to estimate," Retrieved October 2, 2011, from http://chonzfashion.hubpages.com/hub/Chinas-investment-in-Libya-is-more-than-20-billion-and-the-amount-of-loss-is-difficult-to-estimate

11. The author is H. H. Ambassador Sun Bigan, a retired diplomat who served as the Chinese ambassador to Saudi Arabia, Iraq and Iran.

# PART SIX

## Communication, Media, and the Arab Awakening

The Arab Spring or Arab Awakening and its bloody aftermath in the affected countries can be described as the tweeted and blogged revolutions of this era. Arab citizens used everything from the Internet (netizens) and blogs (bloggers) and Twitter (tweeters) to social media (Facebook, LinkedIn) to broadcast the revolution and to inform their own and the outside world of events in their respective countries. Their messages had more credibility than the old government-controlled media. The freedom enjoyed by the Arab netizens contributed to a larger sense of empowerment as people revolted in Tunisia, Egypt, Libya, and Yemen and to some extent in the continued struggle in Syria and Bahrain. Dr. Aman and Tina Jayroe examine the impact of the Arab Spring on state-controlled media in Egypt, the growing citizens' demands for more say in the way they are governed, the end of government corruption, and the end of abuse of power and neglect of people's welfare and wellbeing. Before there was an Arab Spring, Arab bloggers took to the infosphere to express their criticism of their autocratic systems of government and their abuse of human and civil rights of Arab citizens. Blogging was not a safe haven either and was just as dangerous as writing for a local newspaper, or marching in anti-government demonstrations. Arab bloggers have been arrested, tortured, and even killed at the hands of the hated and uncontrolled security forces.

Aman and Jayroe extend the treatment of the Arab media to cover other MENA countries beyond those directly impacted by the Arab Spring. In their paper, they examine the effect and influence the new information, telecommunication, and social media (ITC & SM) have on events preceding and following the Arab Spring. The recent use of the Internet, mobile communications devices, smartphones, and social media like Twitter and Facebook, has demonstrated how access to the newer media has circumvented the established and government-controlled media such as the print media, and radio and television. According to their investigation, while Arab citizens' use of these technologies vary due to economic and education levels, when combined with word of mouth, sermons and gatherings at Friday prayers and Sunday sermons were instrumental in rallying and organizing Muslim and Copt demonstrators against their dictators.

Dr. Wafa addresses the implications of training programs aimed at creating a professional cadré that engages the state-controlled media in Egypt to be a true watchdog for democracy and public interest. Like Aman, Wafa points out that in Egypt, the media played a significant role after the January 25th Revolution in how the public lost trust in the state-controlled media throughout the Arab world. In Egypt, the state-owned and run media continued its support of the Mubarak regime long after his downfall. Wafa points to the fact that, following the Arab Spring, the state-controlled media faced several challenges in gaining public trust, maintaining professionalism, and partnering with the public in demanding transparency and accountability in governance while exposing corruption. There are growing debates among journalists on the proper role of the media in post-revolution Egypt, especially on the issue of freedom of expression and dedication to truth and public service.

Dr. Ivan S. Sheehan uses content analysis to explore how the Iranian dissident organization Mujahedin-e Khalq (MEK) promoted its frames in the opinion sections of major world news publications over nine years (2003–2012) by critically examining arguments for and against supporting the organization and further considers the implications of the United States' embrace of the group for security interests. His research and findings show that by nurturing small opportunities, marginalized political actors can expand media capacity and influence. These effects, he pointed out, are mediated, at least in part, by critical or focusing events that make rival frames less salient as well as implications for American foreign policy in the region.

# ICT, Social Media, and the Arab Transition to Democracy: From Venting to Action

## Mohammed M. Aman
## Tina J. Jayroe

## Abstract

There is widespread use of Information and Communications Technology (ICT) in the Middle East and North African (MENA) countries. Blogging and social media have played an important role in the recent calls for reform and change. Using these new communication systems and devices, citizens have been venting their anger and frustration with their autocratic governments and rulers. Most recently, the venting has turned into action, as shown by the eradication of the old regimes in Tunisia, Egypt, Libya, and Yemen, as well as the ongoing struggle in Syria. The most notable issues include lack of individual freedoms, deteriorating economic conditions, high unemployment, increased corruption, and violent treatment of citizens at the hands of security forces. The Arab Spring, or Awakening, and the events that have since followed have, in part, been promoted by ICT and other means of modern communications. Along with the popular Arab traditions of oral communication as well as Friday and Sunday sermons at mosques and churches, social media were used by organizers of the Arab Spring to call for and coordinate demonstrations against the regimes. Access to this newer media has circumvented the established and government-controlled media such as printed press, radio, and television—outlets bent on appeasing the rulers and misinforming the masses. Arab authoritarian systems have discovered that they cannot simply flip a big red switch to stop the flow of information they would rather keep hidden from the masses. Further discussed are digital democracies that are currently emerging due to the growing population of netizens, bloggers, and social media political activists throughout the Arab world, and the many attempts to silence them.

*Look at what's happening right now in Tahrir Square in Egypt. One of the most spectacular demonstrations of popular activism of courage and determination that I can remember. They are not following leaders. In fact, what's striking, dramatically striking is how self-organized it is. People are forming defense communities to protect themselves against Government thugs, they are forming groups to develop policies, to reach out to others. That's the way things happen.*

—Noam Chomsky, 2011

## Introduction

Since the early part of the 20th century when electronic mass communication media was introduced, it has been managed by Arab governments who realize the importance of controlling and manipulating public opinion. The physical facilities and contents of their broadcasts are strictly controlled; staff have always been employees of the government. Evidence of the vital importance of radio and television can be observed in the physical presence of army and security forces and military tanks guarding the buildings of radio, television, and even major newspaper buildings (CPJ, [Committee to Protect Journalists] 2012). Armed forces and strict access to these buildings without prior authorization and body search of the general public is the norm. There are reasons for this, as most of the previous military coups against Arab governments have targeted these institutions in the same way they targeted royal or presidential palaces, telecommunication facilities, and other important ministerial buildings and military establishments. Cognizant of the ubiquity, importance, and dangers of the Internet infosphere, Arab regimes are trying to catch up with new communication technologies—that is, how to control and censor them.

On January 24, 2010, the Arab ministers of information met in Cairo and approved a joint proposal by the Egyptian and Saudi governments for the creation of a regional office to supervise Arab satellite TV channels (El-Amrani, 2010). The targeted TV satellites for closing by Arab governments included *Al Jazeera*, Hamas's *Al-Aqsa TV*, and Hezbollah's *Al-Manar*. Qatar and Lebanon opposed the plan, while Egypt and Saudi Arabia supported it. One of the most recent examples of a similar type of enforcement is the Arab governments' insistence on installing spyware on smartphones, even before the Arab Spring uprisings (Barrett, 2012).

In order to examine the link between MENA's citizens' demands for democracy and the role of the new media technology, it is helpful to look at the Internet penetration in these countries, which have a combined total population of 367 million, which is 5.2% of the world's population (*Emirates24/7*, 2011).

The MENA region currently has 65 million Internet users (Sajbl, 2012). Statistics published in 2013 predict Internet penetration in MENA countries will be at 150 million users, with 25 million handheld devices expected across the region by 2016 (*Arabian Gazette*, 2013). This increase comes "in response to plummeting charges, improved services, and expanding competition among service providers" (Janardhan, 2011, p. 231). Social networks like Facebook and Twitter enjoy a dominant presence among Arab users. Facebook has more than 34 million Arab-speaking users compared to world subscribers of 800 million (Internet World Stats, 2011).

This rapid penetration of the Internet and blogosphere among Arab netizens in recent years has helped the push for political, social, and economic reform in their respective countries by elucidating the unjust prosecution of bloggers and microbloggers (i.e., Twitter users) by Arab security forces. However, it has also resulted in the government's shutdown of websites and Internet cafés. A 2004 study by the Arabic Network of Human Rights Information reported some 400,000 web pages had been banned and filtered in Saudi Arabia alone to protect "'Islamic values and culture'…. The Saudi government also blocked several Shiite and other Islamic Web sites that offer interpretations different from the official Wahhabi line" (Fisher, 2004).

Although some of the Arab demonstrations demanding change in the status quo have been peaceful, their governments have decided to unleash deadly force in their attempts to crush any uprisings, rather than responding to calls for dialogue and reforms. In the case of Egypt, how new technology played an effective role in the January 2011 revolution and the regime change is well documented (Howard, Duffy, Freelon, Mari, & Mazaid, 2011; Lotan et al., 2011; Maynard, 2013; Neon Tommy, 2011).

Egypt joined Tunisia which ousted its strongman Zein Abedeen Bin Ali in a similar peaceful revolt. In both Egypt and Tunisia, the new media technologies—in contrast to old ones—played a pivotal role in the revolutions. Egyptian and Tunisian netizens constructed e-communities that helped to expose the corrupt political and economic systems in their own and other Arab countries. These e-communities helped to mobilize the demonstrations, disseminate news from inside those events, and attracted global media attention to what was taking place in the countries. A 2003 RAND Foundation Report (discussed in more detail later) had predicted what could and would happen in the Arab world as a result of the impact of media technology on citizens' calls for democratic systems of government in MENA countries.

The infosphere tends to draw young Arabs into the outside world and opens their eyes to a wider global picture different from the one brought to them by their local censored media. Their access to the new media allows them to compare their poor situations and living conditions to those fortunate others among their own countrymen who are members of a privileged ethnic, sectarian, political, or regime-connected group. Such comparisons magnify their unfortunate lot and give impetus to rising demands for a piece of the pie and for the end of oppression, discrimination, government corruption, and misinformation. According to some young Shi'a demonstrators in Bahrain, their anger and resentment grew stronger when they surfed Google Earth and discovered how their fellow Sunni Bahrainis lived in better homes and neighborhoods compared to the cramped and poorer standard of living dwellings in their Shi'a neighborhoods—within the same country (Lubin, 2011). Access to social media like YouTube, Twitter, Facebook, LinkedIn, and others has enabled young Arabs to share and vent their dissatisfaction with like-minded political and social activists. However, this expression often comes at a high cost.

As the short-lived Arab Spring turns into the present Arab nightmare—case in point, Egypt, Libya, and Syria—the development of new media is growing in importance and accessibility to Arabs who continue to be unhappy with the unfortunate turn of events post-Arab Spring. Other Arab rulers watch with apprehension the aftermath of the Arab Spring and the monarchies that are attempting to fend off potential revolts in their own countries by promising reforms, increasing citizens' salaries, subsidizing food stuffs, forgiving mortgage loans, and attempting to persuade their subjects that change should be brought about slowly and without violence. On the other hand, there are internal and external forces that are also bent on pushing their own extreme agendas and hijacking the Arab revolutions that terminated old regimes in the hopes of replacing them with freely elected democratic regimes. Muslim fundamentalists, Salafis, political Islamists, internal anarchists, and sectarianists are equally responsible for political unrest and economic paralysis in the region.

There is no doubt that there is the need for political social change, but there are concerns about how fast and in which direction. The Saudi Shi'a are the agents of political change and liberalization of the Saudi political system. The Shi'a minority have been treated as second class citizens. Their books, websites, and electronic communications are subject to monitoring and censorship (US Department of State, 2004). Religious conservative voices are becoming louder than those calling for political and social reforms and are thus, exerting more pressure on respective Arab governments. Hence, Arab rulers become torn between the push for reform and liberalization, and the pull from conservatives and religious extremists. The latter enjoy more appeal among the masses, the poor, and the illiterate technophobic which unfortunately remain the majority in all Arab countries. In Saudi Arabia, King Abdullah has called for reforms and for giving women limited rights in response to their repeated demands, but there has been a clash with the powerful and extremely organized religious extremists (Tétreault, Okruhlik, & Kapiszewski, 2011).

The conflict between the push for reform and the pull for traditional and extreme Islamic values is expressed by the Grand Mufti of Saudi Arabia who issued a *fatwa* declaring that Saudi liberals are just as dangerous as militant religious extremists (Boustany, 2004). In September 2008, the Islamists called on Saudi leaders to act against "dangerous liberal ideology," and demanded a halt to media campaigns that "promote vice and evil" (Al-Hakeem, 2008). Unfortunately, the post-revolutions' developments in the MENA region are showing clear signs of less tolerance for freedom of expression, free press/media, respect for citizens' dignity, and the rule of law. Arab regimes may have changed, but unfortunately the culture of oppression and suppression of expression remains unaltered, and expectations are that Arabs are taking to the infosphere to force a change.

## The Rise of Digital Democracy

In order to place the Arab Awakening in the context of the digital age, one has to examine the extent of the Internet and social network penetration in the Arab countries. Published sources and statistics such as Internet World Stats Usage and Population Statistics, BuddeCom, and others reveal a growing trend among the young generation of Arabs to use the Internet, social media, wireless communications, and other blogging tools more readily than their parents.

Janardhan (2011) in his chapter entitled "New media: In search of equilibrium" focuses on developments related to the new media in the Gulf Cooperation Council (GCC) countries in the context of media coverage of events in the Gulf, particularly in Iraq. These developments vary by country. Some, like Kuwait, Saudi Arabia, and Bahrain, are actively engaged, while others, like Qatar and the United Arab Emirates, have shown more caution in media experiments. There is a correlation between the economic conditions of an Arab country and the level of Internet penetration (Burkhart & Older, 2003, pp. 48–49). The poorer the country, the less Internet penetration, as the following 2011 figures affirm: Lebanon, 33%; Jordan, 30.5%; Egypt, 26.4%; Syria, 19.8%; Algeria, 13.4%; Yemen, 10.8%; Sudan, 11.4%; Libya, 5.9%; and Iraq, 4.3% (Internet World Stats, 2011).

While the Internet and social media connectivity played a major role in the Arab Spring, wireless communications played an even larger role as mobile and smart phones, texting, and recording are more popular among young Arabs. Of the 30 million Egyptians with Internet access, 70% only use mobile devices and do not access the Web via desktop systems (Internet World Stats, 2012a); in fact, the country has the highest level of mobile-only Internet usage in the world (MobiThinking, 2010). This mobile technology was a valuable and effective communicative tool when the dictatorial regimes blocked Internet access from personal computers.

The combination of communication technology and social media have expanded the already widely used "word of mouth" in the Arab culture of oral communication in addition to the popular rumor and gossip mills among the uneducated masses. Gatherings after prayers at local mosques and churches and major squares—such as Tahrir

Square in Cairo and El-Kornich in Alexandria, among others—have also played a major role in communicating across the then leaderless revolution. Sympathizers around the demonstrations' gathering places collaborated to "re-create" the barred networks using the still-available technologies which consisted of landlines, dial-up modems, and ham radios in order to facilitate communication among demonstrators. Residents around Tahrir Square removed passwords from their wireless networks so protesters could connect and reach the outside world monitoring the events.

New communication technology triumphed over the old-fashioned regime propaganda thanks to satellite TV and a variety of Internet news sources and blogs (Deen, 2004). Such ICTs were also helpful to the protesters. The new electronic media helped liberalize Arab political culture and boost fledgling reform movements. They are also credited with breaking the monopoly of state-owned, government-controlled broadcast systems that have dominated the region. Arab Internet opposition has been transformed into social and democratic reform movements. Conventional media in Arab countries have been engaged in deflecting and ignoring local and regional social and economic problems and by railing against the old-fashioned slogans of American imperialism and the unsolved Israeli–Palestinian dispute. The state-sponsored media was, by design, blind to domestic news: for example, there is no coverage of intellectual developments or human interest stories (Alterman, 1998). Government-sponsored Arab media has continuously downplayed any opposition and ignored opposition leaders or demonized them as foreign agents, enemies of the state, Muslim extremists, terrorists, al-Qaʿida sympathizers, drug addicts, among other labels used by government broadcasters from Tunis, Cairo, Tripoli, and Yemen before their dictators were removed from power.

Prior to the Arab Awakening, ICT provided channels of expression that acted as a safety valve, allowing pent-up frustrations with the regimes and economic, political, and social problems to be vented without adverse political consequences for authoritarian Arab regimes, while opening a space for political participation among the citizens. But when some of the Arab Spring governments showed their bloody hands, the venting turned into action, as we have seen in Tunisia, Egypt, and Yemen.

## Blocking and Blogging

It is no secret that, with very few exceptions, most Arab countries have no working democratic systems of government and the ruling regimes are usually described as the most repressive and dictatorial regimes in our modern times. Tunisian and Egyptian regimes in particular have long been classified as the top providers among Internet users and bloggers of political activists critical of their respective regimes. However, they are also known for blocking access to the Web and blogs. This procedure is an organized, government-sanctioned process that goes beyond religious and moral claims, but is extended to and includes what these governments view as political and social activism, criticism of the internal affairs of the country, its leadership, and any content that government officials and censors consider objectionable on any grounds they choose.

In 2003, the RAND Corporation produced a report on information technology in the MENA countries. The report's authors analyzed the core results of research and conference papers about the state of information technology (IT) in the area and forecast what would happen in MENA countries with regard to catching up with the IT revolution. The main conclusion was that countries of the area—with the exception of Turkey and Israel—"will miss the information revolution" because of the "irregular pattern of ICT diffusion and use" (Burkhart & Older, 2003, pp. ix, x). Because the governing regimes of these countries have such strict regulations on the dissemination of information, and because creating a reliable IT infrastructure is not a priority (except in the United Arab Emirates), as new media communication tools become ubiquitous, the authorities' priority becomes controlling information resources and all methods of information circulation. Thus, as communication satellites and wireless communications spread throughout the region, they move quickly to control the infosphere for fear of rising demands for democracy and the rule of law.

Arab governments, with support from their local Internet service providers, are known to send fake pages in order to attract political activists to log in while government officials monitor users. Political bloggers and Internet activists criticizing their governments are subjected to imprisonment, torture, and death. In 2003, "a Tunisian teacher and journalist called 'Umm Ziyad' was imprisoned for a month because she criticized in a blog the education policy in Tunisia" (Khalifa, 2012). Under Mubarak's regime, the "Muslim Brotherhood" and "al-'Amal Party" sites were blocked for many years. During the January 2011 demonstrations, several sites such as Facebook, Twitter, and *The Original Dostor* newspaper were blocked because of their active role in promoting and organizing the demonstrations.

Former Egyptian president Hosni Mubarak's National Party employed many young people to perform government-sanctioned and financed operations, such as promoting his plan of—upon his death—passing on to his elder son Gamal the presidency of the country. The government was engaged in improving the picture of Mubarak and the governing National Party by establishing thousands of fake accounts, groups, and pages for the purpose of supporting Gamal Mubarak and his political party, and also for attacking leaders of the opposition, such as Mohamed El-Baradei & Ayman Nour. The counter group "6th April Youth Movement" uncovered the fake accounts and published the list to warn Facebook members.

Egyptian authorities have also been engaged in blocking and disrupting telecommunication services, aided by national Internet providers such as TE DATA, the largest Internet service provider in the country, which has been charged with blocking websites. The company offers programs that block sex sites, but it also blocks political blogs. The providers of cellphones and Internet services revealed that their signed contracts with the government require them to cut off services upon receiving official requests/orders from the Egyptian government authorities (Khalifa, 2012).

In Tunisia, many non-Tunisian sites were blocked; among them the Egyptian news site *al-Misryun* and the *Arabic News Network*. For Tunisian sites, there are many examples such as: *al-Kalimah*, *Al Bawwabah*, *Al-Nahdah Net*, and *Tunis News*. The most famous case involved blocking Facebook and YouTube. The deposed Ben Ali's government has had a long history of attacking political opponents and regularly monitoring and hacking opponents' e-mail and their Facebook and Twitter accounts.

These are just a few examples among many reported by various organizations monitoring government corruption and abuses. Next is a survey of specific cases, plus evidence of the governments' extreme measures to prevent the free flow of information, and the people's utilization of ICT in order to identify the governments' abuses.

## The Revolution Was Blogged and Tweeted

Tunisia and Egypt were listed on the 2006 by Reporters Without Borders "roll of shame" as two of the top 13 Internet enemies for repression of intellectual freedom on the Internet (Reporters Without Borders, 2006). Opposition to the respective regimes used the Internet and then later, the increasingly popular Facebook application began in 2008, with Twitter coming shortly thereafter. These were used as the tools of choice for mobilizing and managing demonstrations. Young people especially were able to broadcast the January 25th revolution live on the Web, Twitter, Facebook, and various blogs.

## Tunisia

The Tunisian younger population is growing, with a median age of 30.5 years old, and approximately 23% of the nearly 11 million Tunisians are under the age of 14 (Central Intelligence Agency, 2013a). They rely on the Internet and mobile phones for credible sources of news, information and social connectivity with 93 mobile phone subscribers for every 100 Tunisians. Approximately 25% of Tunisians use the Internet, and some 60% of the Tunisian population stays connected to the Internet throughout the day. Tunisian females are equally active, with more than 30% of Tunisian females reported as active users and contributors to Twitter. Forty-two percent of Tunisian females are regular users of Facebook, and 48% use LinkedIn (Maynard, 2013). Women were among the most active political bloggers, Internet users and critical opponents of the old regime; they posted in French and Arabic lamenting economic corruption, lack of freedom, and demanding a democratically-elected government. They exposed the Tunisian president and his family—such as with the graphically simple video of the President's plane arriving and leaving Europe's elite destinations, with his wife as the only passenger. The uploading of that video to YouTube prompted the Tunisian bureaucrats to crack down, not only on YouTube, but Facebook and others (Howard et al., 2011), and unintentionally accelerated the revolt against their corrupt president.

Mohammed Bouazizi, a street peddler and protester who had had enough with police brutality and humiliation decided to self-immolate himself in public. Sami Ben Gharbia, a leading Tunisian exile and online activist (globalvoicesonline.org/author/sami-ben-gharbia; https://twitter.com/ifikra), and founder of Nawaat (nawaat.org/portail), hosts a Tunisian collective blog which was an aggregator of these events. Together, these acts and activists gave strength to a movement that culminated with the end of Ben Ali's reign on January 14, 2011 (Radsch, 2012). These occurrences in Tunisia were eerily similar to what was to come for Egypt.

## Egypt

Egypt ranks first among Arab countries for Internet use ("List of countries by number Internet users", 2013). Where the median age is 24.8, nearly 33% of Egypt's 84 million Egyptians are under the age of 14 (Central Intelligence Agency, 2013b). The use of IT among that age group is prevalent. Egyptians under the age of 34 (70% of the population) are Internet savvy. Nearly 10% of Egyptians use the Internet, with females comprising 36% of Egypt's Facebook population. Egyptian women made up 33% of the Egyptians actively Tweeting inside Egypt during the revolution. Women like Esraa Abdel Fattah of the Egyptian Democratic Academy became vocal opponents to the regime, and Leila-Zahra Mortada documented women's involvement in the revolution with a popular Facebook album.

The earliest user of the infosphere and blogosphere among the opposition movements was the *Kefaya* (or *Kifaya*) "Enough" movement, a website created in 2004 about Egyptian elections. It preluded the youth revolt of the Arab Spring of January 2011 and "was the first political initiative in Egypt to truly explore and capitalize on new social media and digital technology as its main means of communication and mobilization" (Carnegie Endowment for International Peace, 2010). Egypt's opposition has since relied on blogging and social media to call for reform and subsequently to mobilize the masses and coordinate the revolution.

Active young bloggers have covered the government's abuses of human rights, corruption, and fabricated elections—issues not covered by the obedient, government-controlled, and bankrolled media. The blogosphere and mobile phones became the popular means of physically rallying opposition to Hosni Mubarak's regimes in public squares across Egypt (Sakr, 2007), and many of these bloggers have suffered for their actions at the hands of Mubarak's secret police. In 2007, Egyptian blogger Abdul Kereem Suleiman was sentenced to four years in prison for writing online about sectarian clashes in Alexandria—"The case represents the first time that an Egyptian blogger has stood trial and been sentenced for his work" (CPJ, 2007). "Free Kareem" rallies were held in April 2007 in cities as diverse as Athens, Berlin, Bucharest, London, Oslo, Ottawa, Prague, Rome, and Washington, DC.

In the 2007 article "Egypt's bloggers do it better," the online European magazine *CaféBabel* cited Reporters Without Borders stating that Egyptian bloggers were "not only commentators, but they also engage in investigative journalism" (Sankowska, 2007). The article goes on to mention that in November 2006, Egyptians posted a video on YouTube displaying the torture of Emad al-Kabir under the watchful eyes of police colonel Islam Nabih. According to the article, "The video is one of the first pieces of evidence used to express the government's malfeasances."

Hidden mobile phones were used to uncover and post on YouTube voting frauds and ballot-stuffing during a referendum proposing amendments to Egypt's constitution, further undermining the Mubarak regime. Thus, Egyptian authorities blocked YouTube and DailyMotion for extended periods of time. In 2008, the government blocked Facebook for a month when they realized electronic communication among Egyptian citizens was something to be feared. The state security forces responded in the only way they know how to react to dissent—imprisonment, torture, and death.

Mubarak's security forces in Alexandria tortured and killed Khaled Sa'id a young Egyptian blogger and businessman. Subsequently, a Facebook page was created by Wael Ghonim, a regional executive for Google who wanted to memorialize the young Egyptian blogger. The web page showing his tortured body generated interest—just as Bouazizi's self-immolation generated so much interest—because of the way they lived and died. Reports revealed that the "We Are All Khaled Sa'id" page on Facebook was visited by more than 1.3 million supporters on the Arabic page and more than 100,000 visitors on its English language page. As in Tunisia, a Facebook page became a logistical tool to help organize democracy activists in the country. This and other blogs helped to widely disseminate information on the revolts throughout the Middle East.

One day after the collapse of the Tunisian regime, invitations to a huge Egyptian demonstration were posted on Facebook. January 25th was chosen because it was the "Egyptian Police Day" which is an official holiday in Egypt. The relationship between the police and Egyptians is extremely poor due to the commonly known practices of maltreatment, torture, and killing of citizens by the hated security forces. According to Khalifa (2012), the invitations were posted on the following three popular Facebook pages:

1. *We are all Khaled Said.* Named after Khaled Sa'id, a young Egyptian blogger and professional who was arrested, tortured, and killed by the Egyptian police in Alexandria. This was the most visited Egyptian page on Facebook. By February 14, 2011, the page had 804,000 members.

2. *6th April Youth Movement.* The page had 53,000 members, and the group had 93,000 members. The group was very popular in 2008 and therefore more recognizable on Facebook among Egyptian netizens.

3. *ElBaradei President of Egypt 2011*. The page was created by Dr. Mohamed El-Baradei, Egyptian diplomat and recipient of the Nobel Peace Prize for his work as Director General of the International Atomic Energy Agency (IAEA) from 1997 to 2009 when he returned to Egypt after retiring from his post in Vienna and began his call for political reform. This page had 244,000 members.

The *Rassd News* was also one of the main sources of news and information about Egyptian demonstrations on Facebook. The page had about 250,000 members before being hacked and replaced by a new one. It claimed approximately 150,000 members. *The Original Dostour* newspaper page was another page that covered news of the demonstrations through its journalist bloggers. This page had approximately 110,000 members (Khalifa, 2012).

In addition to Facebook, Twitter played a major role as a tool in managing and disseminating news from and to demonstrations (Maynard, 2013). Twitter was used in 2008 by organizers of the "6th April Youth Movement" which called for a nation-wide strike in all of Egypt on April 6, 2008. The strike was very successful and Twitter became more popular among Egyptian organizers during the January 2011 events. *Rassd News, The Original Dostor Newspaper*, and "We Are All Khaled Sa'id" accounts were the most active on Twitter which carried blogs by famous politicians and challengers to Mubarak, like Dr. Ayman Nour and Dr. Mohammed El-Baradei. Both bloggers and Tweeters served as reporters publishing news, information, photos and videos about the demonstrations and the violent clashes they encountered from the security forces on the streets of Egypt.

Although Egypt had been boiling for a long time as a result of the economic mismanagement and Egyptians' unhappiness with the autocratic and corrupt Mubarak regime (researchers at think tanks, policy analysts, political commentators, and scholars were monitoring the fragile and unstable situation), no one could have predicted how quickly events would unfold.

On Tuesday, January 25, 2011, more than half a million Egyptians filled the streets in eight major Egyptian cities; numbers soon rose to millions, and calls for more demonstrations were renewed on a daily basis. Both Facebook and Twitter were used to announce news and calls for gathering on the "Friday of Anger" January 28, 2011—another day of organized protests where hundreds of thousands of citizens gathered in areas throughout Egypt. According to the activist and technologist Ahmad Gharbeia, the role of the Internet was critical on January 25, as the movements of the protesting groups were arranged in real-time through Twitter. Everyone knew where everyone else was walking, and the organizers could advise on the locations of blockades and skirmishes with police (Elkin, 2011).

Reacting to the massive demonstrations against the regime, the government security forces cut off access to Facebook and Twitter. The shutdown began on Friday, January 28 at midnight, resulting in a total shutdown of Internet connections in and out of Egypt. At 1:00 am, all cell phone networks ceased to operate. At 2:00 am, BlackBerry service was also cut off (*Neon Tommy*, 2011). Egypt was temporarily disconnected from the rest of the world by Mubarak's security forces in their last ditch effort to suppress the Egyptians and crush their demands for freedom and dignity. But by doing this, the government gave the revolution a stronger voice and more support from among the various social and economic strata in Egypt, thereby aiding in adding millions more to the demonstrations which culminated in a total of 10 Egyptian cities participating at the height of the revolution (*Al Jazeera*, 2011).

In the first three days of the demonstrations, January 25–27, 2011, Egyptians were particularly active on Facebook and Twitter managing directions, helping with organizing the demonstrations, and broadcasting audio/visual materials from inside. Some published statistics on the flow of information on social media from January 25 to February 10, 2011 reveal the following: using mobile devices, Egyptian Tweeters were active in and finding each other within an average spacial distance of between 65.2 meters on February 4, 26.7 meters on February 5, and 11.02 meters on February 11 (Walters, 2012). The distance between Tweeters was reduced from day to day and helped with mobilization of crowds, allowing them to find each other and coordinate their activities.

| Date in 2011 | Total Number of Tweets |
|---|---|
| February 4 | 2268 |
| February 5 | 2176 |
| February 11 | 5272 |

*Source*: Walters, 2012

*Rassd News* posted 57 video clips, 400 photos, 367 web links, and 10,584 tweets; "We are all Khaled Sa'id" showed 61 video clips, more than 200 photos, 100 web links; and *The Original Dostor* wrote more than 500 tweets (Khalifa, 2012). On the "Friday of Anger" which was so labeled by the "We Are All Khaled Sa'id" Facebook page, the average increase in membership was about 20 per minute. The page had 400,000 members before January 25, 2011, and grew to 600,000 by February 9, 2011. Five days later the number of members increased to 804,000. This equates to approximately 20,200 members joining the page daily within a span of 20 days (Khalifa, 2012).

Another very popular example of a promotional piece for the revolution was a viral video (http://www.viralvideoaward.com/jan-25th-take-whats-yours/) that served as the rallying cry for the 2011 revolution uploaded on January 27. It has had millions of hits.

# Iraq

In 2003, Burkhart and Older assessed: "In Iraq, the prospects for any development, let alone an information revolution are bleak." Today, a decade later, after trillions of U.S. dollars spent, and over a hundred thousand civilian lives lost as a result of the unjustified invasion of Iraq in 2003 (Iraq Body Count, 2013)—although exact calculations of deaths have been noted to be extremely difficult to estimate and lower than actual numbers—the newly elected government of Nouri al-Maliki has been edging away from democracy. He has taken advantage of the Iraqi constitution's ambiguities to establish personal control over key security institutions, including the Counter-Terrorism Command. His critics have accused him of using these institutions to silence his political opponents (Ross, 2011).

Al-Maliki's government has also been subsidizing journalists and political opponents with cash and land to gain favors with them and the media. Following popular demonstrations in February 2011, Iraqi security forces have reportedly beaten and arrested hundreds of journalists, political activists, and intellectuals (Ross, 2011). As stated earlier, Iraq has one of the lowest Internet penetration rates in the Arab World. According to Facebook statistics, out of a population of 32 million, only about 2.5 million are Internet users (or 8.2% penetration) (Internet World Stats, 2012b). However, as of July, 2013 "a major comprehensive survey" revealed increased use of social media in Iraq, with 77.9% of Internet users having an account with a social media service—with Facebook being the most popular (*Khaleej Times*, 2013). Ironically, the most recent concern for Iraq is that with the rising tension in the country, the social media realm has largely been used as a "place for sectarian hatred" (McEvers, 2013).

# Libya

As with Tunisia and Egypt, Libyan bloggers and social media activists can also be credited with igniting a revolution, and uprising against their former President Muammar al-Qaddafi's 60-year-old regime. For 42 years (1969–2011), al-Qaddafi established a zero-tolerance policy of criticism toward him or his government. Media was strictly censored and controlled. Anyone who defied the President or tainted the nation's reputation could be sentenced to life in prison or receive the death penalty ("Free speech in the media during the Libyan civil war," 2013).

Like most MENA countries, Libya's media is owned and operated by the government which, beginning as early as 2007, has allowed non-government-owned newspapers and satellite TV services to be owned and operated by al-Qaddafi's sons. According to the 2009 data of the International Telecommunication Union, there were approximately 82,500 Internet subscribers and 354,000 users. A single government-owned service provider offered access to an estimated 5.5% of the population (US Department of State, 2011). The government reportedly monitored Internet communications. According to a 2009 report by the OpenNet Initiative, a partnership among several universities to analyze Internet filtering and surveillance, authorities selectively blocked some opposition websites and occasionally blocked others (US Department of State, 2010). ICT penetration in Libya remains modest with 1.1 million fixed-line and 5.0 million mobile-cellular telephone subscribers for a combined fixed-mobile density approaching 100 telephones per 100 persons (Central Intelligence Agency, 2011).

In January 2011, the government began filtering some websites, including YouTube, after the posting of videos of demonstrations by the families of the Abu Salim prison massacre victims, and of videos of al-Qaddafi's family members attending parties (Reporters Without Borders, 2011). Other independent and opposition websites also were blocked that month, including opposition sites Libya al-Youm, al-Manar, Jeel Libya, Akhbar Libya, and Libya al-Mostakbal. According to Human Rights Watch, access was later restored to some of the sites. Libyan political activists used e-media such as *Al-Manar* and *Libya Alyoum*, based in London, to carry statements and reports from inside Libya and were widely credited with spurring support for the protests among Libyans abroad, especially in the United States and Europe (US Department of State, 2010).

Like their fellow revolutionaries in Tunisia and Egypt, Libyans used social media networks as organizing tools and as broadcasting platforms. Libyan bloggers disseminated news and information internally and to the outside world through You Tube, Twitter, and Facebook. But unlike the situations in Tunisia and Egypt, the Libyan regime had to be removed—with help from NATO airpower and military aid.

NATO allied forces used Twitter, Facebook, YouTube, and help from Libyan resistance at home and abroad as part of a wide range of sources of information, ranging from unmanned aerial drones to television news, in order to help determine potential targets for air-strikes in Libya and to assess their success in hitting their targets (Bradshaw and Blitz, 2011). Many remote Internet users contributed to the fight from outside the region of Libya during this struggle. NATO enlisted non-military personnel to help them uncover enemy plans. These "personnel" monitored social media feeds from their home countries; they spent time aggregating messages, synthesizing the data, and then passing it on to officials. At times, the information provided resulted in very precise and accurate accounts about a planned plot or attack—some successfully foiled. "NATO officials have acknowledged that social media reports contribute to their targeting process, but only after checking them against other, more reliable, sources of information" (Smith, 2012).

Since al-Qaddafi's ousting, the first free elections in decades have been held, the freedom of press laws have also been upheld with many newsworthy Arabic TV stations and newspapers covering the ongoing transitional events more objectively, the number of Libyan Facebook users has reached 800,000 (US Department of State, 2012, p. 13), and two of the most popular Libyan youth movement Twitter accounts (@Feb17Libya and @Shabab Libya) together now have 150,000 followers (*BostInno*, 2011).

# Syria

Even though Bashar al-Assad is credited with opening his country for Internet access soon after inheriting the presidency from his father, his country is going through an internal political struggle that has developed into a civil war. Severe measures to curtail personal and political freedoms have been taken away by the Syrian regime, including a ban on social networks. Human Rights Watch reports that the Syrian government tampers with the very fabric of the Internet by blocking access to wireless communication, such as the Internet and social media, restricting the use of the basic electronic protocols that allow people to send e-mail, and constructing websites. Security forces have held online writers incommunicado and tortured them simply for reporting stories the government did not wish to see told (Human Rights Watch, 2005, p. 72). There are about 580,000 Facebook users in Syria, a 105% increase since the government lifted its four-year ban on February 9, 2013 according to Fadi Salem, director of the Governance and Innovation Program at the Dubai School of Government (Bulos, 2013). With foreign journalists barred from the country, dissidents have been working with exiles and using Facebook, YouTube, and Twitter to draw global attention to the brutal military crackdown on protesters that has killed thousands of people, and has led to mass arrests in the last nine weeks. The Syrian Revolution 2011 Facebook page, which now has more than 180,000 members, has been a vital source of information for dissidents (Preston, 2011). Syria is known as one of the most dangerous places for foreign journalists to visit "a pro-Assad Syrian businessman based in Kuwait…announced on Kuwaiti television that he would pay $140,000 to anyone who seized foreign reporters and handed them over to government security forces" (Dettmer, 2013). To quote the Syrian blogger Khaled al-Ekhetyar, "Web tastes freedom inside Syria, and it's bitter," and that for personal safety reasons, "many online journalists used pseudonyms" (Worth, 2010).

Despite these restrictions, Syrians continue to find new ways to circumvent online censorship and surveillance and have rapidly taken to the Internet as a means of getting news into and out of the country. As one prominent Syrian human rights activist explained "the Internet is the only way for intellectuals to meet and share ideas in Syria today" (Human Rights Watch, 2005, p. 66). However, the Syrian government is becoming more clever and advanced in its use of the Internet and social media—it is able to disperse information while blocking local hosts (Chozick, 2012). A recent example of this behavior was in July 2013, when President al-Assad used his Instagram and Facebook accounts to disperse photos of himself acting as a civil leader concerned about the wellbeing of the Syrian people and showing affection and compassion to the injured. The act has been criticized by activists and others as "propaganda" and "a despicable PR stunt" (Karam, 2013). Both social media applications, plus YouTube videos were used to disperse dozens of images which the report claims is "completely removed from the reality on the ground" as more than 100,000 people have been killed since the uprising in 2011 in opposition to the Assad regime (Karam, 2013).

# Yemen

While Yemen's Internet usage has more than doubled from 6.89% in 2008, to 14.9% in 2011 (Internet World Stats, 2012c), Yemen has historically and consistently had one of the lowest Internet penetration rates in the Arab world largely due to the lack of expertise in using technology products as well as the lack of funds to purchase them (Opennet.net, 2007). The country's ICT infrastructure and many (but not all) media outlets have been strictly controlled by the Ministry of Information. Freedom of speech is not freely permitted and journalists are prosecuted for reporting on "sensitive topics" (Opennet.net, 2007, p. 2).

Yemen's Arab Spring piggybacked on the Arab Spring movements in Tunisia and occurred almost simultaneously with Egypt's revolution, partly as a demonstration of solidarity with Egypt, but also in protest of their own repressive conditions. The demonstrations eventually resulted in the end of President Ali Abdullah Saleh's long reign of corruption and economic despair. The Internet was key in getting people to gather in the capital of Sana'a in January 2011 for the initial protests. Twitter was an essential source for real-time information from citizens since many journalists could not obtain visas to report on the up-to-the-minute happenings, even though the use of such tools by Yemeni citizens involved the risk of having their device tracked by the government.

Even under the post-Arab Spring government, Yemen is still considered a country with "pervasive censorship"—meaning it has been classified by the OpenNet Initiative as an entity that censors or filters "political, social, conflict/security, and Internet tools" and invokes imprisonment and other harsh punishments for defying government regulations ("Internet Censorship by Country," 2013).

## Digital Venting in the Gulf States

Arab Gulf citizens are the most cyber-connected in the Arab world. This has recently become a double-edge sword for the rulers of this area due to the fear of following in the footsteps of their counterparts in the Arab Spring countries. Gulf Arab netizens are also calling for political, social, and economic reform in their Gulf kingdoms and sheikhdoms. Twitter's platform for public opinion is emboldening citizens in the Arab Gulf States to exchange views on delicate issues in this deeply conservative region despite the strict censorship that controls old media and extends to new digital media. Unfortunately, these Gulf netizens have discovered that they are not immune from the same mistreatment that befell their fellow netizens and bloggers in the rest of the MENA countries.

# Bahrain

With an Internet penetration rate of 77%, a history of strong government censorship, and complete control over the media, Bahrain has a history of intimidating bloggers and netizens whose views are not shared by the government. The kingdom of Bahrain witnessed its own Arab Spring in 2011, as clashes between the majority Shi'a population (which is about 70% of the Bahrainis) took to the streets demanding social and political rights comparable to those enjoyed by their fellow minority Sunni countrymen. Here again, the Internet and social media were used to organize demonstrations, and also to emphasize the economic, social, and political disparities between the privileged Sunni minority and the Shi'a majority. In order to crack down on the demonstrators, the Kingdom had to rely on the GCC security forces "Peninsula Shield" led by the Saudi forces to quell the mostly Shi'a uprising. King Hamad has recently announced that he is directing his government to establish some form of public representation to give his subjects a voice in the otherwise autocratic rule of the kingdom.

BahrainOnline is a popular blog among members of the Shi'a opposition as well as Sunnis loyal to the ruling family. In 2002, Bahrain's Information Ministry censored Internet sites on the grounds of "inciting sectarian or propaganda lies, sparking activist protests" (*TheAge.com,* 2007). Several other sites were also censored for discussing an alleged plot to maintain Sunni domination. In 2002, the opposition Shi'ite group successfully used the Internet to boycott the national election (Janardhan, 2011, p. 228).

The website "Mahmood's Den" is one of the thousands of blogs that have sprung up across the Arab world and provides a venue for dissent. According to its creator, Mahmood Al-Yousif (a.k.a. "the Blogfather"), the frustration with leadership is at a boiling point and these harassing techniques are symptomatic of the leadership's realization of this fact. Al-Yousif pointed to 13 cases that were brought against Bahraini journalists that showed how the government turned its attention to the Internet. In 2007, he was taken to court for criticizing the Minister of Municipal and Agricultural Affairs, Mansur bin Rajab. Al-Yousif criticized bin Rajab for saying that his ministry did not shirk its responsibilities following the December floods that killed many Bahrainis.

In 2005, the Bahraini moderator of an online discussion forum and two Web technicians were detained for two weeks on charges of defaming King Hamad (*Middle East Online,* 2005). Most recently, bloggers and political activists like Maikel Nabil Sanad post on events that precede and follow the revolution and the persistent conflict between the SCAF (Supreme Council of the Armed Forces), President Morsi, the Muslim Brotherhood and the rest of country. According to Sanad (2011), an important factor in preventing the Egyptian army from shooting at its people was that it was using American-made weapons against a large peaceful protest by an army that had very special ties to its American counterpart. This would not only have serious repercussions on Egyptian–American army relations, but might further damage the American image in Egypt, the region, and perhaps the world. That argument still holds true, even though protestors found that canisters of tear gas used by the Egyptian police were American-made (Wali & Sami, 2011).

In 2011, a Royal decree was issued to rectify previous harsh sentences handed down for some 20 protest-linked suspects, including a 20-year-old woman sentenced to a year in prison for reciting poetry critical of the government's effort to crush a Shi'a-led uprising against the Sunni monarchy (Rebhy, 2012).

## Kuwait

Kuwait ranks among those countries with the highest Internet penetration at 74.2% of the population having access to the Internet and social media (Internet World Stats, 2012d). In spite of its relatively democratic system, it has its own political up-heavals with constant conflict and clashes between the Emir and his Council of Ministers on the one hand, and members of the National Assembly—in particular the ultra-conservative Islamists—on the other. Kuwaitis have used various forms of communication for sound political and electoral objectives, including calls for women's civil and voting rights and inclusion in the legislative and executive branches of government.

Fears of the spread of the Arab Spring movement to the Gulf States have prompted GCC countries, including liberal Kuwait to clamp down on anti-establishment bloggers and online political commentators. Kuwait has jailed several opposition Tweeters and former MPs (Members of Parliament) on such charges, and many others have been tried for a variety of offenses that range from conspiring to overthrow the government to insulting the emir (*News24.com*, 2013). The proposed "Combined Media Law" approved by the Kuwait's Cabinet of Ministers stipulates a jail term of up to 10 years for insulting God, the Prophet Mohammed, his companions and wives, and other prophets. The same penalty applies to those instigating the overthrow of the regime, and stipulates a fine of between $175,000 and $1.05 million for criticizing the emir or the crown prince (*Al Arabiya*, 2013).

This law is in contrast to earlier efforts such as when, in October 2007, a group of Kuwaiti civil society organizations, including the Kuwait Transparency Society, published the "Vision of Kuwait for Reform." The vision called for the endorsement of a bill on the Right to Information in order to achieve transparency in the public sector and a review of the press law to guarantee freedom of media (Almadhoun, 2010). Media watchdog Reporters Without Borders strongly lashed out at the new media law describing it as "draconian" and urged the parliament to reject it (*News24.com*, 2013).Additional efforts to regulate the telecommunication industry prompted some members of Kuwait's National Assembly to pass the first reading of a law to establish a government authority to regulate the telecommunication industry in the country. The proposed new organization, modeled after the Saudi Communications and Information Technology Commission (CITC), would be given the authority to control the mobile and landline phone sectors, as well as Internet providers, including restricting or banning certain services and applications such as the recent blocking of Viber applications—a protocol for smart handheld devices used for texting, sending images, audio files, etc. (Reuters, 2013b).

Yet, fears of a Gulf Arab Spring have resulted in abandoning the spirit of moderation after 2007, and increasing the number of arrests and imprisonments of bloggers and political activists (including a former member of the National Assembly on charges of insulting the emir). The verdicts of these trials produced protests from international organizations like Human Rights Watch and Reporters Without Borders. Most recently, a young blogger by the name of Hamid Al-Khalidi who is part of a growing list of young activists in Kuwait and across the Arab Gulf was targeted for "electronic crimes"—that is, voicing the very same longing for freedom, justice, and opportunity. Just days before Al-Khalidi's sentencing, the Kuwaiti appeals court extended the jail term of another Twitter user, Bader al-Rashidi, who tweeted criticism of the Kuwaiti government. He, too, was sentenced from two to five years on charges that he attempted to instigate a coup and insulted the country's emir. In the past year, Kuwait sentenced some 10 online activists (among them a woman, Huda al-Ajmi) to various prison terms on charges that ranged from Twitter and blog posts insulting members of parliament or the emir, to inciting protests (*Associated Press*, 2013).

According to Mohammed Al-Humaidi, a lawyer and director of the Kuwait Society for Human Rights, "The government of Kuwait and other Gulf governments have begun to feel the danger of Twitter that toppled presidents and governments in the Arab countries and it is clear from the way they are abusing many Twitter users with these false charges" (Salama, 2013b).

On July 30, 2013, in a surprising move, Emir Sheikh Sabah al-Ahmad al-Sabah pardoned every political activist who had ever been sent to prison (some up to 11 years) for insulting him "especially online," and added "By the will of God, we are heading towards a new phase of this legislative term, where the country will witness a promising launch towards progress…and development" (Westall & Lyon, 2013).

## Oman

In spite of calls for democratic reforms during the Arab Spring, the opposition did not gain momentum. The Omani's *Internet Service Manual* details a long list of prohibitions, by which any public Internet service provider must abide, including: 1) defaming His Majesty, the Sultan, or members of the royal family; (2) inconsistency with current laws of the state; 3) undermining confidence in the fairness of the government; 4) containing false data or rumors; 5) anything tending to the hatred of or degradation of the government; or 6) promoting political or ideological ideas conflicting with the country's current system.

Private companies operating in Oman are not allowed to use encoding devices without permission of a competent authority. Bodies governing the censorship process, even the rules governing the methods of censorship, are not readily available to the public. The Omani state-run media outlets do not feature debates or commentaries on political issues. In November 2005, a wave of arrests of protesters calling for political reform was followed in 2006 by government action against bloggers in general, and the online site "Sabla" in particular, on political grounds. In 2012, more than 50 activists were arrested for involvement in online and offline protests, and many received prison terms of up to 18 months.

Omanis are active users of the Internet, more than 68% of the Omani population used the Internet in 2011 (Freedom House, 2012a). The country's public prosecution issued statements threatening to take legal action against anyone publishing "offensive writing" or "inciting protests" via Facebook, Twitter, or personal blog pages. However, Sultan Qaboos bin Said al-Said, who has ruled for 43 years, issued a royal pardon for anyone convicted of "information technology crimes," a move—albeit temporary in nature—that was hailed by human rights organizations. According to the Arab Network for Human Rights Information (n.d.):

> Debate websites such as the Omani network website known as 'Sabla' (www.omania.net) are the only outlet for discussing local affairs. Although the discussions are under pseudonyms, this does not prevent the Omani authorities from arresting and questioning the contributors to these websites, and subsequently sentencing them to imprisonment for one year with a stay of execution. (p. 160)

One such user of influence is the Omani activist Tiba Almauli, a member of the Omani Shura Council who later practiced political activism through the "Sabla" forum by writing a large number of posts using a pseudonym. Almauli was arrested and questioned by the Omani authorities in May 2005 about her writings and postings critical of the increase in the prices of gasoline, eventually leading to an 18-month prison sentence for criticizing senior state officials online. Later the Court of Appeals reduced her prison sentence to six months, and in 2006, she was released from prison. On March 22, 2004, poet and human rights activist, Abdullah Al-Riyami posted an online article demanding the elimination of censorship of the Internet (CPJ, 2004). Banned from appearing in the media, he continued to write online at www.kikah.com and was imprisoned from July 2005 until the beginning of 2006.

# Qatar

In a recent meeting of the Arab Summit held in Doha, some Arab leaders including the then Emir of Qatar urged their counterparts in the region to view the Arab Spring as a wakeup call for social and economic reform, and urged his fellow Arab rulers to use ICT to address some of these issues. In 1995, the same emir abolished the Information Ministry (known for being the formal government propaganda machine in the Arab world) and with it, press censorship. This positive move was followed in 1996 with the establishment of *Al Jazeera*, the first example of Western-style satellite television in the Arab world. It should be noted that *Al Jazeera* came about as a result of ideological and political disputes between Qatar and Saudi Arabia. Even with its Western-style debates of sensitive political and social issues, *Al Jazeera* has to walk a fine line and avoid upsetting its Qatari owners, hosts, and investors.

While these are positive Qatari steps forward, the step backward was the passing of a press law that allows the imprisonment of journalists for work the government finds offensive or politically unacceptable (*Agence France Presse,* 2006). As recently as December 2012, the government sentenced the Qatari poet Muhamad ibn al-Dheeb al-Ajami to life in prison for an Arab Spring-inspired verse that officials claimed insulted Qatar's Emir and encouraged the overthrow of the nation's ruling system. The verdict was passed on this third year college student of literature at Cairo University after spending almost one year in solitary confinement (*Associated Press in Doha*, 2012).

With the younger emir Sheikh Tamim Bin Hamad Al-Thani replacing his aging father as head of the state, it is yet to be determined whether Qatar will follow a more democratic and open path to political reform, or continue on with the old and repressive system practiced by most countries in the region.

# Saudi Arabia

According to the CITC figure for 2012, Saudi Arabia has a mobile penetration of 188% and 15.8 million Internet subscribers (Reuters, 2013b). It has been described as one of the world's premiere blockers of websites. Saudi Arabia, along with Tunisia, Egypt, Iran, and Syria are among the top 13 countries world-wide notorious for Human Rights violations and Internet suppression (*Associated Press*, 2007). It has a national authority responsible for blocking certain sites. Citizens' requests to have a site blocked can file a Web form, and all requests are accepted without any verification to the content of the sites.

The government hand-picks *ulama*, who are given jobs and religious authority by the King and provide a cloak of legitimacy for the rulers under the pretense that under the Al-Saud, religion and state are partners. The Wahhabi clerics have exerted their power to silence the new media by filing lawsuits against bloggers and Internet activists, closing their bureaus, and jamming their transmissions. These religious extremists view the free digital media as a challenge and threat to their authority. The government took different but similar paths by launching its sponsored and financed satellite channels of its own such as *Al-Arabiyya* (The Arab) and *Al-Fajr* (The Dawn), a religious and educational channel intended to combat religion and political extremism in the aftermath of al-Qaʿida's attack on Saudi Arabian installations on May 12, 2003, dubbed the "Kingdom's 9/11" (Tétreault, Okruhlik, & Kapiszewski, 2011).

Incidentally, the freedom conferred by blogger anonymity has encouraged freedom-deprived Saudi women to embrace the Internet, as they consider blogs a safe platform from which women can express themselves and call for change and empowerment. More than half of the Saudi blogs are authored by women, especially on female social issues. Popular Saudi women blogs such as "Farah's Sowaleef," "A Thought in the Kingdom of Lunacy," and "Saudi Eve," among others, are usually critical of male domination in Saudi society and record the experiences of those who dare to challenge established norms. Female bloggers have also posted petitions to the government asking for Saudi women to be given permission to drive their own automobiles (Janardhan, 2011, pp. 228–229).

Fearing internal unrest fueled by cyber communication, the Saudi government has taken draconian measures to limit online activism in the name of national security, including banning web-based communication applications like Skype, WhatsApp, and Viber if the providers do not comply with its requests for surveillance rights (Al-Mukhtar, 2013; Salama, 2013a). A report that ran prominently on the front page of Riyadh-based *Arab News* also stated that Saudi Arabia is seeking to end anonymity for Twitter users by requiring residents to register their national identification numbers to hold an account (Reuters, 2013a). Government officials in the Ministry of the Interior warned that social media websites, including Twitter, have been used by militant groups to incite social unrest, while the country's top cleric described bloggers as "clowns" who waste time with harmful discussions (RT, 2013).

As recently as June 24, 2013, the Saudi Specialized Criminal Court has sentenced seven government critics to prison for terms ranging from five to ten years for allegedly inciting protests and harming public order, largely by using Facebook (Human Rights Watch, 2013).

# United Arab Emirates (UAE)

The UAE has the region's second largest Weblog community. The emirate has one of the most networked and wired digital communities in the Arab Gulf States (Janardhan, 2011, p. 229). It has an Internet penetration of 70.9%, nearly 6 million Internet users, and approximately 3.5 million Facebook subscribers (Internet World Stats, 2012e). The Emirate has introduced a high quality and very modern communication system: the Abu Dhabi-based *Al-Arabiya* satellite TV has drawn large audiences throughout the Middle East, stimulating popular interest in and knowledge of politics and current affairs.

The UAE Constitution guarantees all citizens "freedom to hold opinions and expression of the same" as well as "freedom of communication." In recent years, the government has relaxed its control on the media. The establishment of Dubai Media City drew numerous broadcast and print media to Dubai including the *Middle East Broadcasting Center* (MBC), and Western news services like *CNN* and *Reuters*, in addition to *Al-Arabiya*. The ruler of Dubai, Sheikh Mohammed bin Rashid al-Maktoum, is one of the few Arab rulers to have a Facebook of his own (facebook.com/HHSheikhMohammed). He has used the application on several occasions to reach the public, including answering questions about the 2008 global economic crisis that affected Dubai (*National*, 2009).

The nation's state telecommunication monopoly and sole Internet service provider also plays a major role in suppressing and censoring citizens' blogs. Active bloggers whose views the government considers objectionable are subject to arrest and imprisonment. While the *Etisalat* (Emirates Telecommunications Corporation) has long blocked pornographic and gambling-related sites, it also blocks sites dedicated to the Baha'i faith, and sites with addresses ending in .il—that is, based in Israel (Human Rights Watch, 2005).

Prior to the Arab Spring, the UAE was attempting to liberalize its nationally-controlled media and was responding to calls for free expression. Yet, in spite of the positive measures described above, the UAE has also taken measures against netizens and bloggers. Since December 2008, cyber-police in the UAE have been monitoring the Web and keeping an eye on its users. According to UAE Article 20 of the 2006 Computer Crime Act, "an Internet user may be imprisoned for 'opposing Islam,' 'insulting any religion recognized by the state,' or 'violating family values and principles'" (Reporters Without Borders, 2010).

Since 2009, Colonel Dahi Khalfan, Chief of Police in Dubai, has campaigned by posting on various websites (e.g., www.emarati.katib.org/node/52, www.uaetorture.com, www.Hetta.com, and others). After the Arab Spring, he supported sweeping Internet regulations that allow arrests for a wide list of offenses, including insulting leaders or calling for demonstrations (Rebhy, 2012). He has also been active on Twitter in expressing his harsh criticism of the Arab Spring and demonstrators, and the Muslim Brotherhood (CNN, 2013).

# Iran

For the past decade, Iranians have been turning to the Internet in large numbers. This is evidenced by the increasing number of Iranian Internet users at an average annual rate of 600% between 2001 and 2005, and also from reports revealing that "Iranians 'blog' to an extent unparalleled in the region" (Human Rights Watch, 2005). Still, dozens of Iranian reformist publications have had their licenses revoked. A women's magazine was accused of "threatening the psychological security of society... having weakened military and revolutionary institutions" (*Economist*, 2008). Since 2004, the Iranian judiciary began targeting online journalists and bloggers: "The government has imprisoned online journalists, bloggers, and technical support staff and blocked thousands of websites, including sites that offer free publishing tools and hosting space for blogs" (Human Rights Watch, 2005).

In February 2007, *The Guardian* reported that the Iranian regime had shut down a website "fiercely critical of President Mahmoud Ahmadinejad" (Tait, 2007). Baztab, a Shi'a fundamentalist website that accused President Mahmoud Ahmadinejad of betraying the Iranian revolution by attending a female dance show, was closed for "acting against the constitution and undermining national unity. The order coincided with the confrontation of Gholamhossein Elham" as Iran's new Justice Minister, who previously urged "prosecutors to pursue news outlets that printed 'lies' about Mr. Ahmadinegad's government" (Tait, 2007). His appointment came as the government disclosed new measures to restrict unofficial news websites. The Iranian government has also censored the Farsi-language version of the Reporters Without Borders website RSF.org. The Internet surveillance under the Ministry of Culture and Islamic Orientation is designed to censor and ban websites that the government censors deem unfriendly or spreading false information (Refugee Review Tribunal, 2009).

An example of how issues of politics and participation have recently played out is in the case of the use of Twitter in Iran. In June 2009, in the aftermath of the Iranian election, there was a huge opposition to an election many people believed to be full of irregularities. There were riot police in the streets and a ban of any media reporting in the country ensued. Over the course of 18 days, the protestors turned to Twitter on an unprecedented scale. There were no less than two million tweets from Iran by 500,000 people. At the height of activity, there were 200,000 tweets an hour (*BBC*, 2010). One of the most symbolic historic tweets of Tehran in 2009 summed up the people's protest against the Iranian election fraud. The tweeted picture worldwide of the young girl Neda Agha-Soltan shot in the head by Basji forces became the iconic symbol of how corrupt and morally bankrupt the Iranian government has become. World condemnation ensued and Twitter evolved as an effective organizational tool of protestors around the Middle East.

As recently as 2012, Iran's cyber-police committed the criminal act of killing labor activist, blogger and Facebook user, Sattar Beheshti—who dared to criticize the former Ahmadinejad government. Beheshti died while undergoing interrogation in Iran's notorious Evin Prison just one week after his arrest on national security charges on October 30th. The cyber-police also confiscated his computer and handwritten notes (*Eurasia Review*, 2012). This was not the first time the Iranian former regime has acted violently against netizens.

In the June 2013 presidential election, young people used their smart phones, tweeted, and blogged in support of the moderate candidate Hassan Rouhani who won the free and fair election and provided hope for a new era for Iran and Iranians—one the world hopes will be different from his predecessor's.

## Conclusion

Most MENA governments have recently discovered that the might of the new ICT is much stronger and more threatening to them than any military force that they were prepared to fight. Internet, wireless, and mobile communication devices, coupled with established oral traditions have contributed to the overthrow of a number of authoritarian Arab regimes. The authoritarian regimes failed to quell citizens' anger vented through the digital media available to them. Digital communications moved protestors and information around faster and more efficiently than their governments, with their respective controlled media, could, helping to organize the movements. Egyptian, Tunisian, Yemeni, and Libyan protestors were able to record and broadcast pictures and news messages with their mobile phones by uploading them for the world to see and hear. The mobile devices' global positioning system (GPS) data were particularly useful for tactical and operational support during the demonstrations. As a result, protestors were able to change directions to avoid police barricades and confrontations with security forces. Government efforts to censor, imprison, or murder bloggers have failed to halt the rising tides of protests and the now familiar call: "Ash-Sha'b yurid isqat an-nizam" (*The people want to bring down the regime*) or "Irhal!" (*Leave!*).

There are lessons to be learned by the post-Arab Awakening in the affected countries, and social phenomena to consider in countries with potential for the same unrest. Dr. Ekaterina Stepanova, head of the Peace and Conflict Studies Division at the Institute of the World Economy and International Relations noted:

> If there is a positive pattern to discern in the impact of Internet-based tools and social media networks on recent developments in the Middle East, it may have less to do with fostering Western-style democracy than in encouraging relatively less violent forms of mass protest. (2011, p. 6)

People's demands for reform are ongoing, and are here to stay. While Arab satellite television coverage and political debates like those of *Al Jazeera* inspire Arab activists to call for political and social change, blogs and social networks have become the Arab activists' media tools of choice. Young Arabs in particular now use the blogosphere, not mainstream media, to re-engage and express their own political views which the established Arab media do not allow or provide. Their demands become empowered by these tools and technologies. Netcitizens, bloggers, and organizers of all ages should be prepared to use their sharpened and tested skills to combat and counter their authoritarian governments and force them to adapt to a democratic system—a system that strives toward social justice, peaceful resolution, and clear responsiveness to the massive cries for political and economic reform.

# Challenges of State-Controlled Media in Egypt

## Dina Wafa

## Abstract

The media is considered to be a powerful tool in impacting public opinion, not only in Egypt, but around the world. In Egypt, the media played a significant role after the January 25th Revolution. State-controlled media, however, lacks public trust because of its continual support of the former regime. Today, the state-controlled media is facing several challenges to gain public trust, maintain professionalism, and partner with the public in demanding transparency and accountability in governance while exposing corruption. With the new Constitution and laws in place, there are growing debates among journalists on the proper role of the media in post-revolution Egypt, especially on the issue of freedom of expression. Creating a cadre of professionals to help build a capacity in the state-controlled media based on dedication to truth and public service is of utmost urgency. This paper examines the impact of the Arab Spring on state-controlled media in Egypt, and its implications on training programs aimed at creating a professional cadre that will engage the state-controlled media in Egypt to be a true watchdog for democracy and public interest.

# Introduction

The fast-paced investigative reporting to uncover the turbulent events during the January 25th Revolution, and the need to build a new post-Arab Spring Egypt are posing challenges for the state-controlled media in Egypt. Recognizing the public's demand for truth in reporting, thirst for knowledge, and active participation in the democratic process to safeguard public interests, several organizations in the state-controlled media in Egypt have considered taking active measures in order to reshape the industry and make it comparable to private networks. This notion is of particular importance because of the abundance of information in today's globalized social media and the need for reliable information and creative technology for presenting timely and accurate news and analyses. This paper examines the impact of the Arab Spring on state-controlled media in Egypt and the need of the industry for executive education training programs in order to build a professional cadre capable of reshaping the state-controlled media in Egypt and respond to its many challenges. The research questions are as follows:

- What are the impacts of the transitional period in Egypt after the January 25th Revolution on the state-controlled public administration as a whole, and state-controlled media in particular?

- What are some of the innovative approaches required for shifting the state-controlled media in Egypt toward espousing freedom of expression, truth in reporting, and accountability?

- What are the measures needed in order for the state-controlled media in Egypt to gain public trust?

The survey targeted public administration alumni students, government officials, and civic organizations. It was conducted in Arabic to accommodate those who have not mastered the English language. The questionnaires were pilot tested by a panel of staff working at the American University in Cairo. They were also asked to express their opinions on linguistic phrasing, clarity, and appropriateness of measures. The questionnaires were then modified in accordance with the comments from the pilot test.

Data collection took a total of three months. The sample used was based on purposive selection from the Global Affairs and Public Policy (GAPP) Executive Education network's pool. Next, a snowball sampling technique was used to ensure that all GAPP Executive Education program alumni and diversity of the citizens were represented. Collectively, the sample amounted to 178 participants.

The respondents' ages varied. In the age group 18–24 years, there were 14.4% respondents. In the age group 25–34 years, there were 40.6%. In the age group 35–44 years, there were 28.75%. In the age group 45–55, there were 15%. And, in the age group 55 and over, there were 1.9%. Collectively, approximately 69% of respondents were between the ages of 25 and 45, which correspond to the prime years for receiving public administration training or executive education programs.

The sampled respondents indicated receiving training and executive education on the following topics of public administration post-January 25 Revolution: 42 media-related training; 42 related to monitoring elections; 14 campaign-management related; 5 democracy related; 5 law related; 5 negotiation related;12 strategic planning and performance management related; 1 decentralization related; 1 anti-corruption related; 1 leadership related; 1 Parliament related; and 3 indicated they had received no training or executive education post the revolution.

Approximately 76% of sample respondents indicated that the public administration training or executive education programs they received post-January 25 Revolution were either through a scholarship or free of charge; 6.25% were funded by their work institutions; and 1.25% were personally funded. When asked if their work affiliations encouraged employees for continuing education, training, and development, approximately 84.4% said that their affiliates did encourage the employees, while 15% indicated that their work institutions did not encourage continuing education, training, and development for their employees. Some have mentioned that their work institutions encouraged training and development in principle but did not do so because of budget constraints. Others have mentioned having to search for relevant training programs on their own.

Approximately 79% felt that the knowledge acquired was valuable to their work. Seventy percent felt that the training they received improved their work performance. Among the comments mentioned, the following were emphasized: the importance of practical applications; the added value of international comparisons; the increase in theoretical knowledge; relaying knowledge to performance; better understanding of roles; becoming more aware of the legal framework of the public administration environment; improving fundraising skills; and creating a "new and valuable vision for how to address issues during the transitional phase."

Only 8.75% indicated that they had to discontinue a public administration training or executive education program due to the Arab Spring. Furthermore, only 21.25% of the respondents indicated a change in their development needs after the Arab Spring, while the remaining 25% skipped the question. Of those indicating that their development needs have changed, a few mentioned that the transitional period would require them to search for lessons learnt from other transitions, especially in crises management and understanding change. Approximately 53.75% indicated that the Arab Spring had no impact or change on their development needs. One respondent claimed that his needs were the same, but in the coming phase, they may change depending on the new government.

# The Impact of the Transitional Period in Egypt on State-Controlled Media

In Egypt, as in many other countries in the Middle East, most media sources are controlled by the state. The reason for this is to filter out information deemed to be damaging to public officials and in order to manage public opinion through censorship (Khamis & Vaughn, 2011). Satire and critical reports are examples of topics targeted for censorship. In addition, responsible groups or individuals for such types of reporting are often detained, such as the detention of Abdel Haleem Kandil in 2011 for his critical report of the former regime.

Egypt under Mubarak's paternalistic regime had witnessed deterioration, not only in the media industry, but also in culture, education, and innovation. Such factors resulted in an increase in the level of apathy, cynicism, and depression among the youth (Bassiouni, 2012; Khalil 2012). State-controlled media was among the top industries to be plagued by corruption and lack of professionalism because of its ties with those who controlled the state. Inaccurate news was reported and pictures were altered using Adobe Photoshop in order to glorify the regime and its leadership. For example, a front page picture at the leading *Al-Ahram* newspaper depicted Mubarak in the middle of world leaders during the 2010 Middle East Peace talks, when in fact he was at the end (Shenker & Siddique, 2010). Such fabrications damaged the credibility of the state media and caused a loss of public trust. The aforementioned Photoshop incident was reported throughout social media networks, such as the Arabic Facebook page of "*Kulona Khaled Saied*" or "*We are all Khaled Saied.*" A similar incident took place on April 6, 2008, when striking workers in the city of Mahalla were demanding an increase in wages as well as reinstating their vocational centers for training and development. The strike was significant, not only because it became widespread (to the entire city and neighboring areas), but because it challenged the regime and asked for the resignation of Mubarak while tearing down his pictures. The state-controlled media, however, censored any news on the event as if it did not take place. People outside Mahalla learned about it through the social media channels that reported the event, along with pictures showing the striking workers pulling down Mubarak's posters (Bassiouni, 2012; Radsch, 2011).

Another event censored by the state media was the "Calls for the January 25th Revolution." The event itself was not reported until several days later. Even in its late reporting of the revolution, the state media took the side of the regime instead of those who were demonstrating in Tahrir Square. On 28 January, the Egyptian government made matters worse by cutting all Internet and mobile phone communications in the hopes of ending the demonstrations (Bassiouni, 2012). Yet, the information blackout encouraged ordinary citizens go to the streets and see for themselves what was transpiring. Once they realized the truth, and without state media bias or censorship, they joined the demonstrators in mass (Khalil, 2012).

As cell phone service resumed on January 29, followed by Internet reconnection on February 2, 2011, state media shifted toward presenting the revolution as mere chaos and lawlessness. In doing so it intended to instill fear among the public in order to relinquish its support of the uprising. Volunteer citizen watch groups responded to the fear monger by patrolling the neighborhoods and protecting their homes from any threat. On January 31, 2011, when military jets were flying low over Tahrir Square in order to intimidate the demonstrators, the leading *Al-Ahram* state newspaper printed the news with the following headline: "Mubarak meets his military commanders" (*Al-Ahram*, 2011a; Khalil, 2012). The report was intended to further spread fear among the public.

With the revolution continuing, the gap in reporting the news between state media and other independent media outlets grew wider. For example, while *Al-Jazeera* was broadcasting live from Tahrir Square and interviewing protestors without censorship, the state television and newspapers were campaigning to instill fear of chaos among the public. As more people learned of the true situation on the ground by pouring to the street and participating in the demonstrations, the more the state media lost it credibility.

On February 2, 2011, state media began targeting independent media outlets, professional journalists, and bloggers, accusing them of conspiring with foreign powers. Several international media reporters were detained, including the Bureau Chief of the *Washington Post*, Leila Fadel; *Time* magazine reporter Andrew Lee Butters; CNN anchorperson Anderson Cooper and his crew; CNN reporter Halla Gorani; and ABC anchorperson Christiane Amanpour—in addition to *Al-Jazeera* and *Reuters* reporters (Khamis & Vaughn, 2011; Khalil, 2012). This type of intimidation marked a turning point in international media coverage of the January 25th Revolution, with reporters such as Anderson Cooper, and comedian/commentator David Letterman condemning the Mubarak regime and portraying it as a dictatorship (Khalil, 2012).

Several professionals in the state media started distancing themselves from the industry and resigned in protest. Several of them led charges against their former employers, such as Sabah Hammou, the former Deputy Business Editor at *Al-Ahram* and Shahira Amin, a reporter and administrator at *Nile TV* (Khalil, 2012; Khamis & Vaughn, 2011). The credibility crises intensified when the public started to turn to other media outlets for information.

The credibility crises continued even after Mubarak's downfall—especially after *Al-Ahram*'s hypocritical headline on February 12, 2011: "The People have toppled the Regime" (*Al-Ahram*, 2011b). Until Mubarak's resignation, the state media was anything but a supporter of the Revolution. However, once Mubarak was out of the picture, it quickly turned to save what it has left of its damaged credibility. The credibility issue continued haunting the state media when it was granted the exclusive right to cover Mubarak's court hearings. On August 4, 2011, the *Al-Ahram* front page headline read "The Pharaoh Locked in a Cage" (*Al-Ahram*, 2011c). As a result, state media found itself losing ground to private media outlets and social media networks, and competing for market share, readership, and viewership. The call for objectivity and professionalism in the media also resulted in the abolishing of the Ministry of Information (Khamis & Vaughn, 2011).

## Innovative Practices on Freedom of Expression and Accountability

During the January 25th Revolution, the state media proved incapable of reporting truthful information to the public because of its lack of professionalism and objectivity and ties with power brokers in the state. State media bias was highly exposed during the Revolution and forced the public to look elsewhere for information. Today, the state media is facing a credibility crisis, and is in dire need for genuine reforms. These reforms must be geared toward facilitating accountability and promoting freedom of expression in order to gain public trust and positively influence public opinion. State media may continue to play a critical role in the democratic process, but it has to revamp its vision, rebuild its capacity based on professionalism, champion the public interests, and give voice to the under-privileged in the society. The reforms must also involve legislations that stipulate professionalism in the media and require its autonomy in reporting and analyzing the news without state interference or manipulation. In a word, state media can transform itself into a public media and the voice of citizens rather than the state. Subjecting the state media to the supervision and oversight of state committees, such as the current Shurra Council only undermines the industry's professionalism and autonomy (*Egypt Independent*, 2013).

In an era where the public is no longer an idle receiver of information and in the global world in which we currently live, as interconnected communities, information is available in abundance from many sources. Therefore, controlling information by the state or attempts in managing public opinion through censorship or non-objective information is no longer effective. During the information blackout period after the January 25th Revolution by the state media, or when the state media failed to report the country's economic decline and financial loss, citizens sought innovative measures to acquire information. For example, civic activists set up a project known as "File Transfer Protocol" in order to interact with the rest of the world and gain access to information. When the Mubarak regime cut off Internet services, civic activists maintained the services by connecting with service providers in other countries through landline dialups and satellite phones. When international television channels were shut down by the former regime, citizens managed to access these channels' transmission via Hot-bird and Arabsat.

In their search for alternative media after the information blackout during the Revolution, citizens established neighborhood and community newsletters to keep information flowing and give voice to the public. Blogs, Facebook, and Twitter were also used for communication and information sharing. The average tweets during first quarter of 2011 in Arab region were three tweets per second. The most popular trending hashtag was #Egypt, with 1.4 million mentions (Dubai School of Government, 2011). During the Revolution alone, Internet users in Egypt reached 23 million, and cell phone users reached 65 million (Al-Ahram Center for Political and Strategic Studies, 2011). These simple tools of communication succeeded in keeping the public informed during the January 25th Revolution—a significant part of Egyptian history (Campbell, 2011). What is remarkable about these tools are their low cost, difficulty to censor, defiance of authoritative and traditional media, and inclination to change (Taylor, 2010). After Mubarak's resignation, it became a trend for many public officials to have Facebook pages of their own (Bassiouni, 2012).

## Gaining Public Trust

The former regime's attempt to manage public opinion through the control of state media caused the latter to lose public confidence and trust. The performance of state media during the Arab Spring only magnified the extent of the problem. Freedom House (a non-governmental, advocacy and research group that monitors and reports on political, human rights, and freedom developments) has ranked Egypt among the worst in the world in freedom of information, with a recent improvement from "not free" to "partly free" (Tucker, 2012). Therefore, establishing strict criterion for professionalism and objectivity in state media is critical in order for such an industry to survive.

In the post-Mubarak era, the censoring of Youssef al-Qaeed's article by the *Al-Akhbar* state newspaper which was critical for the Muslim Brotherhood continues to challenge the state media's behavior regarding freedom of expression. The role of the Shurra Council in appointing the chief editors of the state newspapers is also questionable. Adding to this is the ambiguity of the role of the Ministry of Information, which at one point, was abolished and then recently reconstituted. All this adds to public mistrust of the state media and widens the credibility gap. Only by establishing accountability, promoting citizen voices, developing professional standards, upholding freedom of expression, and maintaining autonomy can the state media gain public trust and close the credibility gap. These improvements must be accompanied by proper legislation that does not penalize free and independent public media.

State media, as most public organizations, must follow the principles of public service and serve the public interests instead of the interests of politicians. It must be a voice for the most vulnerable segments in society, and it must defend and uphold objectivity and the truth at all costs and at all times. The administration of state media must also act autonomously and without manipulation or control by politicians, the Ministry of Information, or the new Shurra Council. These steps may make it possible for state media to gain the public's trust again. If not, it is a lost cause as there are numerous other media sources that the public can utilize to access information.

# Changing Training Programs in Public Administration

The Arab Spring pointed to the needs for public administration programs to be re-constructed based on accountability and transparency, and for public administrators to be retrained in order to adapt to the changes demanded by the public for better governance. This requires the establishment of a creative crises management strategy in order to seize opportunities in offsetting challenges. A critical approach is needed in such training programs in order to identify opportunities and match them up against challenges in order to optimize program benefits. The January 25th Revolution has enabled the public to speak freely and demand changes in governance. Public administration must capitalize on these demands and retool in order to deliver the public goods in a better manner, with more efficacy, accountability, and transparency. An effective way for public administration to learn, adapt, and reform is through collaboration with educators and researchers in order to facilitate dialogues, training, and debates among actors in public affairs for better governance. Creating a partnership between public administration, civic institutions, media professionals, and educators is essential for initiating and leading the change.

During the January 25th Revolution, businesses were interrupted due to a communication blackout and imposed curfew. Among those was the Global Affairs and Public Policy (GAAP) Executive Education program. The interruption caused GAPP to abort one of its programs known as the Advanced Public Policy Management, an initiative that was established in collaboration with the Ministry of State for Administrative Development (MSAD).

Per order of Egyptian authorities, Internet and mobile phone communications were shut down during the Revolution. According to Hatem Dweidar, a senior executive in one of the two major operating cell phone services in Egypt, he had received an order on January 23 alerting him to comply with a follow-up order in the next few days regarding shutting down communication lines (Bassiouni, 2012). In doing so, it was difficult for GAPP to continue holding its training sessions. Contacting trainees and trainers for new arrangements with cell phones or via the Internet was a challenge.

After forcing Mubarak to step down, businesses and public administration operations slowly began to resume at some normal capacity. The American University in Cairo was the first educational institution to resume operation while maintaining concerns for safety. Some of the workshops and classes conducted at the AUC Tahrir campus, which overlooked the Tahrir Square, had to be relocated for security reasons and added to the cost of operations.

Returning to school after spending several weeks demonstrating encouraged many students to demand change in the teaching methods. Expectations were high and there was a push for open debates and discussions. Recruitment of new students increased along with petitions for theory and evidence-based courses. The School of Global Affairs and Public Policy became one of the leaders in establishing public discourse in response to political changes. The dialogues were designed to engage members of the media, civic organizations, academia, and political parties with the public in discussing matters important to the citizens. The dialogues took place in AUC Tahrir campus because of its strategic location. Ever since, these discussions became known as the Tahrir dialogues, which are series of public debates focusing on fundamental issues facing Egyptians ("Building a Better Egypt," 2011; M. Haroun, personal communication, February 24, 2011).

GAPP Executive Education programs, which are tailored for mid-to-senior level public administrators and non-profit organizations, were facing challenges to continue operating. Funding the programs was difficult during the transitional period when government was in the process of reorganization and carefully monitoring scarce resources before authorizing new funding. Many other public organizations faced budget cuts which eliminated their training programs. In addition, the Egyptian economy was on decline, which made public funding even more stringent. In September 2011, Egypt's foreign reserves fell to $24 billion from $36 billion the prior year, and a budget deficit reached 9.5% compared to 8.1% in 2010. In October 2011, Standard & Poor's (S&P) downgraded Egypt's rating to BB-, with prospects of lowering it further "...if the political transition falters in a manner that leads to renewed political turmoil" (*Africa Research Bulletin*, 2011a; 2011b). In March 2012 the budget deficit in Egypt reflected a shortfall of £144 billion (*Africa Research Bulletin*, 2012a; 2012b). The economy that had withstood the global economic crises is currently in dire need of a quick recovery operation.

Building a partnership for change is a necessity. With limited sources of funding, whether through the participants' self-funding, or through their affiliates, it is becoming increasingly necessary to turn to other sources for funding public training programs, such as those of the GAPP. Several international agencies and donors are eager to assist and fund such programs. Yet, these organizations have to be approached with caution in order to avoid accusation of espionage for foreign entities (*Ahram Online*, 2012; Feifer, 2011; Torfimiv, 2011). The government has also announced that foreign donors who are willing to fund public programs in Egypt during the transitional period are only interfering in the internal affairs and sovereignty of the country. According to an interview with Fayza Aboul Naga, then Minister of Planning and International Cooperation by the *Wall Street Journal* "I am not sure at this stage we will still need somebody to tell us what is or is not good for us—or worse, to force it on us" (Trofimov, 2011). In addition, the Supreme Council of Armed Forces (SCAF) jumped on the band wagon in criticizing the United States' funding of pro-democracy programs without approval by the Egyptian government. According to Negad Al-Boraie, chair of a human rights organization in Egypt, "We're still ruled by [the] Mubarak regime without Mubarak" (Trofimov, 2011). Accordingly, accepting funding from foreign entities is risky, which forces a new strategy toward diversifying funds based on partnerships between the various public and nonprofit agencies.

Perhaps GAPP can adapt to the new reality on the ground and adjust its operations accordingly. According to Walid Al-Engbawy, General Manager of the Human Capacity Development at the National Management Institute, cuts in expenses, particularly in trainer fees can be adapted by many training agencies and continue to function adequately and survive (W. Al-Engbawy, personal communication, July 3, 2012). The international community and many experts are deeply interested in developments initiated by the Arab Spring, particularly in Egypt. These are encouraging signs. Experts are willing to offer their assistance *pro-bono* and go so far as to cover their own expenses to take part in history unfolding. Soliciting expert opinion and advice to create a comparative learning experience is encouraged by many public training programs. For example, based on expertise of the Venice Commission and Carter Center, the GAPP Executive Education initiated its Free and Fair Elections program through a "Lessons Learnt from Other Countries in Transition" conference (GAPP Execed, 2010). The Free and Fair Elections program expanded to more than 17 governorates in Egypt, providing training workshops in Electoral Monitoring for Civil Society, Effective Journalism for the Election Process, Campaigning for Elections, Empowering Women for Electoral Participation, Lessons Learnt from other Transitioning Countries on Managing Elections, and more. These programs are aimed at creating a cadre of qualified experts in the area of media policy in the region and in helping to build a capacity in state media for professionals. In addition, members of civic organizations and of political parties are also encouraged to take part in the process.

By training approximately 700 members of the civic organizations, media professional and political party members involved in free and fair elections enabled the GAPP Executive Education programs to diversify its funding sources. Despite the added time and administrative costs, the GAPP Executive Education programs are eager to promote its Free and Fair Elections program and maintain its neutrality. Aggressive campaigns and outreach methods for connecting with key stakeholders can yield success in avoiding the traps and rumors of working for outsiders. And by doing so, the GAPP Executive Education is able to position itself as a partner in the change process for building the new Egypt.

## Empowering Citizens as Media Watchdogs

Egyptians had laid the groundwork through their Revolution for basic rights. Egyptian youth went to the streets as an exercise in civic engagement. During the January 25th Revolution, the demonstrators not only demanded basic rights for freedom but also their right for secure homes and neighborhoods, for cleaner streets, and for proper medical care. This demand for "rights" exhibited a hidden sense of pride and belonging that was not diminished by more than three decades of corruption during Mubarak's regime. Harnessing this energy is the duty of all stakeholders in Egypt. This duty consists of providing information to the public through professional media based on accountability and citizen empowerment.

New media and communication technology are leading elements in Egypt's Revolution. They provide a wealth of fast access to unrestricted information. Several public institutions, ministries, the armed forces, political parties, and civic organizations have developed Facebook pages in order to capture the new trend and remain connected with the public. As previously mentioned, Internet users have reached 23 million and mobile phone users have reached 65 million in Egypt. What is more significant is the implication of this trend on the dissemination of information (Taylor, 2010). In addition, new media and communication technology provide rapid access to uncensored information while challenging traditional media methodology in information dissemination (Bassiouni, 2012).

On the other hand, state media in Egypt is facing an identity crises. It has been discredited and regarded as a non-reliable source of information (Al-Ahram Center for Political & Strategic Studies, 2011; Khalil, 2012). With increased competition, media professionals, whether in state or private media, need to develop better skills in meeting the demands of their Facebook-savvy audience. They also need to engage in training workshops in order to focus on building a capacity for professionalism, ethics, administration, marketing, legality, accountability, openness, objectivity, effectiveness, democratization, and civic engagement.

The Executive Education of media personnel must focus on exploiting opportunities through the learning environment. Training workshops must be offered with more flexibility in scheduling and less standardization in order to be able to adapt as trends change. Offering shorter, more focused, and interdisciplinary classes can be more feasible since most professionals cannot take significant time off from their jobs.

## Conclusion

Public admiration and infatuation of technology always increase after significant social upheavals or revolutions. Then the infatuation tends to subside shortly afterward. During the Bolshevik Revolution in 1917, for example, public infatuation with the telegraph as a tool of communication increased, and then gradually subsided. During the 1979 Iranian Revolution, there was an infatuation with tape recordings as a means for communication, and then it faded away. Today, only a few collectors or researchers may be interested in the telegraph or tape recorders (Campbell, 2011). As important a role as new social media played in the Arab Spring, Facebook and Twitter were simply the tools used to express public opinion; they were not the cause for the revolution to take hold or succeed (Campbell, 2011; Dubai School of Government, 2011).

Previously, dictators relied on state media to spread misinformation and exert their control over society. During military coups or social upheavals, state television and radio were always targeted by the revolutionaries in order to broadcast their messages to the public. Today, however, we are witnessing nations removing dictators without bothering to take control of the state media. A major reason for this is the availability of alternative media resources. In addition, the credibility problem of state media has added to its lack of importance and usefulness among the public.

Traditional media, particularly state media, need to adapt to the rapid changes in society in order to remain effective in providing information to the public. This requires it to learn from the new technologies and become more creative, transparent, accountable, and objective. The new media has created a wealth of information through cross-cultural communication methods. Access to information is now available at the click of a mouse or finger. Therefore, state media must abandon its previous practice of censorship and misinformation, and restore its credibility with the public through honest, ethical, and accurate reporting. Its staff and management require new training and development focused on reforms for ethical journalism, autonomous administration, and professional journalism. Continuous training is needed to aide in achieving change, learning new tools and technologies, and remaining active in engaging the public as honest brokers. Since funding for such training programs is scarce, other means ought to be sought through diversification of funding sources. Such reforms must also be accompanied by proper legislations to assure transparency in information dissemination, freedom of expression, and access to public documents. This is in addition to empowering citizens to remain active in expressing their views freely and holding government accountable.

# Challenging a Terrorist Tag in the Media: Framing, the Politics of Resistance, and an Iranian Opposition Group

## Ivan Sascha Sheehan

## Abstract

Scholars have shown that media framing has a powerful effect on citizen perception and policy debates. Research has provided less insight into the ability of marginalized actors to promote their preferred frames in the media in a dynamic political context. The efforts of an exiled Iranian opposition group to get its name removed from official terror lists in the United States, the United Kingdom, and European Union (EU) provides a valuable platform to examine this problem. Using content analysis, I explore how the group promoted its frames in the opinion sections of major world news publications over nine years (2003–2012). I then examine the extent to which journalists aligned to its frames, as opposed to rival official frames, over time in the larger arena of news. The results support research showing that by nurturing small opportunities, marginalized political actors can expand media capacity and influence, but these effects are mediated, at least in part, by critical or focusing events that make rival frames less salient. The study sheds light on the complex relationship between activists, the government, and the media. It has implications for the ability of marginalized political actors to get their frames into public discourse. It also has implications for terror tagging and media coverage of other controversial issues.

# Introduction

In 1997, the U.S. State Department added the exiled Iranian resistance group, *Mujahedin-e Khalq* Organization (MEK), also known as People's Mujahedin Organization of Iran (PMOI), to its list of Foreign Terrorist Organizations (FTO). The purported basis was the killing of six American military personnel and defense contractors 20 years earlier in the 1970s. Two years later, in 1999, the United States went a step further, alleging that the National Council of Resistance of Iran (NCRI), a political organization of several Iranian opposition groups that reject clerical rule, was a front for the MEK and designated it too as a terrorist group.[1] Subsequently the UK and EU followed suit, tacking the MEK/PMOI (although not the NCRI) to their terror watch lists. These listings reflected a shared institutional logic that the group had engaged in terrorist activity in the past and thus constituted a security threat. However, as Friedland and Alford (1991) have observed, institutions can contain contradictions, and individuals operating within them may call on multiple logics. While the dominant, official logic was that the MEK was a terrorist group, there existed a challenger logic (McAdam & Scott, 2005) that presented a very different set of beliefs and premises.

MEK supporters argued that far from being terrorists, the MEK was a legitimate opposition group; that the terrorist listing was based on evidence that even government insiders contested; and that it was politically motivated (to placate the Iranian regime). They contended that the UK and EU listings, occurring in March 2001 and May 2002, were even more direct quid pro quos (the price of opening talks over Iran's nuclear pursuit). In addition, they argued that contrary to "misinformation" orchestrated by the Iranian regime, the MEK had specifically renounced violence as early as 2001 and was dedicated to democracy and freedom in a secular, democratic, non-nuclear Iran. Within short order, they took their case to the courts. They also went public (i.e., they began penning op-eds for the world's major newspapers).

The politics of resistance is predicated on a belief that power is ubiquitous (Foucault, 1980) and as a result resistance must be diffuse (Pickett, 1996)—occurring at micro as well as macro levels (Thomas, 2005). For the MEK, going public was vital to countering a message that stigmatized them as terrorists and made it virtually impossible for them to organize, raise funds, or conduct their mission, namely peaceful opposition to the current dictatorship in Iran.

How did they frame their case in the media and to what extent were their efforts a success? More specifically, to what extent were the frames they promoted in outside commentary picked up in the broader more influential arena of news? While considerable attention has been paid to the effects of media framing, scholars have largely ignored how activists and marginalized political players get their preferred frames into the media in the first place (Callaghan & Schnell, 2001; Rabinowitz, 2010). This may be because of a long held assumption that the media are simply mouthpieces for elite, official government views or it may be because of a belief that the media, because of their own professional norms, are autonomous and impervious to outside influence.

The obstacles activists and policy challengers face in getting their messages inserted into public discourse have been well documented. But there is a growing recognition that activist-media-government interactions constitute a dynamic process in which all players struggle for advantage. There is also a growing recognition that "small opportunities, strategically nurtured by collective actors over time, can expand into bigger opportunities" to improve media standing and capacity and generate more permanent impact (Ryan, Anastario, & Jeffreys, 2005, p. 114).

Most policy issues, for example, have an issue culture dominated by a particular frame. Terrorism, as a policy issue, is dominated by a security frame. But issue cultures often contain alternative frames at odds with a dominant one. These additional frames provide opportunities for activists and policy challengers to redirect the public's attention. Activists can take advantage of other opportunities. Scholars have shown, for example, that critical or focusing events can be catalysts for policy change insofar as they draw media attention and serve as signals of policy failure (Birkland, 1998, p. 55). As such, events also provide a window of opportunity to reframe an issue in a policy debate. Finally, there is a growing recognition that while dominant frames are "difficult to eclipse" (Matesan, 2012, p. 672), they can be vulnerable, especially at times "when the political leaders setting forth these frames lose legitimacy and credibility with the public" (Matesan, 2012, p. 672).

Building on these concepts of political resistance, opportunity, framing, and legitimacy, this paper uses a content analysis to explore the media campaign activists and other political players waged over a decade to get the MEK's name removed from terrorist lists in the United States, United Kingdom, and the European Union. While the focus is on the influence of activist inputs (in the form of op-eds) on journalist outputs (in the form of news), I also examine the role of critical or focusing events in drawing media attention and providing opportunities for policy challengers to shift the debate.

The MEK delisting issue is a useful platform to explore the dynamics of framing and activist–media interactions since it was salient in national and world news for over a decade. Also, like many political issues, it evoked strong emotions and highly polarized rhetoric with one side casting it as sensible policy to contain potential terrorism and the other side framing it as a violation of human rights and justice.

The study has implications for the ability of marginalized groups and political players to promote their frames in public discourse. It also has implications for terror tagging, a phenomenon that is becoming more widespread; has severe contingent consequences; and is much easier "to do than undo" (Gross, 2011, p. 52).

# Historical Background and Context

## The Case of the MEK

To understand the specific struggle of the MEK to get its name removed from terror lists and the obstacles it faced, it helps to provide a little background. The MEK/PMOI was originally formed by three university students in Tehran in 1965. Its mission then was to democratically oppose the regime of Shah Mohammad-Reza Pahlavi, a dictatorship that came to power following a US/UK led coup ousting Iran's first democratically elected government. By the late 1960s and early 1970s, thousands of its members had been arrested and executed by the Shah's secret police for civil disruption. The revolution deposing the Shah in January of 1979 posed a new dilemma for the MEK who, having fought for a socialist-styled democracy, were not ready to accept the theocratic regime by the recently returned Ayatollah Khomeini and actively campaigned against it. These activities earned it the enmity of Islamic clerics who were now in control and attacked the MEK as *elteqati* (eclectic), contaminated with *Gharbzadegi* ("the Western plague"), as *monafeqin* (hypocrites for not aligning with the new Islamic Republic) and *kafer* (unbelievers) for supporting democracy (Moin, 2001, pp. 234, 239). The group and its supporters soon underwent new rounds of arrests and executions, this time conducted by the clerics and Islamic Revolutionary Guards. Subsequently, the leadership fled to Paris, then Iraq where it regrouped and formed a 3,000 strong national liberation army as well as a government in exile dedicated to overthrowing the theocratic regime now operating in Iran and replacing it with a democracy.

The United States did not add the MEK to its list of foreign terrorist organizations until 1997. The purported basis was the killings of six American military personnel and defense contractors in Iran in the early 1970s. The State Department would later allege that the MEK participated in the February 1979 occupation of the United States embassy in Tehran and that after fleeing to Paris, then Iraq in the early 1980s, it conducted terrorist attacks inside Iran. Today, there is good evidence that Iran lobbied hard to get the U.S. and other western governments to designate the MEK as terrorists although the allegations were baseless. Only one day after the United States added the MEK to its list of FTOs in October of 1997, the *Los Angeles Times* reported: "One senior Clinton administration official said inclusion of the People's Mojahedeen was intended as a 'goodwill gesture' to Tehran and its newly elected moderate president Mohammad Khatami."[2] Five years later the same official told *Newsweek*: "[There] was White House interest in opening up a dialogue with the Iranian government. At the time, President Khatami had recently been elected and was seen as a moderate. Top administration officials saw cracking down on the [PMOI/MEK] -which the Iranians had made clear they saw as a menace, as one way to do so."[3]

Across the Atlantic, similar political considerations operated. In an interview with the BBC Radio in 2006, then British Foreign Secretary Jack Straw admitted that the UK designation of the MEK in 2001 was specifically made in response to demands made by the Iranian regime (Safavi, 2010). That same year classified documents, later unclassified by a UK court, revealed that senior foreign service officials were concerned about possible adverse foreign policy consequences if the terrorist designation was lifted since the Iranian regime prioritized "tough legal and political measures" against the organization (Fender, 2007, p. 4).[4] The EU too is now known to have also bowed to pressure in designating the MEK in 2002.

Supporters of removing the terrorist designation soon took their case to courts. These efforts met with strong resistance, not only from spokespersons for Iran, but also from representatives of a new Iran-tilting government in Iraq. By 2006, seven European courts, to be sure, had ruled that the group did not meet lawful criteria for terrorism in the first place. They had also ruled that the terrorist designation should have been moot after 2001, when the group's leadership ceased its military efforts that year to focus on a political and social campaign to bring about democratic change in Iran.[5] Despite these rulings, and the humanitarian crisis that evolved when a new Iran-tilting government in Iraq began threatening to "repatriate" the remaining MEK in Iraq to Iran (where they faced likely torture and execution), it took two to three years for the UK and EU to comply with the courts and delist the MEK. In the United States, where the courts similarly ruled repeatedly in favor of the MEK, and as many as 200 members of Congress signed statements endorsing its cause, the process was also slow and the MEK continued to be proscribed until the end of September 2012. In the interim, a growing number of supporters of the MEK began writing op-eds and letters to the editor in the world's major print publications.

## Terror Tagging as an "Issue Culture"

Terrorism like other policy issues could be said to have a culture. That is, it became a commanding concern evoking a belief set.[6] A characteristic of issue cultures is that there is debate around them and the media can draw on more than one package (Gamson & Modigliani, 1989). After 9/11, the most prominent package was *security* and terrorist designation, designed to prevent terrorist financing and sanction groups thought to be a security risk, fell squarely within that category and package.

Proscription, however, was coming under increasing scrutiny and the media could have called on other packages, although it only occasionally did so. Within the *security* and think tank sectors, critics such as Paul Pillar (2001, p. 150) assailed the process for being too bureaucratic and too slow "to respond to the changes in the international gallery of terrorists." Others noted that the process had become inefficient and "inflexible" (Cronin, 2003, p. 7). As an example, Nathan Stock (2012) points out that as late as 2008—18 years after he was celebrated for ending apartheid—it took an act of Congress to allow Nelson Mandela to enter the U.S. without a waiver and it was not until November of 2011 that his terrorist designation was finally removed.

Sociologists, meanwhile, were raising *definitional* issues. Part of the problem, observed Tilly (2004, p. 5), is that the terms terror, terrorism and terrorist are themselves imprecise since they "do not identify casually coherent and distinct social phenomena." This imprecision allows governments and society wide discretion to decide who gets labeled a terrorist and who does not.

Civil rights advocates weighed in on the *politicization* of the process. As early as 2003, Human Rights Watch's Joanne Mariner noted that all too often individuals and groups appear on terror lists as a "political concession" (Mariner, 2003, para 17). Others attacked proscription for failing to distinguish between terrorism and legitimate struggles for democracy thereby criminalizing self-determination movements and closing off opportunities for negotiation and dialogue around the world (Dudouet, 2011; Gross, 2011; Muller, 2008). The definitional issue (terrorists or freedom fighters) did get picked up routinely in the media, though without much depth. Relatively little attention, however, was paid to the larger argument that the process, whether conducted by the United States, the European Union, the United Nations (UN), or another organization was being used increasingly as an instrument of domestic and foreign policy, e.g., to silence opposition at home and appease allies abroad (Dryfuss, 2002; Muller, 2008; Shapiro, 2008).

In a climate that placed security as the most salient package, *rights* arguments (i.e., that proscription violated fairness, transparency and due process) were also given short shrift, although these arguments were being raised in the legal community (Shapiro, 2008; Sullivan & Hayes, 2011).

In the meantime, proscription, whether applied by the United States, the United Kingdom, EU, UN, or another government or organization was casting an ever-widening net. In the last quarter of 2012, 51 groups were on the U.S. State Department's Foreign Terrorist Organization (FTO) list (U.S. Department of State, September 28, 2012) and there were 126 entries on the Individuals and Entities Designated by the State Department Under E.O. 13224 (US Department of State, December, 2012), many overlapping with the FTO list. Today, nearly half of the State Department's FTOs are based in the Middle East and North African (MENA) region although only 6% of the world's population lives in that region (Stock, 2012). Although not solely a counter-terrorism tool, the Treasury Department's Office of Foreign Asset Control also keeps a list of Specially Designated Nationals and Blocked Persons that now runs to 556 pages (U.S. Department of Treasury, March, 2013). Across the Atlantic, the EU, as of mid-2012, had 25 groups and entities on its primary terrorist list (Eurlex, 2012) and, as of March 2013, the UN had designated over 230 individuals and 63 entities and other groups associated with al-Qaida (UN Security Council, 2013). Taken together, the above listings of these organizations alone include as many as 45% of all non-state armed groups involved in armed conflicts from minor clashes to wars around the world (Themner & Wallensteen, 2011) and a broad range of non-armed opposition movements. The breadth of this net has renewed debate about the legitimacy of proscription, a process that is difficult to overturn (Gross, 2011).

# Theoretical Background

## Media Opportunity

While the court is a valuable forum for policy challengers, there are additional benefits to going public. As Lazarsfeld and Merton observed as far back as 1948 (p. 101), press emphasis confers status on an issue. There are other potential rewards. Media coverage allows activists to expand the debate around an issue. It can also energize a movement by mobilizing a population, and it can increase the legitimacy of a group in the political arena (Gamson & Wolfsfeld, 1993; McCarthy & Zald, 1994; Rohlinger, 2002).

This does not mean that activists challenging a particular policy do not face barriers. Going public does not guarantee media attention. In fact, much of the literature on agenda setting indicates that in a market-driven media environment where reporters are pressured to produce fast, interesting stories, policy issues take a back seat to stories that are more easily dramatized and sensationalized (Hamilton, 2004). Or, as Gans (1979) observes, what is newsworthy is prioritized as what has drama, conflict, novelty, timeliness, and visual appeal. Moreover, when policy is covered, the topics of interest to political elites (decision makers) tend to be favored over those that matter to political challengers (Reese, 1991). Indeed there is good evidence that journalists marginalize activists whose opinions are outside the mainstream (Hooks, 1992; Van Dijk, 1996). This situation makes it difficult for policy challengers to even enter the public debate (Pfetsch & Silke, 2011).

Nor does it necessarily mean favorable media coverage (Terkildson, Schnell, & Ling, 1998). Ideally the media are political watchdogs that stand for truth, balance and objectivity (Bennett, 1990, p. 5). In reality, these expectations are not usually supported (Herman & Chomsky, 1988). In fact, most of the evidence indicates that on policy issues journalists gravitate to insider sources (e.g. government officials and think tank researchers) and either "rally round the flag," slanting coverage towards official views on an issue (Zaller & Chiu, 1996, pp. 385, 399), or create their own spin, reinterpreting messages from either side in a "media generated blend of messages" (Callaghan & Schnell, 2001, p. 184) that may take the form of "issue dualism" (Terkildson, Schnell, Ling,1998, p. 47)—an effort to seek balance by conveying a controversial issue as a political contest, a game or "horse race" in which arguments on either side are made to appear equally valid (Callaghan & Schnell, 2001, p. 205).

For a group tagged with the label of terrorist, the obstacles to gaining what they might consider adequate or appropriate coverage would be further magnified by the stigma of the terrorist label. Still, there is growing evidence that sustained efforts on the part of activists and policy challengers, even otherwise marginalized ones, can improve media capacity and standing although this subject remains relatively understudied (Ryan, Anastario, & Jeffreys, 2005).

## The Role of Frames and Framing

The political process has been defined as a struggle over whose definition of social, political or economic phenomena will prevail (Gamson & Modigliani, 1989). To a large extent, this struggle is played out through language: "If policymaking is a struggle over alternative realities, then language is the medium that reflects, advances, and interprets these alternatives" (Rochefort & Cobb, 1994, p. 9).

A key component of this process is framing. Frames are interpretive schemata (Goffman, 1974) that simplify and condense the "world out there" by highlighting some aspects of reality to the exclusion of others (Snow & Benford, 1992, p. 137). As such they give "inferential cues" on how an issue should be understood and interpreted (Gamson & Modigliani, 1989, p. 143). Frames essentially define problems, diagnose causes, make moral judgments and suggest cures. As Entman has put it:

> To frame is to select some aspects of a perceived reality and make them more salient in a communicating text, in such a way as to promote a particular problem definition, causal interpretation, moral evaluation, and/or treatment recommendation for the item described. (1993, p. 52)

This aspect of political communication is significant since in any policy struggle, all players (activists, politicians, the media) want to control public interpretation; how the media covers an issue has been shown to be a powerful influence on citizen perception (Dalton, Beck, & Huckfeldt, 1998) shaping opinion on topics as varied and controversial as racial politics (Kinder & Sanders, 1996); gun control (Callaghan & Schnell, 2000); hate crimes (Bramlet-Solomon, 2001); the war on terror (Ryan, 2004); affirmative action (Richardson & Lancendorfer, 2004); gay rights (Norris, 2006); legalization of marijuana (Golan, 2010); and European integration (Helbling, Hoeglinger, & Wuest, 2010). Moreover, there is good evidence that policy decisions are frequently made on the basis of how a problem is perceived and defined (Tversky & Kahneman, 1981).

## The Role of Symbols, Rhetoric, and Sources

Frames and framing can be reinforced using other tools of language. Gamson & Lasch (1983) note that public discourse takes place in a symbolic environment that employs images and stereotypes to root positions. Groups with interests at stake may call on metaphors, catchphrases, condensing symbols, or rhetoric to create a positive or negative emotional image that reinforces or offsets a particular frame (Gamson & Modigliani, 1989; Terkildson, Schnell, & Ling, 1998). This can lead to framing contests around an image or even a symbol.

Players with interests at stake can also call on authoritative sources to reinforce or affirm or disconfirm a frame. Journalists are in a particularly strong position in this respect since they need sources "to fill news holes, meet deadlines, provide drama and add issue balance" (Terkildson, Terkildson, Schnell, Ling, 1998, p. 48) but have the unique ability to "choose who speaks (or does not speak) in news coverage" enabling them "to frame news without appearing to do so (Schneider, 2012, p. 72). Journalists have the additional advantage of being able to employ explanatory cues to cast sources on one or the other side in a positive or negative light, and they can influence perceptions by calling on apparently authoritative but unnamed sources to give legitimacy to one or another side of an argument.

## The Role of Credibility and Events

While framing, rhetoric, and selective use of sources play significant roles in policy debates, credibility and critical or focusing events (Kingdon, 1984) can also be key. Scholars have shown that credibility is critical to frame resonance. Frames must be consonant with cultural narratives and larger belief systems (Benford & Snow, 2000). In a word, they need to appear reasonable. The frame maker also has to be credible. But credibility is not a static attribute, i.e., a simple matter of status. Actors can alternately enhance their own credibility and discredit their opponents using tactics such as self-aggrandizement on the one hand and vilification on the other (Wiktorowicz, 2004). Events too can impair credibility. Previous work has shown that critical or "focusing" events (Kingdon, 1984) can be exploited to alter or redirect the content or interpretation of a policy debate and mobilize opinion in new ways (Birkland, 1998; Cobb & Elder, 1983; Callaghan & Schnell, 2001). In addition, parties to a policy debate "can use positive developments to boost their credibility," call on negative crisis situations to damage the legitimacy and credibility of their opponents and "thereby make rival frames more appealing" (Matesan, 2012, p. 678).

# Research Focus

The central focus of this study was the extent to which advocacy inputs on the subject of delisting the MEK were reflected in journalist outputs. Specifically, I examined the extent to which the frames that advocates for delisting promoted in the opinion section of world news publications were adopted by journalists in news coverage. I also examined the role of critical or "focusing" events in drawing media attention and providing opportunities for policy challengers to shift or redirect the debate.

Based on previous research showing that media attention to policy issues increases when there is a compelling story to tell or an event that can be dramatized, I anticipated that the volume of media coverage of MEK delisting would be higher when an event occurred that could be sensationalized. Based on literature indicating that journalists tend to slant towards official status quo positions, but that issue advocates can impact journalist frames, I anticipated that news coverage would incorporate at least some MEK advocacy perspectives, rhetoric and frames over time. However, in view of other literature indicating that journalists create their own "spin," I also expected to find issue dualism and media generated frames (in particular a "horse race" or political contest frame).

# Methods

A content analysis of editorials, op-eds, and news stories was used to examine coverage of the MEK delisting controversy in the opinion and news sections of major world news publications from January 2003 through September 2012.

## Sample Selection

Articles for analysis were retrieved through a LexisNexis search of major world news publications using the keywords "MEK," "PMOI," "NCRI," or "MOK" and terror "designation," "list(ing)," blacklist(ing)," or "proscription."

The year 2003 offered a useful starting point. Although the United States first listed the MEK as an FTO in 1997, the listing became a salient issue in 2003 when the United States used it to rationalize bombing the group's base at Camp Ashraf in Iraq in March and the French subsequently used it to justify raids on MEK headquarters in Paris in June. The year 2003 is also significant since it was in that year, after the coalition bombing of Ashraf, that the MEK voluntarily disarmed, and all individual members then in Iraq signed documents renouncing violence and terrorism.

The time span (2003–2012) was a relevant one, since it covered what Chilton (1987) has called "critical discourse moments" in the struggle of the MEK to get its name removed from terrorist lists in the United States, United Kingdom, and the

European Union. These benchmarks included repeated court filings; repeated court rulings; the eventual reversal in the UK in 2008; in the EU in 2009, as well as the announcement that the United States would lift the designation in September 2012. It also encompassed a sequence of events that affected the plight of the MEK, including the transfer of sovereignty in Iraq in 2004, the gradual withdrawal of U.S. troops from Iraq, and two fatal raids on the group's base at Camp Ashraf—one in 2009 and one in 2011. In addition, it included the period of post delisting discussion after the UK and EU removed the terrorist tags in those jurisdictions and, more briefly, after the United States announced that it too would remove the tag in September of 2012.

I focused on major world news publications since there is good evidence that stories "spread vertically" within the news sector with editors at major newspapers setting news agendas (Nisbet & Huge, 2006). Opinion pieces (editorials and op-eds) were incorporated along with news since, as Hynds and Martin (1979) observe, opinion provides a forum to express political views in a robust market of open debate and competing frames are especially visible in opinion. Additionally, inclusion of opinion allowed assessment of the extent to which journalists in news reporting adopted the frames used by outside commentators for and against delisting the MEK.

To guarantee relevancy, articles that were not substantially related to delisting, were duplicates, or non-articles (summaries) were excluded. A total of 367 articles made up the final sample. Of these, 131 were opinion pieces (op-eds, commentary, or letters to the editor) from outside commentators, 49 were staff-written editorials, and 187 were news or features penned by staff journalists.

## Operational Definition of Framing

Framing, defined by Goffman (1974) as schemata of interpretation can refer to the complete process by which these phenomena are produced, selected, distributed, and adopted, or one aspect of this process. In this study, I focus on the definitional aspect, specifically the *arguments* stakeholders used mobilized to *justify* positions for and against delisting the MEK. In so doing, I rely on literature that suggests that to be effective, policy challengers have to put forward arguments that appear credible and easy to support. In particular, I rely on literature that uses Habermas' (1993) distinction of three types of arguments: utilitarian, identity-related, and rights-based (Helbling, Hoeglinger, & Wuest 2010). This literature identifies utilitarian frames as ones that justify a position by focusing on its ability to achieve a goal or meet an interest that may be political, strategic, or security related. In contrast, identity-related frames focus on ideas and values that matter to a particular community. One category of this frame, as Helbling, Hoeglinger, & Wuest (2010) observe, is a cultural/ideological sub-frame that is invoked to uphold an exclusive cultural, political or religious identity, or heritage. Rights-based frames, on the other hand, refer to moral principles and universal rights that can be claimed by anyone, regardless of their particular interests or cultural identity. Typical examples are humanitarian rights, civil rights, and justice before the law (Helbling, Hoeglinger, & Wuest (2010). However, in view of evidence that journalists employ issue dualism, in which two sides of an issue are treated as equally valid (Terkildson, Schnell, & Ling, 1998), I also examine this category of framing.

## Measures and Coding

The unit of analysis was the individual article. For all articles I coded the following descriptive variables: name of the publication; where it was published (e.g., United States, United Kingdom, Canada); date; LexisNexis classification as news or opinion/commentary; whether the author was a journalist (editor or staff-writer) or outside commentator; and the author's credentials (e.g., editor, staff-writer, activist belonging to formal organization, politician, military expert, representative of international organization such as UN).

## Media Attention and the Role of Events

To track media attention and its relationship to events, I calculated the volume of coverage by year and assessing if coverage frequency waxed or waned with specific events.

## Framing Categories

In examining framing, I focused on what Entman (1993) describes as the problem definition aspect of framing, i.e., the arguments that were mobilized to justify positions for and against delisting. In particular, I focused on utilitarian, identity-related, and rights-based frames as discussed earlier. I also coded issue dualism and an additional frame that crept into news stories in 2012, namely "ulterior motives."

**Utilitarian frame**: I coded a utilitarian frame (either "in our interests" or "not in our interests") if the article invoked an interest to support to support or oppose delisting. Typical interest-based statements in favor of the MEK cause focused on the MEK's role in providing intelligence on Iran's clandestine nuclear program, thereby protecting "national interests," "national security," or the "security of friends, "empowering" or "unleashing" opposition to the regime to promote democracy; diverting regime attention and resources from "mischief making in Iraq," distracting them from their goal of "hegemony in the Persian Gulf," or from their support for terrorists and kidnappers; providing a political alternative or "third way" between military strikes on Iran (to deter their nuclear ambitions) and appeasement. Alternately, interest based statements against the MEK cause stressed its negative effects, e.g., undermining positive engagement with Iran, the possibility of backlash against other opposition groups.

**Identity frame:** I coded an identity-based frame if the article contained a statement or invoked identity or shared values to bolster a position, e.g., if it portrayed the MEK as "someone like us" or alternately as "not like us," appealing to shared or disparate cultural or ideological values, traditions, or beliefs. Typical examples in favor of the MEK claimed the group as a "friend," a "partner," an "ally," presenting the group as "moderate," secular," "democratic," and committed to "gender equality." Such statements characteristically deplored "opprobrium for friends" or "branding friends as enemies." Conversely, identity-based statements on the side of not delisting focused on the "otherness" of the MEK depicting it as "strange," "odd," "bizarre," prone to "cult-like behavior," "violent," "anti-American," and "not a friend."

**Rights frame:** I coded a rights based frame if the article contained a statement invoking a universal moral or ethical principle (e.g., justice), rights before the law, or humanitarian concerns. Typical examples on both sides of the debate included statements invoking legal rights, morality, and justice. On the side of delisting, humanitarian concerns (the possibility of a "disaster," even "wholesale slaughter" in the event the Iraqi Prime Minister followed through on his threat to expel the MEK to Iran) also loomed large and in some ways dominated this frame.

If a writer used or quoted a source articulating two separate frames—for example, arguing for delisting on the basis of strategic (utilitarian) *and* human rights claims—I coded those as separate frames and included both.

**Issue dualism**: For news coverage, in addition to the above frames, I coded for issue dualism, i.e., a "game" or "horserace" frame in which arguments for and against delisting were covered about equally in the same article.

**Rhetoric, sources, and cues.** To capture the role of rhetoric in reinforcing frames, I coded the use of symbolic words and catchall phrases applied to the MEK as a group. In particular, I tried to capture the extent of the use of positive descriptors—words such as "friend," "moderate," "secular," or "democratic" to reinforce a positive frame and conversely the extent of use of negative descriptors such as "strange," "odd," "bizarre," or "cultish" to reinforce a negative frame.

Since journalists rely on sources to shape their story lines, I also documented the sources for any verbatim quotations, whether they were named or unnamed, interest group spokespersons, government representatives, or other experts. I also examined journalist use of source cues, i.e., descriptor words, to add luster to a quote or alternatively to discredit it.

## Media slant

To examine media slant, I assessed whether a given article was for delisting, neutral on the subject, or against delisting. For opinion articles, I coded a pro slant if the editorial or op-ed deplored the terrorist designation, urged delisting, and/or chastised proponents of continuing the listing (e.g., as appeasers); I coded an anti-slant if the opinion piece urged continued listing or criticized proponents (e.g., as paid lobbyists "shilling for terrorists"). On the other hand, I coded a neutral slant if no clear position could be determined. For news articles, I coded an anti-slant if the news report or feature included more attributed statements that favored delisting or slanted the article to indicate that delisting was a sensible choice; a pro stance was coded if the news piece included more attributed statements favoring continuation of the terrorist designation or slanted the article to indicate that delisting was potentially risky or otherwise undesirable; I coded a neutral stance if the news piece contained equal numbers of attributed statements for and against delisting and/or if the overall message was that equally favorable arguments could be made on each side.

## Data Analysis

I ran descriptive frequencies for all variables. For newspaper characteristics and framing, the unit of analysis was the individual article. For rhetorical words and symbols, sources and source cues, the unit of analysis was the number of instances.

# Results

## Overall Sample

The search criteria yielded 401 articles published between January 2003 and the end of September 2012. The final sample, after excluding duplicates and non-articles (summaries), was 367 articles. Of these, 131 were opinion pieces (op-eds, commentary, or letters to the editor) from outside commentators, 49 were staff-written editorials, and 187 were news or features penned by staff journalists (Table 1).

Overall, the retrieved articles were regionally balanced for English language news. One hundred and fifty-seven (43%) were published in major U.S. papers, 113 (31%) in major UK papers, 24 (7%) in Canadian news publications, and 10 (3%) in Australia/New Zealand publications. An additional 42 (12%) were from international publications such as the *Christian Science Monitor* and *International Herald Tribune,* and 15 (4%) were in prominent English language Israeli papers such as *Haaretz.* The U.S. newspaper that published the most articles on the topic was *The Washington Times*

(83 articles). The UK paper that published the most was the London *Telegraph* (39 articles). These two papers tend to be conservative taking hardline, hawkish positions on Iran. However, there was a respectable showing of relevant articles in more centrist/liberal news publications including the *Washington Post* (40 articles), the *Birmingham Post* (24 articles), the *Guardian* (11 articles), and the *New York Times* (11 articles).

My focus in this study was on how rival frames promoted in opinion fared in the news. I was also interested in the extent to which critical events made frames on one or the other side more salient for reporters and how rhetoric and selective use of sources were used to amplify frames. Before examining these topics I want to make a few observations about the opinion sample, the role of events in driving media attention, and the overall slant of opinion and news.

## Opinion Sample

Two observations can be made about the opinion sample. First, most of the outside opinion was penned by advocates *for* delisting the MEK. In fact, the ratio *against* was 8:1. Second, identifiable advocacy groups contributed only about one quarter of all opinion pieces on the topic, and unaffiliated citizens contributed only about 15%. The bulk of the outside commentary came from politicians, academics, and military or security experts. Here, however, there was wide divergence between supporters and opponents in credentials. While all of the political leaders and most of the military experts offering commentary on the pro side of delisting were based in the United Kingdom, EU, or United States, all of the politicians contributing commentary against delisting were based in Iran or Iraq. Moreover, most of the advocacy/interest group representation on the side of not delisting was contributed by individuals affiliated with the NIAC (National Iranian American Council), a group that is known to advocate engagement with Islamic Republic of Iran and has long opposed delisting the MEK. This pattern of authorship was significant since frame credibility has been shown to be a function of source credibility (Chong & Druckman, 2007; Druckman, 2001) and while advocacy groups with known interests command less credibility than politicians and experts, these groups can be vulnerable in a changing political environment.

| Table 1. Credentials in outside opinion (n = 131) | | | | | | |
|---|---|---|---|---|---|---|
| | Delisting supporters N = 117 | | Delisting opponents N = 14 | | Total | |
| | N | % | N | % | N | % |
| Identifiable advocacy group[1] | 29 | 25 | 4 | 29 | 33 | 25 |
| Political leader | | | | | | |
| Politician UK[2] | 32 | 27 | 0 | 0 | 32 | 24 |
| Politician EU | 5 | 4 | 0 | 0 | 5 | 4 |
| Politician US | 3 | 3 | 0 | 0 | 3 | 2 |
| Politician Iran or Iraq[3] | 0 | 0 | 4 | 29 | 4 | 3 |
| Citizen | 18 | 15 | 3 | 21 | 21 | 16 |
| Academic | 17 | 15 | 1 | 7 | 18 | 14 |
| Military/Security expert | 11 | 9 | 1 | 7 | 12 | 9 |
| International organization[4] | 2 | 2 | 1 | 7 | 3 | 2 |

[1] Includes representatives of NCRI, Camp Ashraf residents, and Iranian American Society on the side of delisting and representatives of the NIAC and Foundation for Democracy in Iran on the side of opposing delisting.
[2] Includes op-eds from current and former members of the British parliament with about equal numbers from conservative and labor politicians.
[3] Includes op-eds from representatives of the Iranian embassy as well as office of the Iraqi prime minister.
[4] Includes op-eds from representatives of the UN and the Helsinki Committee for Human Rights.

## Figure 1. Media attention: Volume of articles on removing the MEK terrorist

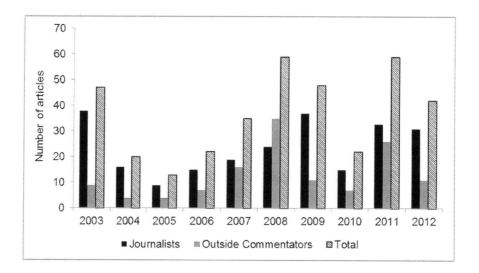

**Table 2. Media attention: Number of articles on removing the MEK terrorist designation by year and key events**

| Year | Number of Articles Retrieved | Outside Opinion | Journalist Authored | Concurrent Events |
|---|---|---|---|---|
| 2003 | 47 | 9 | 38 | Mar: U.S. invades Iraq. MEK headquarters at Camp Ashraf bombed by coalition forces.<br>May: MEK in Iraq voluntarily disarm.<br>Jun: Tehran tries to broker a deal with coalition forces—withdraw its military backing for Hamas and Hezbollah and give open access to nuclear facilities in return for MEK.[1]<br>Jun: 1,300 French police raid homes of MEK dissidents and offices of NCRI in France. |
| 2004 | 20 | 4 | 16 | Jul: MEK in Iraq awarded "Protected Persons" status under Fourth Geneva Convention. |
| 2005 | 13 | 4 | 9 | May: Based on a listing of MEK attacks on Iranian government officials and interests in 1990s, Canada adds MEK to its terror list. |
| 2006 | 22 | 7 | 15 | Jun: 35 members of Britain's parliament apply to UK's Secretary of State to lift ban on MEK.<br>Dec: EU Court calls into question EU's designation of PMOI/MEK as a terrorist organization. |
| 2007 | 35 | 16 | 19 | Repeated appeals to UK and EU governments delist MEK.<br>Nov: UK court rules that PMOI/MEK is not concerned in terrorism and proscription cannot be lawfully justified.<br>Dec: Camp Ashraf responsibility passes from US forces to Iraq.<br>· Iraqi officials threaten to expel MEK from Iraq.<br>· UK court reaffirms November ruling that listing the MEK as terrorist is unlawful. |
| 2008 | 60 | 36 | 24 | Jun: UK removes MEK for its terror list.<br>Oct: EU Court rules that EU was wrong to blacklist MEK.<br>Dec: EU Court rules for a third time that EU was wrong to blacklist MEK |
| 2009 | 48 | 11 | 37 | Jan: EU removes MEK from its terror list. MEK files petition with Washington, D.C. Circuit of Appeals for US delisting.<br>Feb: Iran urges Iraq to expel MEK.[2]<br>Jul: Iraqi security forces raid Camp Ashraf leaving at least 11 MEK dead and 500 injured. The Iraqi government justifies the massacre as cracking down on terrorists. |
| 2010 | 22 | 7 | 15 | Jul: DC Court of Appeals orders State Department to review MEK listing based on finding that the agency violated the rights of the MEK.<br>Nov: A bipartisan group of 110 US Congress members urge State Department to delist MEK. |
| 2011 | 57 | 24 | 33 | Apr.: Iraqi security forces raid Ashraf again leaving at least 33 dead and more than 300 wounded.<br>Dec: US completes withdrawal of combat troops from Iraq. |
| 2012 | 32 | 9 | 23 | Jun: DC Circuit Court rules that the US State Department has 4 months to decide whether to continue to designate MEK as a terror group.<br>Sep 21: Media reports that the US has decided to remove the MEK/PMOI from the list of Terrorist Organizations. |

[1] In 2007, the *BBC News* reported uncovering a letter written after the invasion of Iraq in 2003 where Tehran offers to withdraw military backing for Hamas and Hezbollah as well as give open access to their nuclear facilities in return for Western action in disbanding the PMOI. See BBC News (2007, July 17). See also BBC News (2007, July 18).

[2] See AFP (2009, February 28).

## Designation by year and author type Media Attention and Critical Events

Figure 1 shows the volume of articles by year and type of authorship (outside opinion or journalist authored) over the study period. Table 2 gives more detailed information on the context by year and key events. An important finding in terms of media attention was that, while outside opinion peaked in 2008 (when delisting was an intense topic of policy deliberation in the UK and EU), journalist coverage spiked when events created compelling stories to tell (e.g., in 2003 when the coalition bombed Camp Ashraf and police raided the MEK compound in Paris, and in 2009 and 2011 when Iraqi forces stormed Camp Ashraf killing dozens of MEK then residing there. These results highlight the key role of critical events as potential catalysts for policy debates (Birkland, 1998).

# Media Slant

Table 3 shows the results for media slant. In the outside opinion set, pro-delisting op-eds and letters to the editor outnumbered anti-delisting pieces by a ratio of 8:1. Similar results were found for inside opinion: staff (journalist-authored) editorials for delisting outstripped those against delisting by a ratio of 7:1. These results may say something about the gatekeeping function of editors in opinion sections who, faced with constraints of time and space, tend to favor outside opinion that is consonant with the worldview of the publication (Golan, 2010). In this case, there was a preponderance of publications at the conservative end of the spectrum where more hawkish attitudes towards Iran prevailed. Alternately, the higher number of op-eds on the side of delisting may simply reflect more prolific submission by advocates for the MEK.

A different pattern emerged in the analysis of the much larger set of journalist-authored news and features set (n = 188) where the ratio of articles that could be coded as pro-delisting, against delisting or neutral on the subject was much closer. Overall, 41% of news reportage took a neutral position or presented a mixed stance. Only 27% clearly slanted towards delisting while 32% decidedly slanted towards continuing to list the group—either by using an excess of quotes from sources critical of delisting or by direct commentary.

The aggregate results for journalist-authored pieces, however, obscure changes over time. As shown in Table 3, the percentage of journalist-authored news and feature pieces that slanted against delisting clearly shrunk over the two 5-year periods (from 41% for the period 2003–2007 to 24% for the period 2008–2012), while the percentage that slanted towards delisting almost doubled (from 17% to 33%). These changes, graphically depicted in Figure 2, suggest that journalists began to align on the side of delisting over time, albeit cautiously.

| Table 3. Media slant/position on removing the MEK from terrorist lists (n = 367) | | | | | | | |
|---|---|---|---|---|---|---|---|
| | Pro-delisting (Challenger position) | | Neutral | | Anti-delisting (Government position) | | Total |
| | N | % | N | % | N | % | N |
| **Outside Opinion**[1] | | | | | | | |
| 2003–2007 | 32 | 78 | - | - | 9 | 22 | 41 |
| 2008–2012 | 83 | 93 | 1 | 1 | 5 | 6 | 89 |
| Overall | 115 | 88 | 1 | 1 | 14 | 11 | 130 |
| **Journalist Authored** | | | | | | | |
| *Editorials*[2] | | | | | | | |
| 2003–2007 | 10 | 67 | 4 | 27 | 1 | 7 | 15 |
| 2008–2012 | 23 | 68 | 3 | 9 | 8 | 24 | 34 |
| Overall | 34 | 70 | 8 | 15 | 7 | 15 | 49 |
| *News & Features* | | | | | | | |
| 2003–2007 | 14 | 17 | 35 | 42 | 34 | 41 | 83 |
| 2008–2012 | 35 | 33 | 45 | 43 | 25 | 24 | 105 |
| Overall | 48 | 27 | 75 | 41 | 58 | 32 | 188 |
| *All Journalist* | 82 | 35 | 87 | 37 | 68 | 29 | 237 |

[1] Op-eds from outside commentators and letters to the editor.
[2] Staff written editorials.

## Figure 2. News & feature slant on removing the MEK from terrorist lists for two time periods (n = 188)

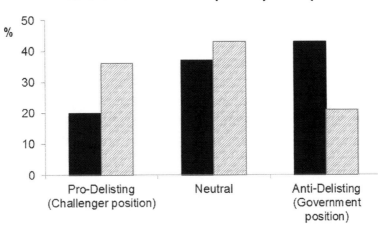

| | Pro-Delisting | | | Anti-Delisting | |
|---|---|---|---|---|---|
| Time | Challenger Frame | % | Time | Government Frame | % |
| 2003–07 (N = 32) | | | 2003–07 (N = 9) | | |
| | Delisting = in our interests | 78 | | MEK are not friends, not like us | 78 |
| | Not delisting = appeasement | 59 | | Utilitarian: not in our interests | 11 |
| | MEK are our friends, allies | 53 | | Simply terrorists | 11 |
| | Human rights/justice | 47 | | MEK advocates have ulterior motives | 11 |
| 2008–12 (N = 82) | | | 2008–12 (N = 5) | | |
| | Human rights/justice | 75 | | Advocates have ulterior motives | 100 |
| | Utilitarian: strategic interest | 46 | | Delisting = politically risky | 100 |
| | Identity: MEK are our friends | 34 | | MEK are not friends, not like us | 60 |
| | Not delisting = appeasement | 29 | | Utilitarian: not in our interests | 20 |
| Overall (N = 115) | | | Overall (N = 14) | | |
| | Human rights/justice | 67 | | MEK are not friends, not like us | 72 |
| | Delisting = in our interests | 55 | | Delisting = not in our interests | 14 |
| | Identity: MEK are our friends | 39 | | Human rights/justice | 7 |
| | Not delisting = appeasement | 37 | | Simply terrorists | 7 |

Table 4. Input: Most frequent frames on removing terror designation in outside commentary

*Note*: Percentages may not sum to 100 since some articles included more than one issue frame.

## Framing

Input (Outside Commentary). There were three key findings in the analysis of outside commentary. First, as shown in Table 4, framing was plainly directional, with advocates for delisting using one set of preferred frames and opponents using another set. Second, delisting advocates were more likely than opponents to use combinations of frames (e.g., utilitarian+identity and/or human rights). In fact, almost half (48%) of the outside commentary opposing the terror tag used more than one frame. In contrast, commentary opposing delisting tended to employ a singular "not like us" (they are "odd," "different," "bizarre") identity frame with only 15% using an additional frame. Third, commentary on the side of lifting the terror designation showed greater flexibility in the choice of frames over time. In particular, there was a clear shift from away from predominantly utilitarian and identity frames to human rights and justice frames. Output: Journalist-authored opinion and news. To what extent did journalists adopt or align to frames on either side of the debate? Table 5 provides the most frequent frames used in journalist-authored pieces, including editorials and staff-written op-eds, on the one hand (n = 49), and news and features on the other (n = 187).

| Time | Editorials/Opinion Columns | % | Time | News/Features | % |
|---|---|---|---|---|---|
| 2003–07 (N = 15) | | | 2003–07 (N = 83) | | |
| | Human rights | 47 | | MEK are not like us, strange | 42 |
| | MEK are our friends, allies | 33 | | Political contest | 28 |
| | Delisting = in our interests | 20 | | Delisting = in our interests | 30 |
| | | | | Human rights/justice | 17 |
| | | | | MEK are our friends, allies | 12 |
| 2008–12 (N = 34) | | | 2008–12 (N = 105) | | |
| | Human rights | 70 | | Human rights/justice | 40 |
| | MEK are our friends, allies | 27 | | Political contest | 34 |
| | Delisting = in our interests | 24 | | MEK are not like us, strange | 20 |
| | MEK are not like us, strange | 15 | | Delisting = in our interests | 11 |
| | | | | MEK advocates have ulterior motives | 10 |
| Overall (N = 49) | | | Overall (N = 188) | | |
| | Human rights/justice | 61 | | Human rights/justice | 30 |
| | MEK are our friends, allies | 29 | | MEK are not like us, strange | 29 |
| | Delisting = in our interests | 23 | | Political contest | 31 |
| | MEK are not like us, strange | 12 | | Delisting = in our interests | 19 |
| | Ulterior motives | 12 | | MEK are our friends, allies | 10 |

Table 5. Output: Most frequent frames on removing terror designation in journalist authored opinion and news

*Note*: Percentages may not sum to 100 due to use of multiple frames.

Staff-written editorials and opinion columns generally adopted pro-delisting frames in both periods, but especially in the second five-year period when 70% of editors called attention to the potential for a humanitarian disaster if the MEK were handed over to Iran. However, compared to opinion penned by outside challengers, lower proportions used additional identity and utilitarian frames to bolster their arguments (27% vs. 39% and 23% vs. 55%).

Turning to the larger set of news and feature stories, a different picture emerges. Human rights/justice frames were relatively infrequent, occurring in only 17% of news reporting in the period 2003–2007. Positive identity frames were even more rare, with only 10% using or quoting sources invoking the "MEK are our friends, allies" frame. An exception is a feature by *New York Times* writer Douglas Jehl who quotes Yleem Poblete, staff director for the House International Relations Committee's subcommittee on the Middle East and Asia 2003:

> They are our friends, not our enemies. And right now, they are the most organized alternative to the Iranian regime, and the fact that they are the main target of the Iranian regime says a lot about their effectiveness. (Jehl, 2003, B1)

More typical in news reportage were frames conveying the "MEK are not like us," "they are strange," or "they are not liked," infusing as much as 42% of news reportage in this period. Two examples, the first from *the Australian*, and the second from *The Guardian*, are shown below:

> Welcome to the quixotic world of the Mujahedin-e Khalq (MEK), the principal Iranian resistance organization which blends a strange mix of Marxism and Islam in its long-running quest to overthrow the Islamic republic in Tehran. ("Freedom fighter or foe," 2003, p. 9)

> [It is] a bizarre revolutionary army. (Leigh 2005, p. 9)

Some journalists went a step further characterizing the group, not only as strange but also as "cultish." Citing an Iranian journalist, Graeme Hamilton of Canada's *National Post*, for example, penned these words:

> Their ideology is strange. Internally, they are profoundly undemocratic and cultish and bizarre. (Hamilton, 2012. p. A1)

These results show the considerable hurdles MEK advocates faced in seeing their frames published in news and features.

Still, there was a clear reduction in the "not like us/they are strange" frame over time (from 42% of news stories in the period 2003–2007, to 20% in the period 2008–2012), and a corresponding shift in journalist reportage towards human rights/justice frames (from 18% of news stories to 44%). This shift quickened in 2008 as the reins of power in Iraq were passed to a new Shi'ite controlled government that took its cues increasingly from Iran. By the year's end, journalists such as Steven Edwards of the *Gazette* (Montreal) were quoting human rights advocates who warned that a "disaster in the making" loomed for thousands of Iranian dissidents in Iraq's Camp Ashraf (Edwards, 2008, p. A16). The summer of 2009 confirmed these fears as video footage circulated showing Iraqi troops, backed by Humvees and armored personnel carriers, storming Camp Ashraf and shooting at unarmed civilians, killing 36 and wounding hundreds more. Reporters, covering this development, gave weight, to be sure, to the U.S. government stance that the raid was "the legitimate act of a sovereign government" (LaFranchi, 2009; *Christian Science Monitor*, USA, p. 2.), but many also noted that human rights activists denounced it as a violation of international law and the Geneva Convention.

This was a time when election protests, following the disputed victory of Iranian President Mahmoud Ahmadinejad, were also in the news. In op-eds and letters to the editor, MEK advocates called attention to the Iranian regime's use of the designation to justify arresting and executing its opponents. News reporting began incorporating this theme. Quoting European lawmakers, *Washington Times* journalist, James Morrison, for example, noted that:

> … the [terrorist] designation provides justification for the Iranian regime to execute its opponents under the pretext of 'Moharb' (waging war against God) and 'terrorist.' …By maintaining the MEK/PMOI terrorist designation, "the United States is alienating the pro-democracy Iranians who yearn for a democratic and nuclear-free Iran. (Morrison, 2010, p. A8)

Journalists continued to insert human rights themes into their stories in 2011, a year that saw the "Arab Spring," but also witnessed Iraqi security forces bulldozing their way once again into Camp Ashraf, opening fire and leaving as many as 33 unarmed civilians dead and hundreds more injured. In a feature for *The Guardian* that displayed photos of Iraqi soldiers patrolling near burned trailers at Camp Ashraf, journalist Kate Allen, for example, asked the world to take notice of this "massacre" of Iranian exiles suggesting that it will provide a window on the country's "human rights progress":

> …the world should start paying attention to this forgotten story. How Iraq treats the residents of Camp Ashraf will provide an important window into how far Iraq has come in respecting human rights. (Allen, 2011)

Overall, these results suggest that over time, news reporters and feature writers moved, if cautiously, in the direction of frames used by delisting supporters. This may be because they needed frames that were more salient. It may also be because a cascade of events had damaged the credibility of those promoting alternative frames. At the same time, almost a third (31%) of the journalist authored articles conveyed issue dualism. Moreover, about one in ten (10%) opted to highlight new opposition complaints designed to cast doubt on the credibility of politicians on the side of delisting—they had "ulterior" motives, they were "paid lobbyists."

## Symbols and emblems

The analysis of symbols showed that news and feature reporters adopted symbols and emblems from both sides of the debate in about equal numbers. The word "cult" or "cult-like," an evocative negative descriptor culled from a now discredited 2004 Human Rights report (Safavi, 2009), was used to describe the MEK as many as 242 times, mostly without source attribution or only with attribution to unnamed Iranian officials. The term "sect" was used at least 10 times and the terms "violent" or "violence" (as in the MEK's "history of violence") were used 150 times usually without sourcing or explanation. Other negative descriptors (e.g., "radical," "extremist," and "leftist"), designed to evoke an undesirable image, were also common. But reporters frequently used positive words to convey a different image. For example, the word "democratic" was used as many as 244 times, the word "secular" 65 times, and the word "moderate" at least 34 times.

## Source quotations

Since reporters are expected to avoid expressing personal opinions, they rely heavily on visible, influential, and convenient sources in constructing news and stories. Visible sources, defined as spokespeople for interest groups and carriers of expertise, and influential ones who hold positions in hierarchies, help them add an air of legitimacy to news coverage, while convenient ones help them cope with quick deadlines.

Overall, 75% (140/188) of the news articles contained at least one sourced quotation. As shown in Figure 3, the most common sources of the 384 identified quotes were pro-delisting political leaders in the United States or the United Kingdom (26%) and spokespersons for the NCRI (24%). Surprisingly, considering their direct role in the controversy, relatively few quotes were attributed to official representatives of the U.S. government (16%), the UK, or the EU (5%). However, 11% were attributed to representatives of the governments of Iraq or Iran. The remaining quotes came from military experts (4%), intelligence sources (2%), former MEK members (4%), "experts" from academia or think tanks, representatives of international organizations (4%), and MEK opponents in the NIAC, a group that is thought by some to be a pro-Iran lobby (2%).

# Figure 3. Breakdown of quotation sources on delisting the MEK in news and feature stories

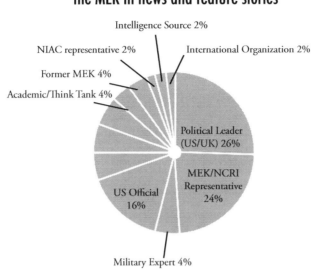

Intelligence Source 2%

NIAC representative 2%

International Organization 2%

Former MEK 4%

Academic/Think Tank 4%

Political Leader (US/UK) 26%

MEK/NCRI Representative 24%

US Official 16%

Military Expert 4%

## Source anonymity

MEK/NCRI sources,[7] political leaders,[8] and military experts,[9] all quoted in support of delisting the MEK, were uniformly named. Iraq government sources,[10] usually critical of delisting, were also named. In most cases, however, quotes attributed to "official" United States, United Kingdom, and European Union government and intelligence sources were anonymous—that is, direct or paraphrased quotes to unnamed persons.[11] Quotes from government sources within the Islamic Republic of Iran were similarly anonymous. On the other hand "experts" in think tanks and former MEK members making statements on the subject were sometimes named and sometimes not named.

This anonymity granted almost exclusively to critics of delisting, allowed journalists to attribute blanket negative opinions to "official" or expert sources without sourcing them. Two examples of sourcing to *unnamed* authorities, both from Scott Peterson of the *Christian Science Monitor,* are shown below:

> The Islamic Republic's policy toward the MKO is very clear—there is nothing hidden,' says a foreign ministry official who asked not to be named. 'In our opinion they are a terrorist cult. (Peterson, 2008, p. 6)

> Yet current US officials and many Iran experts—hawks and doves alike—question the MEK's ability to change in light of the group's unique history and its cult-like characteristics. They say the fact that it is widely despised inside Iran makes it a dangerous tool to change Iran's Islamic regime. (Peterson, 2011, p. 3)

## Source cues

While the proportions of quotes for and against delisting were similar (54% vs. 46%), this was not the case for cues to interpret these quotes. Beyond the words "official" and "expert," descriptive cues never preceded quotes attributed to government sources, intelligence or think tank sources, or sources in international organizations or in the NIAC, a group that opposes the MEK. In contrast, news reportage frequently parenthesized quotes from Maryam Rajavi, the acknowledged head of the MEK and president of its parliament in exile, with negative descriptors characterizing her, for example, as "autocratic," "cult-like," "charismatic," "zealous," "a self-styled leader," "a self-declared president-elect." Similarly, quotes in support of the MEK from political leaders were routinely prefaced with negative cues (e.g., "star lobbyist," "high profile lobbyist," "well-financed lobbyist"). These cues allowed journalists to cast a distinct cloud on the credibility of MEK supporters while adhering to a journalist norm of quoting sources.

# Discussion

This study attempted to examine the interplay between efforts by activists and political players to gain media visibility and journalist coverage of the MEK listing debate. The data allowed comparison of inputs, using opinion from interest groups and political players, with outputs in the form of news and feature reportage. My expectations, based on the literature, were: 1) that news coverage would be greater when there was a dramatic event to cover; 2) that supporters and opponents of delisting would both have preferred frames; and 3) that journalists in news reportage would generally slant to official perspectives (i.e., take the side of delisting opponents) and align with government frames. But in view of other literature indicating that journalists create their own "spin," I also expected to find issue dualism and media-generated frames and in particular a "horse race" or political contest frame.

The results largely supported these expectations. There was clear evidence that reporters paid less attention to delisting when it was purely a policy matter and more attention to it when it could be connected to events that had story-telling potential. These results support earlier research highlighting the role of drama plays in news agenda setting (Hamilton, 2004). Other research on agenda-setting has shown a strong correlation between the emphasis the mass media place on an issue, based on amount of coverage, and the importance attributed to it by mass audiences (McCombs & Shaw, 1972). While the results shown here cannot tell us the degree of importance the public attributed to the issue at hand (that would require a different study), they do suggest that the media played a role in orchestrating a sense of importance by virtue of selective coverage.

The results for media slant were more mixed. Over the entire time period, about 4 in 10 (41%) news articles conveyed neutrality or issue dualism, as if both sides had equal merits. About 3 in 10 (27%) took the side of delisting supporters, while another 3 in 10 (32%) took the side of delisting opponents. These results support theories of press independence (Callaghan & Schnell, 2001). Still, there were distinct changes in slant over time with the percentage of articles slanting towards approval for delisting almost doubling from 17% for the first period (2003–2007) to 33% for the second period (2008–2012), while the percentage slanting against delisting decreased from 41% to 24%.

These changes paralleled changes in framing. In particular there was a clear shift towards humanitarian/justice frames, and a shrinkage in the use of the "they are not like us," "they are strange" frames from the first 5-year period to the second one. These changes in journalist output may have been, in part, a function of changes in advocacy group input. Analysis of opinion arguments indicates that MEK advocates not only used a greater range of arguments, but also adapted their arguments over time and in relation to events. This was especially evident in the way they shifted towards a greater use of humanitarian arguments, which would have had more mainstream resonance after 2007. In contrast, opponents tended to promote a singular hostile identity frame based largely on the "otherness" of the MEK. This frame, one that lent itself to hyperbole, was the chief one adopted by journalists in the initial phase of coverage. Over time, however, it appears to have had less resonance in the context of events and journalists began to align more with the human rights frames that had greater salience.

There are at least two important limitations to this study. First, the content analysis is limited to major world newspapers in English. Different results might have been obtained if the study had been extended to a wider range of sources (newsfeeds, TV and radio media, daily papers, and blogs) and non-English language news sources. Second, advocacy group influence is known to vary depending on the visibility of a campaign and on the ideological cast of an issue (Kingdon, 1995). The ability of MEK advocates to influence media framing may not be generalizable to policy debates featuring a less visible campaign or a different ideological component. Third, we cannot prove that frames promoted in op-eds and other opinion pieces or critical events influenced journalist frames although the evidence appears compelling.

Despite these limitations, the study provides several insights for policy challengers. First, for groups that want to get a message into the media, policy context makes a difference. The delisting controversy received relatively little attention from journalists *per se* when the policy process was mainly administrative or a matter for the courts and there was little opportunity to dramatize a story. On the other hand, critical or "focusing events" provided an opportunity for activists to help the media reframe and draw attention to their cause.

Second, framing can make a difference. Outside commentators commanded more attention (more opinion articles published) when they began to frame delisting as a humanitarian issue as they did from 2008 onwards.

Third, human interest matters. While journalists tend to slant towards official policy (in this case against delisting the MEK), there was evidence that a change in stance occurred when human interest was at stake. This was the case in 2009 and 2011, when residents of Camp Ashraf were under siege and dozens were killed and hundreds more were wounded. Under such dramatic circumstances, journalists may be more inclined to take the side of an interest group that is at risk.

Fourth, persistence and flexibility in framing can make a difference. There was clear evidence that journalists drew more on pro-delisting frames as time went on. As a result journalist framing became less one-sided in the latter period. Still, the obstacles were high. Most journalists gave equal weight to both sides of the debate and even though MEK supporters routinely made themselves available as sources for quotes, journalists tended to go more often to unnamed government sources who bolstered the case against delisting. Finally, critical events matter in that they can damage the credibility of one set of frames or make them less salient.

## Conclusion

The study findings show that the media took a visibly active role in directing how the MEK delisting story was told. In its selective use of frames, rhetoric, symbols, sources (named and unnamed) and leading source cues, it constructed a story that at first aligned mostly with input from delisting opponents who cast the MEK as odd, strange, bizarre, or "not our friends" and thus, as somehow undeserving of removal from terror lists, no matter the merits of the case. As time went on, however, and a cascade of events damaged the credibility of rival frames and their articulators, many journalists began building a new storyline that adopted the frames and rhetoric of delisting advocates who cast the issue in humanitarian and rights terms. While journalists caged their bets, often conveying the controversy as a contest with equally valid points on either side, it is clear that even marginalized actors who persist and strategically nurture small opportunities can exert influence and expand the discourse.

## Notes

1. The National Council of Resistance of Iran (NCRI), founded in 1981 in France, is the "parliament in exile" of the "Iranian Resistance." It is a political umbrella coalition of five Iranian opposition political organizations, the largest organization being the People's Mujahedin Organization of Iran (MEK). The NCRI was originally formed by MEK head Massoud Rajavi and former president of Iran Abolhassan Banisadr, who were joined by National Democratic Front and Kurdistan Democratic Party of Iran. During the Iran–Iraq War the NDF and Banisadr withdrew from the NCRI (Keddie & Richard, 1981, p. 256).

2. See Norman Kempster (1997, October 9, p. A4).

3. See interview with Martin Indyk, Assistant Secretary of State for Near Eastern Affairs in Isikoff (2002, p. 2).

4. BBC Radio 4, Today Program interview with British Foreign Secretary Jack Straw, February 1, 2006, cited in Safavi A. (2010, March 31). See also Benjamin James Fender, Britain's Foreign and Commonwealth Office, Second Witness Statement to Proscribed Organisations Appeal Commission, POAC, p. 4, June 25, 2007.

5. The evidence showed that the contractor killings that formed the basis of the original designation were carried out by a splinter group, not under the control of the group's leadership; that there was no credible proof that the MEK participated in the 1979 embassy takeover; and that the military operations, carried out by the MEK from Iraq, were the activities of a liberation army against military targets not terrorist acts against civilians. MEK advocates also noted that the leadership had specifically renounced violence and ceased all military operations in 2001 and that all of its members had voluntarily disarmed and renounced violence in 2003 following the coalition invasion of Iraq.

6. Issue cultures have been defined as "cognate sets of social problems that become a commanding concern in society" (Ungar, 2007, p. 81).

7. The most frequent named source for MEK/NCRI-attributed quotes in news reportage was Maryam Rajavi, president-elect of the NCRI. Attributions, however, were also made to other named spokespersons, e.g., Ali Safavi and legal representatives of the group, e.g., Allan Gerson.

8. Quote attributions to political leaders were made, among others to: John R. Bolton (UN ambassador), Andrew Card (former White House chief of staff), Louis J. Freeh (FBI director), Tom Ridge (Homeland Security secretary), Howard Dean (Vermont governor), Bill Richardson (New Mexico governor), and Togo D. West Jr. (Secretary of the Army), Edward Rendell (Pennsylvania governor), Rudolph Giuliani (former mayor of New York), Patrick Kennedy (Senator, Rhode Island), Howard Dean (former DNC chair), Bill Richardson (UN envoy); Lords David Alton, Robin Corbett and David Waddington (MPs or former MPs in British parliament); and Lord Peter Archer (former Solicitor General).

9. Attributions to military experts were made, among others to: Gen. Wesley Clark, Gen. Henry Shelton (Chairman of the Joint Chiefs of Staff), Gen. James T. Conway (Commandant of the Marine Corps), Marine Gen. Peter Pace (Chairman, Joint Chiefs of Staff), Marine Gen. James L. Jones (National Security Adviser), and Gen. Richard Myers.

10. Attributions were made, among others to Nouri al Maliki (Iraq's Shi'ite prime minister and Adnan al-Shamani (a Shi'a lawmaker).

11. To be sure there were exceptions. Pressed by reporters, then National Security Advisor (later Secretary of State Condoleeza Rice) was specifically quoted in *Newsweek* as saying that the United States was not working with the MEK, and as acknowledging a lack of agreement in the administration on Iranian policy (Dicke, Hosenball, and Hirsh 2005, 30). Similarly, Secretary of State Hillary Clinton was specifically quoted in the *Washington Post* in March of 2012 as stating that the MEK's cooperation in a planned relocation of its base in Iraq "will be a key factor in the delisting decision" (Associated Press, 2012).

# PART SEVEN

## Policy and Public Administration

It has been said that one of the major challenges facing MENA (Middle East and North Africa) countries is a leadership and public administration crises. Most MENA countries are known for government corruption, and too much inefficient bureaucracy that stifles economic and human development. Leading efforts to up-grade, educate, and train civil servants on management organizational innovations and introduce them to best practices based in these fields are too little and perhaps too late.

Peter Mameli examines leadership in MENA countries and how the ongoing effects of the Arab Spring highlight the importance of leadership training and the adoption of best practices of better public administration at all levels of governments. Clearing a path toward establishing the necessary cultural congruence among administrative processes, tools, solutions, and people is a prerequisite to success that rests on identifying, in particular, indigenously acceptable approaches to change. Engaging authentic leadership to guide successful achievement of new public management and new public governance goals offers one way to both, envision and construct ongoing balance in the future. Mameli points out how the Arab Spring signifies a desire for change in the region that is anchored in values of public sector accountability, transparency, and ethical competence. He argues that the phenomenon that has swept through MENA countries creates an opportunity to embrace and shape leadership research for MENA countries. He concludes his paper by pointing to the importance of a focused empirical study of leadership which is required to unearth effective, Arab-centred understanding of the issues in these settings.

Mameli's argument regarding leadership and public administration in MENA countries is supported further in other papers selected for this book from the first conference of the Association for Middle Eastern Public Policy and Administration (AMEPPA) which was held at Al-Akhawayn University in Ifrane, Morocco and chaired by Dr. Alexander Dawoody, member of the International Editorial Board of the *Digest of Middle East Studies (DOMES)*.

Dr. Slaoui-Zirpins' paper combines theories of decentralization and interest mediation in order to address the issue of decentralization in the MENA region. Accordingly, progress in local and regional governance means effective participation through the implementation of subsidiarity. He attempts to combine theories of decentralization and interest mediation in order to explain formal and informal processes in the interactions within the bureaucracy as well as between the state, civil society, the market, and citizens. Using the example of economic policy for the promotion of offshore services in Fez, Morocco, the author applies these theories within this case study and emphasizes the strengths and the weaknesses of the process.

Iraq is another case study that was investigated by Dr. Alexander Dawoody in his paper "Observing the Failed Nation-State of Iraq: A Perspective." Dawoody examines the Iraqi nation-state as a foreign entity imposed from the outside on people who were strange to its paradigm, the eventual deterioration of the model, and the possibility of its complete collapse. In doing so, he explains how Iraqi societal components since the British creation of the new Iraq in 1921 remained fragmented, while a manufactured Iraqi identity emerged through coercion in order to justify the legitimacy of the new nation-state. Among Iraq's social components, the Sunni Arab tribes benefitted the most from political and economic power by contributing the most to the governing administrative cadre at the expense of other social groups, especially the Kurds and Shi'a. Dawoody attributes such a notion to the Baa'th regime, which ruled Iraq from 1968 to 2003. With the United States' led invasion of Iraq in 2003, the formula was turned upside down by empowering the Kurds and Shi'a at the expense of marginalizing the Sunni Arab tribes. Thus, for the first time in nearly 80 years, the Sunni Arab tribes found themselves outside the political formula in Iraq. Dawoody concludes "… with the exclusion of the old Sunnis from administration and with the new governing groups' lack of administrative experience, post-Sunni governing Iraq started to decay in its infrastructure and lack of public services."

In their paper "Building capacities in public financial management in a post-conflict country: A practice from the Ministry of Finance and the Institute of Finance of Lebanon," El-Ghandour, Hatem, Bissat, and Rihan, highlight the potential role that a leading training institution can play in post-conflict reconstruction. They draw on the experience of the Institut des Finances Basil Fuleihan, in supporting and complementing the Lebanese Ministry of Finance's policies and reform goals with capacity development. The authors touch on the importance of public financial reform in the MENA region and emphasize the positive role that training and capacity development can have on such reforms. According to the authors, their findings aim to provide elements of response to the following questions: 1) What is the most suitable administrative and financial set-up and recommended organizational culture required to effectively run a capacity-building institution? 2) What is the role of political leadership? 3) Is the successful reform of core governance institutions of a country both a necessary and sufficient condition for overall governance improvement? 4) What is the role of donors? and 5) How can the country make its homegrown agenda prevail?

Dawoody and Marks address the need for adapting complexity paradigms such as forecast, subjectivity phase shift, collapse dynamics, interconnectedness, mutual causality, and chaos in observing the complex nature of the Middle East. In their paper entitled "Abandoning Predictions and Control: lessons for the Middle East," the authors based their study on the rationale that by learning from complexity, avoiding arguments for prediction, control, and stability, researchers could offer more realistic solutions to Middle Eastern problems, learn from other countries cooperative experiences and models such as those of Brazil, Russia, India, China, and South Africa (BRICS), and hopefully help move forward Arab aspirations toward sound governance.

# Under New Management: What the Arab Spring Tells us about Leadership Needs in the Middle East and North Africa

## Peter Mameli

## Abstract

Leadership analysis examines how political heads and managers of public sector organizations can employ styles that will dovetail with the aspirations and energy of their country's inhabitants. Uncovering leadership models capable of channeling growth and productivity in this manner within Arab MENA (Middle East and North Africa) settings is essential to the stability of the region. Turbulent change in a globalizing environment continues to deepen this realization, and the ongoing effects of the Arab Spring highlight the importance of such an undertaking. Clearing a path toward establishing the necessary cultural congruence among administrative processes, tools, solutions, and people is a prerequisite to success that rests on identifying indigenously acceptable approaches to change. Engaging authentic leadership to guide successful achievement of New Public Management and New Public Governance goals offers one way to both envision and construct an on-going balance in the future.

# Introduction

As the effects of the 2011 Arab Spring reverberate across the MENA (Middle East and North Africa) region, analysts, practitioners, and theorists continue to calculate its impact. To date, there have been significant regime changes in Tunisia, Egypt, Yemen, and Libya, and another regime change still possible in Syria. Many Arab MENA countries are contemplating, or enacting, policies that would lead to a reinvigorated private sector. Some are even attempting to grow a civil society. At the same time, large public sectors remain a conundrum to be confronted if the efficiency and effectiveness of government services are to grow. Corruption control, accountability, and transparency discussions are also in the forefront of government concerns, even if improvements in form are only slowly followed by actual changes in behavior. These sector-specific issues are intertwined with questions of how to adequately address unemployment among youth, underutilization of the educated, and an imbalance in gender relations where men dominate many roles and activities.

Managing these problems while facing the multiple influences of globalization, western engagement, the role of Islam in the region, and the need to modernize institutions and the workforce across sectors and domains, remains a daunting set of challenges. The additional dilemmas of finding ways to increase citizen involvement, participation, and power provide a continuous undercurrent of warning to both political and organizational leaders that the time of waiting for transformation is drawing to a close.

Events from the last two years demonstrate a region and people that are ready for change now. Public organizations and societies, in general, are full of energetic and creative individuals who have interests and desires that are not being fulfilled within current structures that inhibit their ambitions. If anything, the future requires a means of channeling this energy toward effective use, rather than impeding it further with combustible effect. Building trust and confidence in government is required for this purpose (Newell, Reeher, & Ronayne, 2012; Terry, 2003). Fortunately, part of the solution to this problem is known in general terms—leadership matters. Today Arab MENA states are at a crossroads requiring deft leadership that can ensure safe passage to a more secure environment in the years to come (Jreisat, 2009b).

The definition of leadership relied on here is as follows: "Leadership is a process whereby an individual influences a group of individuals to achieve a common goal" (Northouse, 2013, p. 5). This paper applies an examination of leadership theory and leadership styles to the study of improving organizational performance in Arab MENA public sectors. It begins with an examination of global and regional context affecting such efforts. From this base, theoretical pillars for moving the public sector toward an increasingly productive future are set within discussions of New Public Management and New Public Governance concepts. These pillars enable constructive reflection on leadership practice to take place.

# The Landscape Encountered by States and Citizens

The Arab Spring must be understood in terms of the times and pressures that generated it. Consequently, these times and pressures must also be considered when crafting the means to resolve the problems that have developed. The landscape to be traversed in order to find a productive way forward through this crisis consists of factors external to the region, as well as internal to it. How leaders address both is critical to achieving success. In addition, both sets of circumstances must be confronted in a coordinated fashion. Prior to examining internal MENA concerns, it is necessary to situate its larger world environment. The current time period's foremost characteristics, players, sectors, levels of response, and policies must be visualized as a holistic system. Only after this is completed can the MENA situation in relation to the Arab Spring be properly deciphered, for it is forged within this crucible. And the proper centering of this crucible can best be located within the forces of globalization that exist in the 21st century.

Globalization's tentacles are long, and it can be discussed from the perspective of multiple domains simultaneously or separately (Held, 2000). Since many of the elements that have been difficult to capture in a definition of globalization relate directly to the discussion of MENA regional development and progress, it is important that they be unpacked early in this discussion. Figure 1 offers a necessarily incomplete image of just how broad is the playing field engaged.

## Figure 1. Levels of response and six primary domains of impact

| Level/Domain | Politics | Economy | Health | Cultural | Environmental | Technology |
|---|---|---|---|---|---|---|
| Global | | | | | | |
| International | | | | | | |
| Transnational | | | | | | |
| Regional | | | | | | |
| National | | | | | | |
| Community | | | | | | |
| Individual | | | | | | |

Since the end of the 20th century, the general study of globalization has become of central concern to many scholars from the social sciences for just the reasons stated above. For these same reasons, the field has proven to perplex many trying to understand its contours and parameters. As Harris (1993) noted in the 1990s: "Terminology in this whole area seems designed for obfuscation" (p. 757).

This might very well have been due to the fact that there are a variety of perspectives competing to paint a picture of globalization and define it. Serrano (2002, 23-27) captures three distinctly different threads. At the same time Cochran and Pain (2000, pp. 22-25) refer to this same general terrain as "The Big Debates." And Klingner (2004, p. 739) finds it difficult to separate the meaning from the ideological overtones of its definers. As a result, globalization is a term that remains in flux. Indeed, there are some theorists who do not believe globalization is occurring at all. At the same time, some people speak of the world as if it is globalizing as a whole. Giddens (2002, pp. 7–10), refers to these two groups as the "skeptics" and "radicals," respectively. Then there is a camp that sees twin developments occurring side by side. A globalization process and a return to local traditions and structures in reaction to it are noted here (sometimes referred to as "Glocalization"). Others see the world globalizing, but in a variety of contradictory and complex ways—with some places being affected faster than others. This staggered process has opened space for both advocacy and resistance (Roddick, 2001). Finally, there are those who see the phenomena as already completed, and discuss it in the past tense, having determined that the world is already globalized.

The truth of the matter seems to be that there are elements of old and new processes of globalization in existence today. The changes associated with these phenomena have more influence in some domains, and on some countries, more quickly than others. That said, while globalization as a set of processes has been around for quite a while, it is still very different today than it has been in the past. Modern globalization processes display characteristics of greater impact, magnitude, and speed than ever before (Held & McGrew, 2000, p. 4). These facts, therefore, change the complexion of globalization in today's experience as opposed to its character in decades past. So, how should the concept of globalization be defined here? A basic definition provided by MacEwan described globalization this way: "The international spread of capitalist exchange and production relationships" (1994, p. 1).

While this definition does expose some of the powerful players and structures at the heart of the economic aspect of the globalization explosion, capitalists and capitalism, it does not completely cover the matter (Carroll & Carson, 2003). Early on, Held and McGrew offered deeper insight with the following comments:

> On the one hand, the concept of globalization defines a universal process or set of processes which generate a multiplicity of linkages and interconnections which transcend the states and societies which make up the modern world system: the concept therefore has a spatial connotation. On the other hand, globalization also implies intensification in the levels of interaction, interconnectedness or interdependence between the states and societies which constitute the modern world community. (1993, p. 262)

Many of today's writers have made significant headway in coming to terms with what globalization, in fact, is (Kennett, 2010). For the most part, capitalists, entrepreneurs, and nation-state power elites are identified as the practitioners (and essentially the winners) of globalization in civil society and government circles. However, until recently, fewer people were terribly concerned with the negative aspects of globalization. The liberalized global economy that allows free market success to some is said to leave many more in varying forms of degradation. Problems such as growth in the trafficking of human beings, increasing poverty, advancing dispersion of diseases such as the Human Immunodeficiency Virus/Acquired Immune Deficiency Syndrome (HIV/AIDS), or who the winners in uncivil society might be, are now regularly coming on to international, regional, national, and local agendas. Caring about those who have become the losers in this global experiment, or what they have been experiencing, is finally part of the ongoing debate. Advocates for this class of people represent a growing wave of non-state actors seeking to make their voices known across all levels of political response.

As these changes have developed, one byproduct of globalization's march forward is the curious impact it is having on the traditional structures of international relations. In particular, this is true of the positioning of the state on the international stage, and its socially constructed system of global governance. States were once considered dominant players in the study of international relations. Theorists who held sway in global political discourse assigned to them qualities of internal and external sovereignty, as well as abilities to handle their own affairs without interference or support from outside parties. But this romancing of the state was always more of a fiction than a reality. Now, states are routinely discussed as something less than invincible organizational forms. This is the result of influences that tug at their security and power by exposing their lessening ability to carry out their business in an independent manner. Indeed, states are feeling pressures both internally and externally as a result of global and transnational influences that tax their ability to respond to borderless issues and concerns.

The internal pressures manifest themselves in areas of service delivery, where states no longer find themselves able to provide goods without support from entities beyond government. Externally, pressure builds from the increasing power that non-state organizations, and even individuals, are gaining in the international milieu. As a result, multiple players often bring power to bear on resolving problems that were once believed to be the sole domain of governments.

States have created some of the players within this web of relationships. For example, international governmental organizations have always been used to coordinate and manage problems that multiple states are engaged in at once. Others are not controlled as closely. Private sector businesses, and multi-national corporations extending their business practices through political engagement, offer such examples. Others still, however, represent a human centered influence. These international, regional, national, and community based nongovernmental entities are engaging topics of global interest more today than ever before, with an interest in furthering the public good—however they may define it. Finally, there are select instances (thankfully) where members of uncivil society can be found manipulating, eroding, and sometimes even controlling governmental resources. In all cases, the point of this discussion remains the same. The state no longer solely controls policy, implementation, and program development. These are shared experiences now more than ever, particularly where global issues are involved.

## The Landscape Encountered by Public Sector Professionals

Public sector employees function within this increasingly complex work setting in all countries to varying degrees. The internal and external influences on their productivity have become intricately connected. Conceptualizing their world through an image of concentric rings that expand outwards from the individual can help to illustrate the interwoven nature of these pressures (see Appendix, p.18).

The inner ring depicts the human capital brought to bear on governance concerns (Ring A). This first ring can be seen as comprising street level bureaucrats, front line staff, analysts, policy professionals, and managers who both implement and guide service delivery. The second ring considered (Ring B) represents the organizational housing within which the public sector employees operate. The structures, rules, goals, technology, and culture of the organization exerting force on the individual employees can be found here. The third ring of influence (Ring C) includes external entities comprised of organizational and individual actors. These stakeholders can span policy domains, levels of political engagement, and sectors of interaction.

The outer ring in this scenario captures sweeping external effects for which the preceding rings must adjust. Whether it be processes of globalization, social and political upheavals like the Arab Spring, or emergent shifts in the physical environment such as those resulting from global warming or pandemic surges, Ring D completes the framework outlining the world of the public sector employee. Further, it illustrates the proximal location of the public sector employee to these events. The public sector professional is at the center of this whirlpool. Such a turbulent system requires steady leaders to navigate its waters. The means by which leaders stabilize the system must take into account changes within all of the rings at once, and respond to them with coordinated vision and action.

## The Arab MENA Context

Responding to globalization differs from region to region, and country to country. The resulting approaches are flavored by variations in culture, political structure, economic development, and an openness to change among the people themselves. In the Arab world, globalization takes on three competing images based on: (a) views highlighting economic factors; (b) perspectives on information and technology; and (c) a comprehensive assessment of its processes that captures multiple domains and levels of response, as discussed earlier in this paper (Jresiat, 2009a, pp. 37–50). Individuals and groups in the Gulf, Levant and North Africa have struggled to assess proper ways to encourage change, often being prodded by outside forces. Some have even attempted to maintain an ill-advised isolation (Dubai School of Government, 2008, p. 10). With the advent of the Arab Spring, the struggle has turned into a full-fledged battle in some corners, while widening opportunities to leverage peaceful change in others (Akhtar, 2011; el-Massnaoui & Biygautane, 2011, p. 6; World Bank, 2012, pp. 6–7). Regardless of the road taken, however, the Arab Spring provided an opportunity to actively seek change.

Among the issues requiring immediate attention in Arab MENA states are those of growing youth unemployment, gender imbalance in the workforce regarding small numbers of working women, and the underutilization of educated citizens (Chaaban, 2010; World Economic Forum and Organization for Economic Cooperation and Development, 2011). Add to this the possibility that weakened countries can provide a foothold to terrorist organizations or extremist ideologies (Fukuyama, 2008, pp. 11–12; Mantzikos, 2011), and a sense of urgency should take hold quite quickly. The chronic problems of a sluggish public sector and a weak private sector complicate matters further still. A lack of creativity connecting education and training to technology and process advances, accountability failures, transparency and participation weaknesses, corruption, and perhaps what amounts to rampant workplace discrimination—*wasta*, rounds out the picture (Beschel, Jr., 2010).

Despite the problems noted, indigenous solutions exist as well. Khodr (2012) tells us that the specialized cities of the Gulf Cooperation Council (GCC) are likely to end up largely peopled and run by women. Indeed, this is an interesting change in narrative from what we are accustomed to hearing about MENA worker and leadership gender deficits, regardless of sector. And certainly there are innovations of note in problem areas specific to public sector organizational management being surfaced as best practices too (Department of Economic and Social Affairs, 2007; Middle East and North Africa Vice Presidency, 2010). Identifying and learning about these advances is not a challenge being ignored in MENA, but a coordinated response is still emerging. At the present time there are a growing number of Public Service Training Institutes in the region, and there will likely be more in the future to take up this charge (GIFT-MENA, n.d.). But they require more support for empirical research to guide their recommendations.

Unpacking Arab MENA settings to get at the heart of response patterns is no small undertaking. There are societal players of importance that all impact a country's progress. Categories for those who are politically ensconced, religious elite (*ulema*), established business and land owner classes, existing and former nobility, military and bureaucratic power centers, important families, professionals, and the rank and file citizens, must all be accounted for. And the fact that the mix of these elements differs from country to country must be properly understood (Andersen, Seibert, & Wagner 2012, pp. 182–202).

In addition, capturing distinctions at the regional and national level is also important. Examples addressing the emergence of new technologies are instructive. Mahmoud (2003) discusses the slower path the MENA region as a whole took in exploring Internet usage, as compared to other regions of the world. Mishrif and Selmanovic (2010, p. 913) offer an example of how this dynamic played out in relation to more specific experiences with e-government in Egypt and Morocco—the point here being that both regional and national contexts are important to grasp when grappling with such topics. All of these conditions make generalizing for the sake of broad regional analysis problematic, but not impossible (Chaaban, 2010; Saif, 2012).

To date, the limited number of public sector leadership studies struggle to achieve such nuance. Whether the government is depicted as traditional and autocratic, evolving towards modern, technical and bureaucratic in nature, or led by charismatic men of the people, it is rare that an authoritarian image is not associated with political leadership style in MENA (Andersen, Seibert, & Wagner, 2012, pp. 203–233). The impact this has on the subsequent conduct of public sector officials is no doubt important. When public sector leadership is considered within countries, it is sometimes viewed as cascading in form from political heads through to administrative officials, with minimal variation in application due to setting (Common, 2011). But, of course, there must be more to the story than what we see after this initial cut at the issue. To better understand actions of public sector leaders in the region, the tensions they labor under must be more closely examined.

## Figure 2. Eight tensions inherent in the MENA public sector experience

| Global Context Impinges | Local Context Maintains Hold |
|---|---|
| Change in Views of Population | Inflexibility in Political Sphere |
| Western Views About Public Sector | Indigenous Views About Public Sector |
| Perceived Theory "Y" or "Z" Worker | Perceived Theory "X" Worker |
| Merit Driven Public Sector | Wasta Driven Public Sector |
| Desired Leadership | Practiced Leadership |
| Participative Engagement | In Groups/Out Groups |
| Inclusive Workforce | Limited Engagement of Women, Youth, and the Educated |

Figure 2 juxtaposes tensions in the MENA region that impact public sector leaders. These conditions need to be considered when meeting the policy challenges of the 21st century. The first tension illustrates the conundrum of addressing global shifts while maintaining local traditions. This pressure exists the world over, no doubt; but in the MENA region, it specifically reflects conflicts that develop when forces of modernization strain the boundaries of traditional worldviews involving Islamic and ethnic tribal cultures (Abdallah & al-Homoud, 2001; Sarayrah, 2004). Finding a balance between these forces is essential, and currently unresolved in many of the countries of the region. As a result, public sector performance suffers, and public administrators are challenged to achieve a stable footing to carry out their jobs.

The second tension is a result of the first. While the struggles between global change and local traditions occur, some elements of society strive to move toward change while others attempt to hold firm to time tested stabilizing influences. This stress has been furthered by information technologies that raise expectations in the general population while creating new skill sets. The resulting gap is found to be threatening to those who are not ready, willing or able to make the leap. When political systems fail to modify their goals and abilities for too long, difficulty mollifying segments of the populace that seek change shrinks. This scenario is playing out to differing degrees across MENA settings (Jreisat, 2009b, p. 9). Public sector organizations and officials are left standing at the center of the maelstrom.

As the battle between change and stability continues (Abdallah & al-Homoud, 2001, p. 518), it impacts the public sector in terms of its structures and forms of service delivery. Here there are numerous issues that impact performance—not the least of which is the conflict that exists between Western views of public administration (discussed further in the next section), and indigenous expectations for the public workplace. Chief among these differences is the view of the purpose of the public sector (Abdallah & al-Homoud, 2001, p. 510). The imagery from the West has moved over time to focus on efficient and effective service delivery. Its methods and approaches have retooled for the current era of globalization accordingly, although remaining a work in progress. MENA country views of the public sector are tinged with expectations of decent employment at a decent wage, and job security that is relied on to stabilize the society. While the two views are not anathema to each other, finding a balance that allows them to productively coexist in a non-Western setting is part of the ongoing story that is uncovered below with the discussion of additional tensions (Abrahart, Kaur, & Tzannatos, 2000).

An image of workers being inherently unproductive, or productive, colors the fourth tension about Theory "X," Theory "Y" or Theory "Z" individuals. Essentially, the social construction of the MENA workforce seems to rely primarily on the first of these descriptions. McGregor's Theory "X" argument is woven into narratives on public sector performance to what appears to be damning effect (Hammoud, 2011, pp. 146–147). The notion that Arab workers suffer from a poor work ethic, that they are complacent, and that their primary interest is in having a comfortable job where they are told what to do is an unfortunate mindset expressed in many commentaries (Tompkins, 2005, p. 301). The resulting conditioning makes it difficult to move forward with advancing towards more productive images of highly motivated Theory

"Y" workers (Tompkins, 2005, p. 302), potentially existing in Theory "Z" environments (Tompkins, 2005, p. 369). While this image appears to persist in many MENA countries, and is sometimes referenced as a reason to turn to non-native workers, the non-natives often include Arabs from other MENA states (Abdallah & al-Homoud, 2001, p. 510–511). The implicit suggestion being that while Theory "X" is being applied within MENA countries to some Arab workers, it does not refer to just any Arab worker. Rather, it appears to reflect Arab workers with whom the employers within that country are familiar. The question raised in such circumstances is, "why?" Is this really all about skill assessment or something quite different as well?

The fifth tension presents itself as quite possibly the ultimate cause of the Theory "X" stereotype that is applied to many Arab workers. The existing informal structures associated with wasta, or connections, that echo back to familial and tribal lineages often create a stifling environment for many who are not from more privileged backgrounds (Subotic, 2011). Essentially, public sector leaders are dealing with an external influence creating an internal organizational culture. In such settings some workers receive favored positions based on nepotism, and promotions, as well as power follow suit throughout their careers. This occurs to the detriment of other workers who might be more capable. Further still, even though the member groups will differ from country to country, wasta seems to be ensconced throughout MENA public sectors as practice. It is not a heavy lift to assume that those who believe they are shut out of effectively improving an organization, or having a true say in its operation, will stop trying terribly hard to achieve at a high level.

Recognized as a limitation on personal growth, worker ingenuity, and worker creativity, the development of merit-based personnel systems have been seen as a potential remedy to the more insidious characteristics of "*wasta*." However, experience with breaking the grip of wasta on public sector organizations in MENA has proven difficult (Subotic, 2011). What could possibly be at work on some undetermined level is a thoroughly engaged system of workplace discrimination, carried out by networks of linked power figures.

The sixth tension flows from the assertions identified about Arab workers in the fourth and fifth. Public sector leaders in MENA are depicted as relying on authoritative approaches and styles of leadership in the practical application of their duties. This image is precisely linked to views of how to manage getting things done with the people at hand. The Theory "X" characterization of Arab workers has little hope but to result in Theory "X" leadership techniques as a self-fulfilling prophecy (Bell and Smith, 2010, pp. 68–75; Hammoud, 2011, pp. 146–147). This situation is complicated by an underutilization of those that are being trained for advancement as well. The mismatch of human competencies to organizational needs can defeat efforts to improve performance, even when they are being made (al-Yahya, 2008).

More in depth leadership analysis, such as what was included in the Global Leadership and Organizational Effectiveness (GLOBE) research program report from 2004, points us toward specific aspects of the problem. Here it is noted that a penchant for "in-group collectivism" is a defining element of leadership in the MENA culture cluster of states studied (Northouse, 2013, p. 392). The report also notes important findings in other areas. Part of the desired leadership model identified by GLOBE focuses on participative and consultative management with all followers, or as much as can be achieved. The results for MENA show a lower ranking of these leadership qualities than those relating to being humane, autonomous and self-preserving (Northouse, 2013, pp. 402–403).

Regardless of the theoretical structures of desired models of leadership, MENA examples consistently display an arraying of small in-groups and large out-groups within organizations, establishing stark tiers of involvement. The implication being that wasta results, not just in creating connections for privileged groups of people, but also in creating barriers to those on the outside. In a classic construction of leader-member exchange theory, leaders and managers would strive to increase positive dyadic linkages with all workers, thereby expanding in-groups. However, there is no indication that this takes place to any serious degree in MENA settings even though it appears to be recognized as important by some. The resulting condition reinforces a stagnant public sector environment further. Therefore, the seventh tension involving the reliance on limited in-groups becomes the standard. Participative leadership, where consultation extends beyond this trusted core, is not easily identified in the literature.

Interestingly, the GLOBE research brought forward some competing ideals to those just mentioned as being acted on by leaders in the MENA culture cluster that offer some hope for change in the future (Northouse, 2013, p. 403). This idealized model runs counter in some key respects to the real world experience of leadership on the ground (Abdallah & al-Homoud, 2001, p. 523). For example, the emphasis placed on leaders being humane and sensitive to their followers seems at odds with established norms in the region that likely do not reflect such treatment beyond in-group participants (Northouse, 2013, p. 395). Additionally, a localized study of leadership utilizing GLOBE measures in Qatar and Kuwait found a strong desire for consultation to be practiced between leaders and followers (Abdallah & al-Homoud, 2001, p. 522). One possible reason for these differences is that the GLOBE project inquiries about leadership may not have been fully reflective of indicators relevant to the Arab MENA region (Dastmalchian, Javidan, & Alam, 2001).

Leading in the MENA public sector is inhibited by additional forces external to organizations that prevent an inclusive workforce from being fielded. This is the final tension discussed. First, part of the desire to maintain traditional cultural values inside MENA public organizations' lack of opportunities made available to women in the workplace. Women who could add value, well educated or not, find their road to employment rocky. In essence, this is the biggest in-group/out-group relationship of all in the Arab working world, and it is a reality that operates to the detriment of individual organizations, countries, and the region as a whole. As the Arab Spring clarified the aspirations of unsatisfied people in the region, it also elevated issues involved with women's rights.

The growing unemployment of youth is a further aspect of MENA's problems in this regard. Finding a means to provide employment for this population, and enable them to see a path to a prosperous future is essential to ensuring peace and stability. An expanding youth demographic without gainful employment does not bode well for countries seeking to develop and grow. It will only be a matter of time before that energy turns in directions that are ultimately unhelpful to achieving these goals. The question, of course, is where to find the jobs? And what can an overburdened public sector hope to achieve in this regard?

A last part of this eighth tension involves the highly educated within Arab MENA countries. These are often individuals who have acquired academic skills associated with the social sciences that are not a fit with current employer needs. These individuals tend to wait for jobs they consider to be worthy of their effort, and expect good pay for their engagement. Often they desire public sector employment because of the decent salaries, work structure, and stature within society (Saif, 2012). Even though wasta threatens growth and ambition for many, they still prefer this setting to less secure employment.

## Considering New Public Management and New Public Governance as Paths to Crafting Improved Leadership

One area of growth in public administration theory at the close of the last century involved the study of organizational performance. Central to discussing the accountability of government organizations and programs is the question of how they perform—and how that performance is controlled and scrutinized (see Kettl & Fesler, 2009, pp. 9–12, for a useful description of the layers of government accountability). Activities such as audits, inspections, program evaluations, and the establishing of ongoing performance measurement and management systems, can all aid in this effort (Mameli, 2011; Osborne, 2010, pp. 3–4). These methods are exercised within the larger concerns of achieving "efficiency, downsizing and decentralization, excellence, and public service orientation" (al-Yahya, Lubatkin, & Vengroff, 2009, p. 17). This movement became known as the New Public Management (NPM). Observers note that Arab MENA bureaucracies continue to struggle with successful implementation of these concepts and mechanisms (Jreisat, 2009b).

Underpinning NPM efforts has been a drive to dramatically improve the efficiency of the public sector, often looking to the private sector for ideas. During this same period, another area of review, aimed at understanding the broader context of public administration through governance, has examined the importance of networks, partnerships, and coproduction in public service delivery (Lynn, Jr., 2010, p. 109; McQuaid, 2010; Pestoff & Brandsen, 2010). New Public Governance (NPG) theory takes increased aim at decoding public sector effectiveness by better understanding the public organization within a complex external environment (Osborne, 2010, p. 10).

Studying networks among a growing plurality of actors has been preoccupying academics for the last 20 or so years across a wide array of disciplines. The topic came into vogue for public administration theorists in the 1990s, when there was an undeniable blurring of boundaries taking place between government agencies and the non-profits they often employed for the delivery of services. But, networks were not a topic for such cross sector studies alone. The concept also became prominent in the study of criminal activity. Whether discussing terrorism or organized crime, the topic gained traction quickly. As a result, loose organizations of actors that connected to carry out a task in either the licit or illicit worlds suddenly became important to better understand in many different settings. The world increasingly came to look like a spiderweb of nodes and lines of communication. If you wanted to govern better, you needed to understand how to respond to the entire milieu.

Clearly then, with the advent of increasing globalization at the close of the 20th century, and the disintegration of a variety of different types of barriers with new technologies, this flexible mode of organization became attractive to many different types of actors. What this meant for the topic of public sector leadership was multifaceted. Certainly, all our prior knowledge was being impacted by the changes in the real world, and certainly, approaches to leadership had to accommodate these shifts. But shifts in leadership to these changing circumstances had to be properly attuned to the circumstances first. Like adjustments made for the findings of NPM primarily within organizations, application of leadership to a world recognizing NPG outside of public organizations had to make sense of its finer characteristics too.

## Figure 3. New Public Management (NPM) and New Public Governance (NPG)

| Quadrant One: NPM HIGH/NPG HIGH | Quadrant Two: NPM HIGH/NPG LOW |
|---|---|
| Quadrant Three: NPM LOW/NPG HIGH | Quadrant Four: NPM LOW/NPG LOW |

The above matrix displays different result patterns public sector leaders can achieve as they respond to challenges of globalization and regional context, using the administrative and managerial logic of our time. The more a country reaches a level of competence in both areas (Quadrant One), the more it is expected to be able to control both its external and internal influences with reasonable success. The result is a public sector that can run in both an efficient and effective manner—maximizing tools for improving performance and leveraging network linkages to accomplish even more thorough outcome achievement.

Quadrant Two identifies situations where countries have demonstrated an ability to integrate the tools of NPM into their service delivery organizations and activities, but are struggling with managing the networks so important to NPG. In this scenario, establishing on-going coproduction activities that ensure cohesive realization of missions and goals continues to vex public sector practitioners. Quadrant Three of the matrix represents a reversed image of Quadrant Two. Here, country public sectors have dealt reasonably well with engaging networks of players from differing sectors and levels of the globalized system they operate within. However, they have failed to put into place reliable mechanisms for guiding and growing performance.

The final quadrant of the matrix, found in Figure 3, highlights settings where both NPM and NPG concerns have not been achieved to any serious degree. In these locations, deficiencies are present that seriously compromise outputs, outcomes and overall missions attainment. Further still, the severity of these failures can be translated into assessments regarding a country's stability, as the public sector's activities are so critical to survival. Failed and failing states provide examples for such a crosswalk.

Utilizing this matrix in order to characterize strengths and weaknesses that countries need to overcome can be useful. Parsing out the elements of NPM and NPG that need to be achieved can set the stage for focusing leadership to deal with problems. But structuring how to best depict these categories for assessment is a much larger project than can be addressed within this particular discussion. However, it is a necessary step in a more rigorous march toward clarifying what must be done for MENA countries to both endure and thrive in turbulent times.

## Developing Leaders and Leadership Skills to Meet MENA Needs

Leading the public sector of MENA countries in pursuit of NPM, an NPG result is a joint task for key players across levels of response, domains of activity, and sectors of society in which to engage. Achieving networked governance that improves service delivery by heightening the use of tools and techniques designed to empower public administration professionals are both required steps to meet this overall goal. Developing public sector leadership capable of reaching this destination is a critical element for success (Jreisat, 2009b, p. 10–11; Newell, Reeher, & Ronayne, 2012).

Unsurprisingly, interest in the development of leaders, and the practice of leadership, has grown in MENA over the last two decades. However, while interest has been raised, indigenous empirical studies of the topic extending past political heads of state to public administrators are few and far between (Abdallahh & al-Homoud, 2001, pp. 507–508; Common, 2011). Indeed, a lack of study relating to matters of the public sector is true for a host of analytical interests that are required for a better unpacking of the MENA context (Boumarafi, 2009; Chene, 2007; Khodr 2012;

Khouri, 2008; Lee, 2000; Perry, 2000). Adequately formulating approaches for moving the application of leadership forward are best built atop such a foundation.

Whether seeking to recommend policy changes in broad or narrow corridors, establishing leadership that displays cultural congruence across regional, national, and organizational levels is necessary (al-Yahya, Lubatkin, & Vengroff 2009; Kalantari, 2005; Mameli, 2011). Carefully accounting for differences across Gulf, Levant and North African countries within MENA, whether it involves economic development or cultural distinctions, will no doubt be improved with heightened involvement of Arab academics and practitioners (Smith, Achoui, & Harb, 2006, p.8).

Past leadership research on politicians, private sector managers and public sector administrators from Arab MENA countries has often focused on authoritarian styles and models (for one discussion see Hammoud, 2011, pp. 146–147). As noted earlier, the argument supporting this approach to leadership in public sector settings seems to have turned on a belief that Arab workers were essentially characterized as Theory "X" personalities—hard to motivate and exhibiting a poor work ethic (Abdulla, 2010; al-Yahya, 2009; Crotty, 2010; Tompkins, 2005). As such, authoritarian approaches to management were not only implicitly justifiable, but also necessary by those implementing them. During the end of the last century, and on into the mid-2000s, a more nuanced understanding of leadership in the region began to emerge. A prime mover in this area was the GLOBE study that spanned roughly a decade, and attempted to flesh out regional models of ideal leader characteristics across the world. A small sample of representative states from the MENA region was included in the initial analysis, and an idealized picture of desired leadership was constructed. What subsequent reviews of the region have demonstrated, however, is that the desired form of leadership does not tend to find steadfast footing in the actualized practice of leadership. This duality holds true in political, private and public sector settings (Common, 2011; Hammoud, 2011; Sarayrah, 2004).

More recent studies of MENA leadership that focus on public institutions specifically recognize the need to grow human capital and administrative technology as a means to advancing country goals. But problems remain in matching skill sets to needs, and assuming that untargeted training and general technological improvement necessarily complement each other has not been born out. Furthered by problems with integrating youth, women, and the educated into the workforce successfully, a complex understanding of the problems leaders need to overcome has gradually been coming into focus, although the most productive approaches for leaders to take remain debated. Therefore, lasting positive change has been elusive. Worse yet, as societies grapple with these dilemmas, expectations of the population are unmet. This creates a circumstance of relative deprivation (Gurr, 1970), seeding the ground for continuous unrest.

Leadership analysis is a subsection of organization theory studies which can be helpful in addressing these issues. What has been learned over the years in all areas of organization theory is that we tend to start with the most basic of theories first, and then continually open them up to learn more about the world being examined. Leadership theorists consistently moved from a logically intuitive approach of trying to understand leaders from their traits, to looking more deeply into their skills, abilities, behaviors, and relationships. When you open the black box of leadership and look inside, you start to realize that a surface understanding of the topic simply would not do. Ultimately, what is left to the student of the field, as well as the practitioner, is that there is more than one answer about how to lead. The problems come with choosing from what we already know regarding appropriate application, while also continuing to grow our knowledge base. In discussing MENA contextual issues, in conjunction with NPM and NPG, some of the broad thicket has been cleared in terms of end outcomes sought. Finding means to attain these outcomes is partly the task of leadership analysis.

## Figure 4. Leader Development (LD)/Leadership Development Skills (LDS)

| Quadrant One: LD HIGH/LDS HIGH | Quadrant Two: LD HIGH/LDS LOW |
| --- | --- |
| Quadrant Three: LD LOW/LDS HIGH | Quadrant Four: LD LOW/LDS LOW |

Leader Development (LD) and Leadership Development Skills (LDS) training capture the internal and external dynamics of leadership analysis, respectively (al-Dabbagh & Assaad, 2010a; 2010b). The former examines issues of individual ethics and morals, while exploring personal cognitive awareness of core strengths, weaknesses and biases. This internal growth sets the stage for successful external application of additional leadership skills. For example, contemplating one's own understanding of gender relations and cross-cultural interaction in the context of creating a just work setting within a specific environment helps set the stage for constructive relationship building within organizations. The latter concept of LDS focuses more on the second step of such a process, the actual interactive communication and engagement. These social skills, once deployed, can be of value both internally to an organization as well as external to it.

Arguably, LD and LDS are two halves of the same coin, and they should be seen as such. As these competencies are strengthened within a leader, they will be more likely to improve the efficiency and effectiveness of their organization as well. While it is not an easy link to the earlier discussion on NPM and NPG, it seems undeniable that LDS enhancement is essential for surviving in a world struggling with the multitude of effects brought on by globalization. Networking to develop solutions is at the heart of NPG, and requires such abilities to be employed. Additionally, without responsible grounding in LD, efforts made by leaders to achieve core values of NPM, such as corruption control, transparency, and accountability, will ultimately fall flat.

The quadrants in Figure 4 take a first cut at explaining the preparation required for public sector leaders to succeed in addressing problems within MENA countries. Quadrant One offers the best-case scenario. Here, leaders have highly developed internal and external skill sets. Theoretically, such individuals would be in the best position to approach issues from both NPM and NPG vantage points in order to guide public sector organizations through turbulent circumstances. Of course, ultimate results are dependent on many more things as will be discussed later. However, when considering the leader alone, well developed LD and LDS abilities place them on the firmest ground for completing their tasks. It is arguable that there is no strong example of an Arab MENA country to fit into this cell at this point in time.

Quadrant Two presents an image of a leader with high LD and low LDS capabilities. In such scenarios, you would expect to find situations where training has exposed leaders to the importance of focusing on constructing a reliable moral compass with commensurate management capacities, but has left them without the ability to guide change easily in a highly interactive setting that involves players both inside and outside of an organization. There is an argument to be made that this is where many MENA public sectors now find themselves. Over the last decade, an understanding and desire to create change, along the lines of NPM, has taken hold. But bringing the task to fruition remains a work in progress with many of these countries (Meraj, 2009).

It is possible that an undervaluing of LDS has contributed to this situation. With weak civil societies and private sectors, networking abilities in the region external to public organizations are often limited to contacts with actors from international governmental organizations and/or international non-governmental organizations. In both cases, MENA public sector leaders are at power disadvantages. The need to deploy LDS competencies may have seemed limited. Internal to public sector organizations the problem is somewhat reversed. In this context, LDS skills are utilized, but appear to not be employed with vigor due to a focus on in-group relationships. This is likely due to authoritarian approaches built on perceptions of Theory "X" employees, and the barriers to participation that have developed over many years. The need to improve on LDS competencies, by tailoring them to the MENA context and individuals of the region, could be central to alleviating the problems at hand for countries within this quadrant of the matrix. Leveraging LDS so that leaders can apply it successfully within organizations, while networking with those outside as well, is a critical element of securing both NPM and NPG goals. Accomplishing this will further unleash abilities of public sector workers.

Quadrant Three depicts a setting where LD is low and LDS is high. In such circumstances, you would expect to find public sectors that are somewhat directionless in terms of efficient service delivery. It is likely that leaders would be involved in public sector settings where internal mismanagement is the norm, and the leaders themselves may be part and parcel of the condition. Having well developed interactive and networking skills can easily be misapplied without ethical and moral balance employed to the situation being addressed. Where LDS is high, and LD is low, this would be one expected result.

The last cell identified, Quadrant Four, provides the image of a public sector leader who has the least development of both LD and LDS. One would assume that such leaders would be in the worst position to achieve either NPM or NPG goals, regardless of whether or not they have been sculpted for cultural relevance. Public sectors in decay or that have outright collapsed, fall into this category. In these settings, public sector fraud, waste, mismanagement, and abuse, as well as an inability to apply relational skills to positively address these conditions, would be expected to run rampant.

## Discussion: Leadership Theory and Mena Leadership Practices

Conversations about globalization, the Arab MENA context, NPM, NPG, LD, and LDS help clarify where public sector leaders need to end up to improve their organizations and countries, as well as the road they must travel to get there. However, specifics about how the road can best be travelled remain incomplete. A review of the existing work on leadership theory needs to occur in order to move this discussion forward (see Daft, 2008, pp. 20–23 for a concise presentation of the trajectory to date; Northouse, 2013 offers in-depth review). As such, this section of the paper will identify some of the more durable leadership approaches uncovered by theorists. It is important to note, however, that authentic Arab contributions on the topic of leadership are essential to flesh out this dialogue and make it more applicable to MENA settings. Potential inadequacies of Western models have been highlighted in the past when being applied to non-Western countries (Smith, Achoui, & Harb, 2006). In short, to better target applicable leadership skills to the MENA region, and achieve cultural congruence that can yield increased usefulness, Arab understandings of the topic must be fully incorporated (Hofstede, 1980; 1984; Dubai School of Government, 2007, for one positive example attempting to explore the role of women and leadership in the United Arab Emirates).

Trait theory is where the study of modern leadership set its primary flag. The logic being that common traits could be identified that enabled leadership. Theorists started their analysis with straightforward ideas about the topic, and then used the resulting construction of reality as a "straw man" to punch holes in when moving forward. As they learned more when new information became available, trait theory was modified, and new theories were also spawned. The debate about whether leaders were born or made began to be hammered out in this arena. There are both compelling and confusing elements to this approach to leadership. The suggestion that one size fits all was understood long ago to be too simplistic, and the inability to clearly articulate what that one size in fact was, made adequately applying these ideas to the hunt for leaders all the more problematic. So, while the debate continued to rage, the field also moved forward.

While it may be helpful for MENA leadership theorists to think in terms of identifying desired traits, it is only an initial stepping stone on a much longer journey since it never provides a full answer about how to lead. Indeed, this has been recognized by the few who have taken this path so far. The empirical study of Gulf leadership traits has been explored in an attempt to begin unlocking some of the broader puzzle (Abdallah & al-Homoud, 2001). But focusing on traits is understood as being only a part of the process of understanding leadership.

Recognizing limitations within trait theory, researchers became more interested in nuance, and deepened their studies. They continually opened up their viewpoints to learn more about the topic being examined. As could be expected then, the study of leadership grew both in the number of theoretical approaches to the topic as well as in complexity. The study of the topic is therefore constantly moving from more closed approaches to more open ones. Few have been completely discarded, leaving a tool kit of theories to draw on available. Individuals can mix and match the theories, or come up with just one that fits a setting and/or leader. But, ultimately, the more that there is to work with the better the analysis becomes.

The Path-Goal theory and Leader-Member Exchange (LMX) theory provide valuable windows into basic truths about leadership that resonate with MENA experience. Ingrained in both discussions is the reality that leadership depends on a good many things. The leader, the follower, and the situation, to name the big-ticket items, are all essential components.

With the Path-Goal theory, the notion that a leader must define a goal, clear a path, remove obstacles, and provide support seems self-evident no matter what traits a leader has, or what style may be employed. The question is not whether they should do these things as part of being leaders, but whether or not the individual leader has the actual ability to. Similarly with LMX theory, it seems patently obvious at this point in time that leaders do not exist in a vacuum, and in fact the roles that followers have in the relationship between the two are critical to the process becoming a success. As a result, examining followers in conjunction with leaders more closely is a critical element in understanding whether or not a leader has the ability to succeed in creating change. These are not difficult concepts to grasp, but they can be to implement. As noted earlier in this paper, the Arab MENA experience shows incomplete application of LMX logic that no doubt inhibits successful achievement of Path-Goal intentions. In fact, autocratic, inexperienced leaders with limited vision and social skills were seen as inhibitors to success (Abdallah & al-Homoud, 2001, p. 522).

Team leadership theory suggests that leadership can be shared among leaders and followers. Even when followers were recognized as part of a process (such as in LMX) they were seldom considered as being true partners in leadership, to the extent that they would actually be responsible for making some leadership decisions and assessments. If anything, when subordinates were considered as achieving leadership roles, they might have been seen as more of a threat due to "emergent" leadership characteristics and not as support to the identified authority figure. This appears to be the case with at least one examination of leadership carried out in Oman (Common, 2011, p. 221). This finding, though limited to one setting and observation, suggests the difficulty that such a style would have finding traction within MENA public sector environments. It also offers further evidence that weaknesses inherent in LDS competencies prevent effective enhancement of LMX principles that could lead to team activities. The historical yielding of ground to Theory "X" perceptions, and wasta sensitivities, appears to have had a direct impact on moving in these directions.

Team leadership theory suggests that the identified authority figure in the team, the actual leader by assigned role and power, should be open to having team members assume control and decision making over certain areas of the leadership process. And, as long as things are going well, the assigned leader should be comfortable stepping back and letting the process run in this fashion, without feeling the need to put their stamp of approval and leadership on every little thing that gets done below them. To accomplish this successfully requires leaders who are very secure in their abilities, and in their own inherent self-worth. In this regard, team leadership theory broke new and interesting ground. In essence, the team itself becomes the leader in the best functioning scenarios. All participate in leadership, and all also participate in the following— with varying degrees of involvement and responsibility. While participative and consultative traits and styles may have been identified as desired for MENA region leaders in some past studies, moving to this level of engagement with followers would be a remarkable achievement given the current limitations already discussed in this paper (Abdallah & al-Homoud, 2001). But it is a necessary part of any answer to bolstering future productivity within the public sector.

A relatively understudied area that can help move MENA leadership practice in a new direction includes the topic of Servant Leadership. From this viewpoint, altruistic leaders and their fundamental desire to empower and grow followers' abilities, as well as give back to the community, are examined. This is an unusual twist on matters since we tend to think of leaders as wielding power, not sharing it or giving it away. But in this theory, selflessness is the central feature of the leader. Interestingly, one review of historical leadership patterns in the MENA region identified Servant leadership as an approach once employed in Bedouin-Arab culture (Sarayrah, 2004). This effort attempted to ground the values of consultative leadership in tribal practice, and thereby legitimize a reason for returning to such efforts now. The role of the past should not be discounted when trying to forge a path into the future. As such, this study is useful in terms of providing infrastructure to prior Arab leadership practice. It should be examined in greater detail when attempting to blaze a new trail ahead.

Transformational leadership theory excited many academics and practitioners at the end of the 20th century, and continues to do so today. It suggests that leaders can move followers to achieve desired ends with an exceptionally high level of commitment. The primary tools involve application of a leader's vision, and engagement in the creation of social architecture associated with building organizational cultures. However, an indispensable part of the process is associated with the leader's own charisma. It is the personal charisma of the leader that engages and energizes followers beyond their normal willingness to perform. Almost bringing us right back to trait theory, and adding a new twist on an old question: Can charisma be taught? If not, can anybody really become a transformational leader?

It is true that activities such as creating trust can be taught, and leaders can learn how to be the type of people that others may want to emulate and follow. But this is still somehow different than the way these same characteristics fold together when combined with charisma, which seems to many to be a natural trait for a transformational leader. It is also true that leaders can be made, but transformational leadership suggests something more is present as well. So the question is posed yet again, but slightly altered. Are transformational leaders born or made? And more importantly to the discussion at hand, how can these skills be imparted to MENA settings in a productive manner?

A compelling theory to consider at this stage of the discussion is that of Authentic Leadership (George, 2003; Terry, 1993). This approach seems to be wrestling with fusing elements of transformational leadership, servant leadership, ethics, and LMX theory to explain how exceptional leaders achieve their goals. The importance of a profoundly internalized ethical and moral structure within the individual is key to their performing well as authentic leaders. This inner base connects them to their followers, and their societies, in a clear and focused manner. Once followers understand what a leader's ethical and moral attributes are, and where they come from, they can then see these attributes externalized in the way that the leader acts. As a result, a powerful bond can develop. The notion that you should not just "talk the talk," but also "walk the talk," is central to an authentic leader being able to command respect from followers. Moreover, this type of conduct builds trust between the parties going forward (Northouse, 2013, pp. 253–270).

There are several core constructions to Authentic Leadership theory and practice that have already been briefly noted above. However, one element yet to be discussed is crucial to the Arab MENA experience. An essential aspect to developing authentic leaders is the existence of a "critical life event" (Northouse, 2013, p. 266). This event, or events, can serve to actualize the individual's depth of self-propelling them forward as leaders. It also cements the relationship with external parties and worldviews when they display and communicate their experiences. In short, this part of the path they travel actually establishes confidence in their ability to carry out their role.

Authentic leaders in MENA would be able to connect with both the societal culture and external stakeholders. In addition, they would connect better to immediate followers within the public sector setting. These are necessary beachheads to secure (Nahavandi, 2009, pp. 33–59). The ethical and moral base suggested would drive the desire to expand in-groups and minimize out-groups by serving follower needs. Concentrating on building ethical linkages between the leader's actions, character, goals, power, honesty and values will strengthen the odds of success in public sector management (Northouse, 2009, pp. 157–168). Authentic leadership characteristics, therefore, become a requirement for the overall effectiveness of a leader's efforts.

Given the wide-ranging and dramatic events of the Arab Spring, it is reasonable to assume that a number of potential authentic leaders have been spawned throughout the MENA pool. But they need to be cultivated in a positive manner so that their energy and drive are not wasted, or turned to destructive ends. Central to the Authentic Leadership argument is the position that these skills can be both taught and learned (Northouse, 2013, p. 268). A combination of structured LD and LDS competency enhancements would gear individuals to become future authentic leaders. With LD focusing on ethical, moral, and inner core strengthening, and LDS building intercommunicative networking abilities, leaders to come could be prepared to take this road. Ultimately, such competencies would position leaders to better meet the realities of both NPM and NPG challenges in the Arab world.

## Conclusion

The Arab Spring signified a desire for change in the region that is anchored in values of public sector accountability, transparency, and ethical competence. The phenomenon that has swept through MENA countries creates an opportunity to embrace and shape change. Moving to more open, engaged and inclusive leadership models in government is essential to securing better public policy and public management for the region in the future. However, as has been noted several times in this paper, leadership research for MENA countries has been limited (Common, 2011; Leung & Bond, 2004; Smith, Achoui, & Harb 2006). As such, it is clear that, first and foremost, a more focused empirical study of leadership is required to unearth an effective, Arab centered, understanding of the topic in these settings.

Tied to improving public sector efficiency and effectiveness through better leadership means, therefore, establishing the importance of focusing on Arab sensitive solutions to a host of interconnected MENA problems. Issues of unemployed youth, gender imbalances in the workforce, the underutilization of educated individuals within societies, and creating better functioning civil society and private sectors, while managing rising expectations brought on by globalization processes, can be addressed by a plethora of policy initiatives. But the ones most likely to secure success in implementation will be those that are stamped with an authentic Arab understanding of a proper path forward. This does not mean starting from scratch to resolve problems that have as many internal causes as external ones. Indeed, examining models of improvement from other parts of the world is a necessary step to crafting lasting change. But it is not a sufficient one (Abrahart, Kaur, & Tzannatos et al., 2000; Abdallah & al-Homoud, 2001). The corrective actions that will survive the test of time will be those honed with the people of the region and countries in mind (Biygautane, 2011; Coleman, 2011; Kalantari, 2005; Khodr, 2012).

Arab constructed solutions must be identified and implemented by authentic leaders who can achieve desired results in MENA settings. For successful public sector management in MENA to be deployed when meeting these challenges, leaders must exercise internal and external skills in a way that achieves NPM and NPG goals within a globalized environment. This means galvanizing followers to achieve at a high level. In order to do this, images of Theory "X" Arab workers must first be cast off, and wasta must be challenged as though it includes elements of discriminatory practice—and not simply painted as a relatively benign form of "connections." Both of these plateaus will likely be reached when authentic leaders step to the fore with ethical norms that are honed to address the local realities of MENA countries, and the region in general (Jreisat, 2009b, p. 11). The pursuit of crafting authentic leaders for this purpose, through coordinated LD and LDS preparation today, is an enabling approach that can yield large dividends tomorrow.

# Appendix

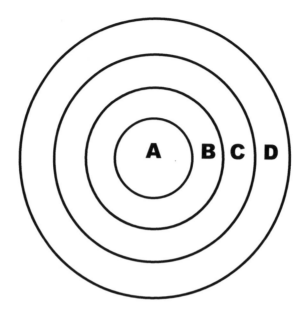

APPENDIX: RINGS OF INFLUENCE IMPACTING PUBLIC SECTOR PROFESSIONALS

<u>Ring A</u>: This first ring can be seen as comprising street level bureaucrats, front line staff, analysts, policy professionals and managers who both implement and guide service delivery.

<u>Ring B</u>: The organizational housing within which the public sector employees operate. The structures, rules, goals, technology and culture of the organization exerting force on the individual employees can be found here.

<u>Ring C</u>: Includes external entities comprised of international, national, organizational and individual stakeholders, competitors and tangential actors. This array of players can span policy domains, levels of political engagement and sectors of interaction.

<u>Ring D</u>: The final ring captures sweeping effects that the preceding rings must adjust for. These effects can include processes of globalization, social and political upheavals like the Arab Spring, or emergent shifts in the physical environment such as those resulting from global warming or pandemic surges. Ring D completes the framework outlining the world of the public sector employee. Further, it illustrates the proximal location of the public sector employee to events in their external environment.

# Decentralization Needs Interest Mediation: The Moroccan Development Strategy and Partnering with Non-State Actors for the Promotion of Services Offshore

## Stefanie Slaoui-Zirpins

## Abstract

This article combines theories of decentralization and interest mediation in order to address the issue of decentralization in the region of the Middle East and North Africa (MENA). Accordingly, progress in local and regional governance means effective participation through the implementation of subsidiarity. Combining theories of decentralization and interest mediation, one can explain formal and informal processes in the interactions within the bureaucracy, as well as among the state, civil society, the market, and citizens. Using the example of economic policy for the promotion of off-shore services in Fez, Morocco, this article will apply the mentioned theories within a case study, while emphasizing the strengths and the weaknesses of the process.

# Introduction

Theories of decentralization provide many advantages for the study of local and regional governance in the Middle East and North Africa (MENA) region by focusing on changes in the policy process. Indeed, their limitation in focusing only on the policy process is problematic since such a process in the MENA region is often not well defined. On the other hand, theories of interest mediation, although not widely used by researchers, can be useful for policy evaluation and assessing whether a particular policy is suitable for the region and other emerging economies (Alhamad, 2008; Heilmann, 1999; Kennedy, 2005). Because of this, researchers interested in the MENA region find theories of interest mediation particularly interesting in examining the role of non-state actors and civil society. Examples of these researchers are Lust-Oskar and Zerhouni (2008), Heydemann (2004), Harders (2009), and Bellin (2000). Analyzing the policy process in the MENA region, they not only describe formal processes but also answer questions about who effectively influences policy choice. This article examines research strategies that combine formal and informal aspects of the policy process and uses Morocco's efforts to establish a new economic program for offshore services as a case study. It elaborates on assumptions presented by theories of decentralization and interest mediation, and by analyzing the processes applied to the Fez area.

## Theoretical Approach: Decentralization, Interest Mediation and Policy-Analysis

## Terminological Clarification

In order to understand decentralization in context, perhaps it would be useful to understand terminologies such as De-concentration and Devolution.

**De-concentration:** According to a definition used by United Nations in 1962, Deconcentration refers to the "Deconcentration of decision-making authority to dependent field units of the same department or level of government, that is the delegation to civil servants working in the field of power to make decisions in the execution of central politics (also referred to as administrative or bureaucratic decentralization)" (Reddy, 1999, p. 16).

**Devolution:** According to a definition used by the United Nations in 1962, Devolution refers to the "Devolution of decision-making authority to relatively autonomous regional or local governments, or to special statutory bodies, that is the cession to power to make decisions (including restricted policy-making power) to representative (usually elected) authorities, or to more or less autonomous public or voluntary enterprises (also referred to as political or administrative decentralization)" (Reddy, 1999, p. 16).

De-concentration, thus, refers mainly to the bureaucratic sphere. Devolution, on the other hand—as well as concepts such as privatization, denationalization and de-regulation—refers to political and economic issues. These terminologies can be particularly measured through administrative efficiency, participation/democratization, and economic development (Polte, Steinich, & Thomi, 2001, p. 313). While administrative efficiency pays more attention to the vertical dimension of decentralization, participation/democratization and economic development pay more attention to the horizontal dimension of the concept.

Although decentralization may have broader meaning, many studies still use it to focus on the "classical" vertical dimension within the state, or on the horizontal dimension between the state and civil society. An example is the work of Rather. He sees Tunisia as a virtual centralized political system with only some de-concentrated elements (Rather, 2001, p. 117).

In these studies, vertical decentralization from the state to the market attracts little or no attention. Although there are counter examples, such as by Rondinelli and Nelli (1986), changes in economic structures are frequently studied from a more macro-oriented perspective of economic liberalization. The latter studies often are conducted by the so-called "pure" economists, while studies on bureaucratic decentralization are conducted by public administration scholars who pay little or no attention to the fact that decentralization is always a political process that can have unintended consequences and may be influenced by many actors (Manor, 1999, p. 41). Other researchers include economic perspectives but criticize decentralization strategies as neoliberal and as consolidating authoritarianism (Bergh, 2012, p. 308).

## What is Necessary to Make Decentralization Processes Successful?

The processes of decentralization and centralization as well as institutional arrangements require several answers. For example, to determine if a decentralization policy is successful, one has to look at administrative efficiency, participation/democratization, and/or economic development (Polte, Steinich, & Thomi, 2001, p. 313). Some researchers, such as Manor (1999), use political economy perspectives on decentralization to describe informal structures by focusing less on horizontal and more on vertical decentralization. An example would be the structure of the World Bank.

Combining theories of decentralization with theories of interest mediation is uncommon. Yet, the combination enables researchers to have a detailed understanding of the decentralization policies' impact on governance. In particular, it makes it possible to comprehend interactions and adjustments between the spheres of the state and the market. Hence, subsidiarity and interest mediation play important roles in achieving goals generally associated with decentralization.

The underlying idea of the principle of subsidiarity is that government can promote citizen participation and economic efficiency while operating with smaller administrative units. Subsidiarity also defines interaction between public and private actors as well as between higher and lower levels within the same class in a society. According to the principle of subsidiarity, the state ought to:

- abstain from becoming involved in anything that is better accomplished by smaller units;

- provide help and support to empower smaller units and encourage self-help; and

- become involved only when the next smaller unit is unable to perform (Reddy, 1999, p. 14-15).

The principle of subsidiarity does not, however, take a position on the size of an administrative unit to perform a certain task. Hence, empiric evaluation is needed to find out if subsidiarity is truly required. Because of the political nature of the decentralization process, however, this issue cannot be answered hypothetically or in a technocratic way. In fact, answering this question has to take into consideration the interests and the capabilities of the different actors involved in the performance of a task, and theories of interest mediation are the ideal candidates to guide such an approach.

Interest mediation is more than "interest representation" in terms of influencing governmental decision-making process as explained by theories of pluralism (Albrecht, 2008, p. 17). According to these theories, actors and structures involved in decision-making processes other than the "state" are neglected. This study, on the other hand, supports interest mediation as described by Molina and Rhodes (2002) and their explanation of decision-making as an exchange process. Such an exchange takes place among different actors and from different parts of society, including the state, civil society, the private sector, and citizens. The exchanges express power relationships among the actors involved in the decision-making process (Jansen & Schubert, 1995, p. 95).

Interest mediation can be heuristic, used to structure research. Like many other research studies, this article distinguishes between pluralism, corporatism, clientelism and monism (Kennedy, 2005, p. 6). Policy analysis in this sense is not considered in light of how to solve a particular problem, but how to analyze a situation. In order to make the political process transparent, the actors must be allowed to participate effectively (Héritier, 1993, p. 11), and move from the state-centered approach in examining decentralization. As a consequence, there are continuous interactions between different actors within one sphere (vertically) as well as between different spheres (horizontally) (Thomi, 2001, p. 19). These interactions are parts of decentralization.

# The Establishment of an Offshore Sector in Fez

## Economic and Political Needs for the Upgrading of the Regions

Realizing that top-down economic development and planning is no longer suited for Morocco, and recognizing that the Moroccan economy is not growing fast enough to reduce unemployment and poverty, the Moroccan government is finding itself in a difficult situation. On the one hand, centralized industrialization policy seems to be necessary because of the immense developmental disparities between localities in Morocco. Shifting decision making to localities and aspects of public service to the private sector, on the other hand, is also being considered.

Regionalization (vertical decentralization) is becoming part of the governmental strategy, especially since Mohammed VI's accession to the throne in 1999. This approach is gaining more importance after the 2011 constitutional reforms. Progress in regionalization may also lead to solving the conflict regarding the Western Sahara. Consequently, there is a broad consensus that local and regional actors should play an important role in the planning and implementation of economic development.

Despite the fact that the prevailing economic ideology in Morocco has always been pro-business, public actors had intervened heavily in the economic processes for many decades. Therefore, horizontal decentralization also seems to be necessary in this aspect. To date, the public sector in Morocco remains relatively influential in directing the country's economy. In addition to public enterprises, the Moroccan state intervenes through various developmental projects and investment subsidies. The development projects are run by public and private actors who set economic goals for development in industry, agriculture, and tourism, such as Plan Emergence, Plan Maroc Vert, and Plan Azur. Because of the cooperative character of these development plans and their emphasis on private investments, they are designed to be distinguished from the typical public economy projects.

The costs of the Plan Emergence which is designed to encourage industrial development in Aeronautics, Agribusiness, Automotive, Craft Industry, Electronics, Offshoring, Seafood, and Textile are 1.1 million Euros for 2009–2015. The largest segment of funds goes to education. The developmental plans are designed on local levels. At these levels, tripartite negotiations play a marginal role. The drafting of plans is usually examined by research offices that make political discussions difficult. However, more and more local actors, such as unions, and chamber of commerce show interest in shaping the plan. These factors are now encouraged by new constitutional reforms (Slaoui-Zirpins, 2011, p. 10).

The construction of an offshore park in Fez and the establishment of a sector on offshore services in the Moroccan regions exemplify how strongly intertwined politics and the economy have become. In observing this we can also gain a better understanding of local governance in MENA as a whole.

## The Different Types of Public Actors

The Moroccan state has five levels of government: the central state, the regional governments (the wilaya), the prefectures, the municipalities, and the districts. There are also subdivisions within the districts level—although they are not influential in designing the economic policy. The principle of subsidiarity is referenced in article 140 of the Moroccan Constitution of 2011. On nearly every governmental level, de-concentrated structures coincide with self-government and the cooperation with the special interests and their representatives.

Until 2011, the municipalities were the only political subdivision with no parallel structure to the central state. On this level, the president of the directly elected city council was also the head of the municipal administration. On the levels of the prefectures and regions, the councils and their presidents did not have discretionary power over the administration. Additionally, these councils were elected indirectly from the members of the city councils. Accordingly, presidents of city councils have relatively extensive authority. In retrospect, the governor of the prefecture as a de-concentrated authority controls the activities of the city council. Yet, municipalities do not have sufficient funds to finance large projects on their own (Chabih, 2005).

At the regional level, there are two types of de-concentrated state authorities: the administration under the control of the *wali* and the regional delegations of the ministries. The wali is subordinated to the Ministry of Interior that has been serving as a controlling agency for decades. Until 2011, the king appointed the five principle ministers. One among them was the Ministry of Interior. The administration under the authority of the wali conducts several general administrative tasks at the regional level, such as issuing of passports. In addition, there are several regional delegations of the other ministries whose ministers are appointed by the prime minister. These delegations perform administrative tasks in their respective fields. There are also provincial delegations of the ministries.

The transfer of power to lower levels of government in Morocco has a longer history than Morocco's political parties, trade unions, and business associations. Even prior to the Protectorates, the government in Morocco was decentralized. There was also no trained cadre of local officials, and the system only merely attempted to cope with conflicts between pacified crown land, the *bilad al-makhzan* (tribes in rural areas) and the *bilad as-sā'iba* (tribes in towns). The main problem was that many tribal groups accepted the king as a religious leader, but avoided paying taxes (Chabih, 2005, p. 50;

Eisenstadt & Roniger, 1984, p. 95). As a consequence, the lower levels of state government had to de-concentrate, partly for devolution. The first elections after the Moroccan independency were, in effect, the local elections of 1960 (Vermeren, 2006, p. 6).

The current municipal code was adopted in 2002 and modified in 2003. Since 1971, the territory was divided into seven regions to improve governmental planning. In 1992, the regions gained the status of a territorial authority. In 1997, a reform augmented the number of the regions to 16, enlarged their competences, and imposed an indirectly elected regional council. The southern provinces gained more autonomous status in 2007 and the Moroccan king held several discourses on advancing regionalization, especially as of 2008 (Rousset, 2010, p. 9). A consultative council on regionalization was inaugurated in 2010 that presented its report in 2011, proposing a model of 10 regions.

Concretizing the regionalization process is one of the most important challenges to the Benkriane government elected after the adoption of the new construction in 2011. The dispositions in the new constitution concerning local authorities are general. More specific issues, such as the election of representative councils, division of competences, and finances ought to be articulated by regulations. Even at regional levels, there are still state organizations acting to delegate tasks to public and joint enterprises. Examples of organizations with tasks delegated from the central state are OFPPT (Office Nationale de la Formation Professionell et de la Promotion du Travail)—an office that provides vocational training for the public—and the national employment agency ANAPEC (Agence Nationale de Promotion de l'Emploi et des Compétences). These organizations are under the supervision of the Ministry of Labor and Vocational Training, but organizationally they are relatively independent (Slaoui-Zirpins, 2011, p. 23).

Although the role of the state in economic processes was considerably cut back throughout the structural reforms of 1983 and onwards, the public portfolio remains important and a major factor in economic planning and development. The administration of these entities and their privatization is through the Ministry of Economy and Finance. Privatization issues, however, are concluded by Parliament. While denationalization and privatization are still at an early stage of development in Morocco, the number of public programs that have been privatized are increasing. The state, however, temporarily retains shares during a privatisation process in order to exert its influence (Slaoui-Zirpins, 2011, p. 9).

The implementation of Moroccan development plans is primarily conducted by state-owned companies—in particular, subsidiaries of the Caisse de Dépôt et de Gestion (CDG). For example, the CDG subsidiary MedZ that was created in 2002 organizes the construction and administration of the offshoring zones as a result of the Plan Emergence. Although the organization is 100% public, it nevertheless uses several modern private sector strategies to increase its response to the market.

While the relation between public organizations and state regulatory authorities is relatively explicit, the relations between these authorities and other actors are less clear. For example, it is easy to distinguish between actors who receive state support and those who do not. "State-supported" actors receive privileges from public authorities, and these privileges often include subsidies. Such relations are best explained by theories of clientelism or theories of corporatism.

## The Project FezShore: Ambitions and Reality

## The Moroccan Offshoring Strategy as an Innovation

Currently in six Moroccan cities, there is an offshore park project under construction: Casablanca, Rabat, Fez, Marrakech, Oujda, and Tetouan. Most of the tasks performed are less knowledge intensive, except in Rabat where knowledge intensive tasks were applied. Actualizing offshore parks, however, is not the first trial for an offshore enterprise in Morocco. The call center operator "Web Help" that has been successfully functioning in Morocco since 2001 is an example. Also since 2001, the Casablanca Technopark has been in operation. It is owned by the Moroccan Information Technopark Company (MITC), a joint-venture with 65% of its shares held by a consortium of banks and 35% held by the Moroccan state.

The construction of the Casablanca Technopark is an important milestone in the change of the Moroccan economic strategy. In comparison with other newly industrialized countries, technology-based development played less an important role historically in Morocco than, for example, in Korea or Brazil. Awareness of strategies for developing low-cost labor did not materialize in Morocco until the 1990s (Djeflat, 1996, p. 32). This may be partly due to the fact that, since then, unemployment among young graduates has become very high in Morocco. Today, however, there is more emphasis on low-cost labor and cooperation between the public and the private sector to control cost, especially in export-oriented branches (Eddelani, 2009, p. 133). Figure 1 shows the sphere of the state in Morocco with entities that have close connections to the state. It illustrates the difficulties in conceptualizing actors relations based on theories of decentralization. Thus, the figure does not include the processes of interest mediation between segments of society or between actors.

In the offshoring parks, innovative settings are designed to encourage enterprises in Morocco and increase GDP in order to generate jobs. Enterprises that follow up on such design may purchase or rent bureaus in well-equipped, closed-industrial areas for low rates. Within these complexes, administrative procedures are facilitated. Alternatively, enterprises that receive investment subsidies have to establish themselves through services to the cities.

## Figure 1. The Sphere of the State in Morocco

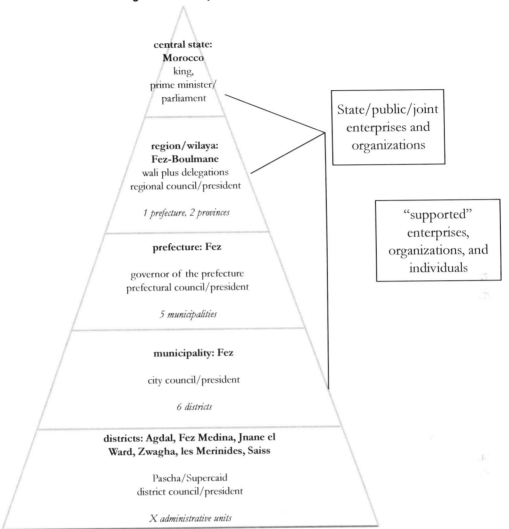

**central state: Morocco**
king,
prime minister/
parliament

**region/wilaya: Fez-Boulmane**
wali plus delegations
regional council/president

*1 prefecture, 2 provinces*

**prefecture: Fez**

governor of the prefecture
prefectural council/president

*5 municipalities*

**municipality: Fez**

city council/president

*6 districts*

**districts: Agdal, Fez Medina, Jnane el Ward, Zwagha, les Merinides, Saiss**

Pascha/Supercaid
district council/president

*X administrative units*

State/public/joint enterprises and organizations

"supported" enterprises, organizations, and individuals

Offshore enterprises are exempt from corporate tax for the first five years of their operation. For each new employee with Moroccan nationality, these enterprises get training grants for a period of three years. Additionally, they can use a special employment contract for labor market entrants that are publically supported for 24 months. Moreover, a more general reduction of the income tax is permitted. Generally, it is evident that the Moroccan state intervenes through its offshoring strategy to encourage private investment rather than to create state-owned economic entities. To reach the goal of creating an innovative setting, there are efforts to involve different actors in the development of these projects.

Outsourcing means the externalization of a business process outward by shifting aspects of the organizational operations conducted from within the organization to outside through another enterprise that can do the same function but with less cost involved. This can be done onsite or offsite. Offshoring, on the other hand, means the delocalization of business processes to a foreign country. This may occur within the same enterprise (if the enterprise has subdivisions abroad), or from one enterprise to another. Outsourcing offshoring becomes possible only when an organization outsources aspects of its operation from within the organization to another enterprise. All forms of offshoring may be undertaken onshore or offshore. Such clarification is important in order to avoid confusion because official Moroccan documents use French word for externalization. It is also confusing because Moroccan offshoring parks host enterprises that undertake services outsourced to multinational entities that often do not utilize outsource as a process.

## Development and Implementation of the Project FezShore

From a theoretical perspective, it is important to investigate how a Moroccan offshoring platform is constructed and how it is been made operational. The construction of such a platform can be understood as an expression of will to overcome economic problems and lack of innovation. Simultaneously, these processes take place in a time when the general discourse is geared toward privatization and regionalization.

The FezShore project exemplifies Moroccan efforts to implement offshore platforms in regions with structural deficits. Thus, not only is the offshoring platform itself important but also the establishment of a sector for the offshoring services within the region. The project is one important development in "offshoring" in the course of implementing the Plan Emergence and encouraging industrial development in Morocco. Industrial development itself is an aspect targeted by various plans. In addition to Plan Emergence, there are plan Azur (in tourism), plan Verte (in agriculture), and plan INDH (Initiative Nationale de Développement Humain/National Initiative for Human Development). These plans, particularly Plan Emergence, include coordination between the public and private actors. Because of this, many actors refer to the Plan Emergence as "pact" Emergence.

The basic idea for project FezShore is the generation of investment incentives instead of completely relying on public economic activities. To enable suitable incentives for local needs, the regional level had identified an important role in the project. Additionally, on the central-state level, strong efforts were made to emphasize the network character of the project. It is still evident that the state plays an important role in the impacted and effected economic activities created by the project, but the decentralization efforts on the vertical and horizontal axe seem to be incomplete.

To explain this further, let us attempt to answer the following questions:

1. Is Plan Emergence a real pact between the public and the private sectors?

2. Is project FezShore locally realized?

## Is the Plan Emergence a True Contract?

The Plan Emergence is completed by the following: different state ministries, the employers' organization "Confédération Générale des Entreprises du Maroc" (CGEM), and the Moroccan organization of banks "Groupement Professionnel des Banques du *Maroc"* (GPBM). Through their involvements, these organizations arranged for a new type of cooperation, like a neo-corporatist arrangement where state and non-state actors come together to find common solutions for problems.

Regarding the number of actors involved in the plan, it is evident that public or quasi-public organizations have a majority of actors in the plan. The GPBM, for example, is a quasi-public organization because its membership is mandatory and subject to banking regulation. The bank's tasks are transferred through delegation and its actors are supported by privilege granted to them by the state, thus enabling the bank to enlarge the size of its actors.

The CGEM is the most important Moroccan association of employers in terms of impact and notoriety on the political stage. Members of the confederation are enterprises (regardless of their form and their field of activity), associations, and liberal professions. The CGEM has about 2,000 members, but most of them are small enterprises. The organization is often criticized for its lack of representativeness. Specifically, most members of the organization do not pay their fees and there is a large overturn. For example, 560 companies were recently closed and lost their membership status. In the first trimester of 2011, 200 companies joined as new members (Slaoui-Zirpins, 2011, p. 22). Although CGEM has federations on different economic branches, its involvement in the political processes is routine and general. The development plan can be improved through the involvement of a wider set of actors, particularly relevant business associations and trade unions. Although the vast majority of tasks are controlled by the state, having additional players in these tasks can make project FezShore more feasible to achieve its targets.

# Is the Project FezShore Locally Realized?

Project FezShore is described as a project realized through a network of actors. The official project partners are listed below. The list creates the image of a local network of (public) actors contributing to the realization of the project FezShore:

1. The wilaya Fez-Boulmane as a de-concentrated institution of the central state;
2. The regional council of the region Fez-Boulmane as an institution for devolved self-government;
3. The Ministry of Industry, the commercial sector, and new technologies as de-concentrated institutions of the central state;
4. The regional investment agency as regionally organized public institution with delegated tasks close to the wilaya;
5. The vocational training provider OFPPT as regionally organized public institution with delegated tasks;
6. The public employment agency ANAPEC as a regionally organized public institution with delegated tasks; and
7. The local university Sidi Mohammed Ben Abdellah as a public institution with delegated tasks.

The decisions limiting the scope of local action are mainly due to the orientation of many local actors on the guidelines of the central state written down in the Plan Emergence, and the country's prime minister circular letter concerning offshoring. According to the author's interviews, these papers constitute again and again, the main reference frame of at least the public actors mentioned in the list above. The decisions taken in these papers are heavily intertwined with the second limiting factor for local action: the transfer of the planning, construction, and operation of the offshoring platform FezShore to the project developer MedZ.

MedZ, on the other hand, is a subsidiary of the public Caisse de Dépôt et de Gestion (CDG). MedZ was created in 2002 and oversees the construction and administration of the offshore zones as a result of Plan Emergence. Until now, there has been high demand for the capabilities of the bureaus in the offshoring zones and techno parks. A French study attested that synergy affects innovative working conditions in these parks rather than in the overall economy (Assens & Abittan, 2010, p. 157). Despite these achievements, however, the transfer of the planning and the construction and operation of the platform FezShore to MedZ had depoliticized the actualization of FezShore. Now, it is no longer a political issue of importance here, but rather an issue on how the private sector can escape public scrutiny when matters are related to public funding. Without determining the role of the state in the economic process, it would be better if the operation of entities such as MedZ were made more transparent.

The other factor that limits the activities of local actors in offshore enterprises is lack of capacities on local and regional levels. Local actors primarily function through the regional investment commission—a commission located at the regional investment center and established to supervise the realization of the project. Regional delegations of involved ministries often negotiate certain issues, such as rent. Successful negotiations depend on the issue and the skills of the negotiators. Elected officials both on municipal and regional levels do not have good knowledge of the issue or skills for negotiation. Hence, members of these councils have to describe the construction of the project FezShore as a governmental undertaking in order to enable the elected official to understand the project.

Accordingly, the vertical aspects of decentralization are not realized in the actualization process of the project FezShore and aspects of the horizontal decentralization are even more lacking. Due to the impact and role of MedZ, potentials for the private sector's actors to influence the realization of the project FezShore are relatively small.

The fact that enterprises operating in the branch of offshoring services already exist, they may (in the long run) have an indirect influence on the private actors. This is witnessed by statements made by various entrepreneurs. Some of these enterprises are networking intensively with public officials. Others tend to keep a distance from public administration, and focus on the business at hand. In contrast, larger companies have closer relations with the state and receive official recognition for job creation. It is obvious that the Moroccan way of mediation between the interests of state-actors and market-actors do not completely fit with the pluralistic ideal. The fact that some economic actors have stronger ties to the state than others may be attributed to the notion that the separation between the public and the private sectors in Morocco is incomplete; in order to progress, horizontal decentralization must be taken into consideration.

## Conclusion

Exemplified by the project FezShore, this article addressed the Moroccan policy-process at regional and local levels. Applying theories of decentralization and interest mediation helped to identify what these theories can explain. In combination, they become a good forum for conceptualizing public policy process, especially in emerging economies. Being successful in decentralization instigates the ability to reach the assigned goals with efficiency, participation/democratization, and economic development. The study shows that there is not one specific way to achieve goals—mediating between different interests in society is essential. The example of project FezShore shows that the Moroccan development strategy in general, and partnering with non-state actors for the promotion of the offshoring of services specifically, can be successful.

# Observing the Failed Nation-State of Iraq: A Perspective

## Alexander Dawoody

## Abstract

Since its inception in 1921 by Great Britain, the new state of Iraq utilized state apparatus to engineer many aspects of Iraq's tribal, ethnic, and sectarian society. This phenomenon along with wealth generated from oil exploration led to the emergence of a new cadre to run the machinery of the newly constructed state and administer its public affairs. The manipulation of this cadre of the state enabled it to accumulate vast experience in governance and transform the society through the state's regulatory systems and political and economic spheres into tribally-infused urban and rural communities. Although societal components remained fragmented, a manufactured Iraqi identity emerged through coercion in order to justify the legitimacy of the new nation-state. Among the social components, the Sunni Arab tribes benefited the most from political and economic power by contributing the most to the governing administrative cadre at the expense of other social groups, especially the Kurds and Shi'ites. This notion was emphasized during the Baa'th regime of 1968–2003. After the 2003 U.S.-led invasion, however, the formula was turned upside down by empowering the Kurds and Shi'ites at the expense of marginalizing the Sunni Arab tribes. For the first time in nearly 80 years the Sunni Arab tribes found themselves outside the political formula in Iraq. Inversely, the U.S invasion of Iraq had provided a kick to destabilize the socio-political and economic structures in Iraq that had held the nation-state intact for eight decades. Owing to the new governing groups' lack of administrative experience, post-Sunni governing Iraq started to decay in its infrastructure and lack of public services. This paper examines the Iraqi nation-state as a foreign entity imposed from outside on people who were strange to its paradigm, the eventual deterioration of the model, and the possibility of its complete collapse.

## Introduction

This paper observes the structure of the Iraqi political formula and challenges facing the nation-state as model from inception to date. The methodology of the research is qualitative, relying on content analysis of political and historic literature, focused studies, and field observation. Emphasis will be on the devolution process induced by the U.S. occupation of Iraq in 2003 and the question of legitimacy facing the continuation of the nation-state to remain in power within the format that was introduced by Great Britain in 1921.

## A Brief Historical Background

In recorded history, humanity's first cities were created in southern Mesopotamia (modern-day Iraq) around 3500 BC. With the birth of civilization in Sumer, Ur, Akad, Nainava, and Babylon, writing was also discovered in the form of cuneiform, in addition to the concept of the state as introduced by Sargon the Great of Akad in 2270 BC. Other significant contributions included the first codified law in history by King Hammurabi of Babylon in 1792 BC and public administration in the form of scribes who were entrusted with the task of recording and auditing temple offerings, a cadre that later was developed into a full professional class who was in charge of administering public affairs (Tripp, 2007).

During the Islamic Abbasid Caliphate the city of Baghdad was built in 762 to become the cultural capital of the world. It housed universities, such as Dar al-Hikma and Al-Mustansaryia, hospitals to quarantine the sick and advance medical science such as that by Al-Razi, and translation centers that translated Greek philosophy texts to Arabic and encourage Islamic thinkers such as Al-Farabi, Al-Ghazali, Avicenna and Averroes build on the Hellenistic civilization (Kennedy, 2006). Important discoveries were achieved in mathematics, algebra (which is itself an Arabic word), chemistry, physics, astronomy, and medical science. Libraries were established and learned scholars arrived from around the world to study in Baghdad (Bennison, 2009).

Unfortunately, these scientific achievements came to halt in 1258, when Baghdad was sacked by the Mongol herds and its libraries, schools, universities, hospitals, and irrigation systems were destroyed. Iraqis consider the Mongol invasion as the single most devastating event in their history (Tripp, 2007). The only other event that many Iraqis compare to the 1258 Mongol invasion is the U.S. occupation of Iraq in 2003 and the subsequent destruction that had been brought with it.

After a series of foreign invasions, Iraq became part of the Ottoman Empire (1534–1917) and was ruled by three governors appointed by the Ottoman Sultan in Istanbul. The three governors respectively administered Ottoman rules in the three provinces of Mosul in the north, Baghdad in the middle, and Basra in the south. Ottoman administration, however, was inept and ineffective, with the exception of few governors, such as Medhat Pasha in 1869 (Haj, 1997). As a consequence, the previous prosperity and achievements of the Abbasid era did not resurface.

After the defeat of the Ottoman Empire by Allied Forces in World War I, the three provinces of Mosul, Baghdad and Basra were combined in 1921 by Great Britain to form a new nation-state called Iraq (Marr, 2011). Hence, it is worth noting that despite the fact that Iraq had witnessed the birth of the first state in history in ancient Mesopotamia, and despite the fact that the seat of Islam's greatest empires, the Abbasids Dynasty was in Iraq, the country, nevertheless, has no experience in constructing its own form of organic nation-state. The country and nation-state that we know today as Iraq did not exist prior to 1921 and it is completely a foreign invention, created and enforced by Great Britain. Therefore, the concept of Iraqi identity is inorganic and has no prior historic roots and it is a mere British invention. This identity was then forcefully imposed on the tribal inhabitants of the land in order to create a new manufactured identity.

The British relied on tribes from the Sunni Arab region in mid-Iraq to lead the new nation-state. They did so because of the Sunnis' long administrative experiences during the Ottoman and Abbasid periods, and for not participating in revolts against British rule, as was the case with the Kurds and Shi'ites (Haj, 1997). The British, however, did not trust the Sunnis and did not choose any of them to be king of the new state. Therefore, they imported Faisal, one of their allies in Hijaz (located in modern day Saudi Arabia) to bestow the title on him. Although Faisal was foreign to Iraq's societal construction, he proved to be astute in learning how to form tribal alliances and anchor the foundations of the new state (Dodge, 2005). Strife, nevertheless, continued to exist between various Iraqi tribes and ethnic, religious, and sectarian groups (Batatu, 2004). The tension further intensified with the discovery of oil, the Sunni domination of the state, and through it, wealth generated from oil production and sale (Kent, 1976).

Along with oil exploration/production and the administrative apparatus, the British also created the Iraqi army to safeguard the interests of the new state (Mahdi, 2011). The army became an important organ to maintain internal order and enforce stability in order for the state to function. Reflecting competing interests among the army's officers that further translated competing interests among the tribal factions that dominated the state, the army became a vehicle to seize political power and enforce the hegemony of one group over other. The series of military coups, beginning with that of Bakir Sidqi in 1936 which marked the beginning of military interferences in the political process in the Arab world, had anchored a long period of governance dominated by paranoid regimes that did not hesitate in exercising the most naked form of political tyranny in order to remain in power (Batatu, 2004).

The second major military coup in Iraq was in 1958, led by Abdul Karim Qassim. It overthrew the monarchic regime and established the Republic of Iraq while pulling Iraq out from under British influence and moving it toward the former Soviet Union. Power struggle among the coup's leaders, however, resulted in the assassination of Qassim and the Baa'th Arab Socialist Party to take control of the political power, first in 1963, and later in 1968. The Baa'th regime of 1968 remained in power until the U.S. occupation of Iraq in 2003 (Dawoody, 2006b).

The Baa'th emphasized a centralized state bureaucracy aimed at reconstituting all aspects of Iraqi society and tribal affiliations, ethnic relations, and sectarian behavior. The state became a vehicle to promote the Baa'th's plan for the population's complete submission to authorities, anchoring a cult of personality around the regime's leader, and augmenting the ideology of Pan Arabism that centered on the notion of creating a unified Arab state in the Middle East (Makiya, 1998). Within the massive and elaborate state bureaucracy at its disposal, the Baa'th developed public administration to carry out its social, economic and political programs and to re-engineer Iraqi society in order to fit with the Baa'th's blueprint for Iraq. Selected Sunni Arabs tribes were chosen to take prominent position in the Baa'th regime and to direct state machinery toward the Baa'th goal (Dawisha, 2009).

In 1979, the Shah of Iran was toppled and replaced by a revolutionary, Shi'a Islamic Republic (Marr, 2011). Energized by its colossal victory in overthrowing the regime of the Shah, the Islamic Republic sought to extend its influence beyond its borders and encourage Iraqi Shi'a to overthrow the Baa'th regime and establish a similar model to the new regime in Iran. This, of course, agitated the Baa'th regime and led it to respond to the Islamic Republic's threat by declaring war on Iran in 1980, an event that lasted for eight years (Hiro, 2001).

The Iran–Iraq War ended with a stalemate. Neither warring countries was able to score a decisive win and both suffered as a consequence. To rescue its war-tarnished economy, the Baa'th regime annexed Kuwait in 1990 and used it as a cash cow to help support state functions (Springborg, 2007). Iraq's action resulted in a U.S-led war in 1991 that expelled Iraq from Kuwait and placed Iraq under a heavy economic sanction. The Baa'th regime, however, was spared from being overthrown because of fear that a power vacuum could lead to instability in the entire oil-rich region and would empower Iran to fill the gap. This was recalculated after September 11, 2011 as the United States deemed the continuation of the Baa'th regime in Iraq more of a liability (Naylor, 2009).

Hence, the United States invaded Iraq in 2003 and overthrew the Baa'th regime after it spent more than three decades in power. Along with the invasion arrived a new Iraqi political group from exile that exacerbated the flawed nation-state model inherited from the British by exchanging Sunni domination rule with Shi'a–Kurdish rule (Allawi, 2007). The Iraqi army was disbanded in order to safeguard the new political regime from threats of military coups. The Ba'ath Party was also de-rooted in order to rescue state machinery from the ideology and indoctrination of the former regime. The elimination of the Iraqi army, however, resulted in the state losing its main organ to maintain order and enforce legitimacy. The process of "de-Ba'athification" deprived the administration from the expert cadre that ran the bureaucracy and administered public affairs. As a consequence, the nation-state fell into chaos and its true ingredients as a failed model began to clearly appear (Agresto, 2007).

## Inherent Problems in the Iraqi Nation-State Model

Since its inception in 1921 by Great Britain, the Iraqi nation-state has contained chronic ailment embedded in its systemic construction. From the start, the state's model was foreign to the tribal people who had inherited the formula. In addition, only one segment of the population, the Sunni Arab tribes, were entrusted with leadership positions in the state while the majority of the population, such as the Shi'a, Kurds, Christians, Jews, Turkoman, and other religious and ethnic minorities were excluded (Dodge, 2005).

Because of such inequality in assigning state functions and leadership positions, the political and economic lot of most Sunni Arab tribes improved at the expense of the rest of the population. This factor was further enhanced once the state began producing and selling oil (Alnasrawi, 2002; Mahdi, 2011). Public administration and leadership positions in the newly created Iraqi Army were also entrusted to elements from the Sunni Arab tribes (Haj, 1997).

As a result, the Sunni Arabs developed far more experience in managing public affairs than other segments in Iraqi society and used coercive measures in order to subjugate the population (Marr, 2011). Examples of coercive measures included control of information channels, censorship, political oppression, economic intimidation, and torture (Batatu, 2004).

State repression continued, modified periodically from one regime to another based on public submission to the enforced mantra. Within the ruling factions, however, conflicts were also emerging over the share of power and manipulation of state-generated economic opportunities that often were exercised through military coups (Dawisha, 2009). This notion reached its peak during the Ba'ath regime from 1963 to 1968 (Makiya, 1998). The Kurds and Shi'a presumed with their own internal tribal conflicts but united in their struggle against the Sunnis in order to gain access to the organs of political power (Hegener, 2010).

With the U.S. occupation of Iraq in 2003, the foundation of the nation-state was disassembled and reassembled in a new fashion that placed the Shi'a and Kurds at the helm of state leadership while disempowering the Sunnis. The format of the model itself as inherited from Great Britain, however, remained intact with slight modification in fragmenting the state's centralized function into a decentralized mood within a limited form of federalism based on regionalism and semi-autonomous provincial structure (Allawi, 2007).

The Sunni tribes traded places with their former adversaries and resorted to organized armed opposition of the modified model. Their goal was not in devising an organic state model for Iraq, but to rescue the existing formula from modifications and regain their position in power (Agresto, 2007). The Kurdish, Shi'a, and other minority groups, on the other hand saw opportunities in the devolution of the nation-state model to advance their interests, even at the expense of the model itself and the possibility of its gradual disintegration. By refusing to share power with their former adversaries and the continuous internal strives among them, the Iraqi nation-state model may indeed be heading toward a gradual disintegration, with the possibility of morphing toward a complete collapse from within.

The inability of the new leading groups in Iraq to share power, especially the Shi'a, is caused by their long history of opposition. For them, power is not to be shared, but to be grabbed and held on to, as the Sunnis did prior to 2003. Hence, power is either controlled completely or not at all (Charountaki, 2010). The consequence of these actions is more emphasis on tribal, sectarian, religious, and ethnic identities instead of a unified national identity known as "Iraqi." With tribalism, regionalism, sectarianism, and ethnic identities taking hold, the prospect of maintaining Iraq as a unified nation-state grows weaker and the push toward autonomous regionalism within a fragmented Iraq based on ethnic and sectarian affiliations grows stronger.

With the Kurds benefiting from the economic prosperity of their region in northern Iraq and the potentials for new oil explorations in Kurdistan becoming more realistic, their Shi'a counterparts in governance may push toward doing the same in having their own sectarian-fused region in southern Iraq. Such a prospect is especially promising, since southern Iraq is already benefiting from a rich oil field in Rumela (Mahdi, 2011; Springborg, 2011). The Turkomon may also be encouraged by these developments in pushing for their own autonomous region in the oil-rich city of Kirkuk. This will leave the Sunni Arabs at a disadvantage as the only social group without any political or economic prospect, especially when their region in mid Iraq lacks any natural resources to sustain its autonomy (Anderson & Stansfield, 2009; Mahdi, 2011). Their only hope is to prevent regionalism from further materializing and in keeping the Iraqi nation-state model as introduced in 1921 intact.

The United States' intention in revising the nation-state's model in Iraq and introducing a new form of limited federalism based on regionalism was not intended to push toward the disintegration of Iraq, but rather to correct its model. However, these very revisions to the model had stripped it from its coercive measures to remain intact, and "delegitimized" its manufactured Iraqi identity for the benefit of the inhabitants' organic, ethnic, religious, and sectarian identities. This very notion is emphasizing the model's inherit flaws and inversely exposing it as a failed model. Figure 1 illustrates the formation of the Iraqi nation-state model as a political formula, first as introduced by Great Britain in 1921 with the Sunni Arabs at the helm of political power, and later after the injection of the United States' occupation to the equation as a kick, as fragmented and disintegrated formula. The entire trajectory is an illustration of a failed model from inception to date.

## Figure 1. The Devolution of the Iraqi Nation-State

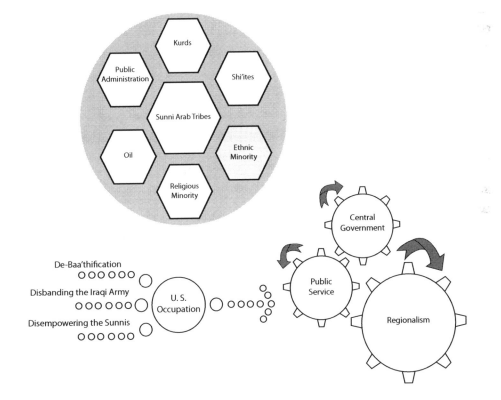

# Erupted Symptomologies of the Failed Model Since 2003

## The Constitution

The Iraqi Constitution prevents separation of power between the legislative, executive, and judicial branches of government, and has little or no effective mechanism for checks and balances. Instead, it amalgamates the legislative and executive branches together, with the former acting as a pool for selecting the executive branch (Arato, 2009). The problem in mixing these two branches together undermines accountability and renders one branch as the extension of the other.

Voters do not vote for individual candidates for seats in the Parliament. Instead, they vote for political parties or blocks. The winning coalition in Parliament will then form the executive branch of government. Accordingly, voters do not get to choose the Prime Minster or members of Parliament; winning coalitions of political parties have that opportunity (Mingus, 2012). This formula undermines democracy and voters' choice. In a country that is divided along ethnic and sectarian lines, procedures will emphasize social divides instead of promoting the manufactured national identity known as "Iraq."

Political parties, in return, form alliances based on ethnicity, religion, and sectarianism while advancing their own narrow interests at the expense of the entire population (Dawoody, 2006a; International Crisis Group, 2011). Often, the winning margin of political coalitions is too narrow, leading to continuous power struggle between the political parties and resulting in the formation of a weak national government that is susceptible to the Parliament's threat of no-confidence vote. Backdoor maneuvers then take place in order to trade votes based on exchanges in favors in order to form a weak coalition government. The April 2010 national elections in Iraq for Parliament, for example, resulted in the victory of a coalition headed by Ayad Allawi. However, the margin of win was thin and a group headed by Nuri al-Maliki won the elections and the opportunity to form the national government through the support of Shi'a and Kurdish blocks.

Another problem in the Iraqi Constitution that threatens its flawed nation-state model is its institutionalization of the quota system. Based on such a system, power allocation in the Iraqi government is based on ethnic and sectarian quotas. The result of this system is each social group emphasizing its strata as the genesis for representational democracy at the expense of a national unity (Arato, 2009).

When it comes to public funding, the quota system also targets allocations of public funding by insisting on expenditure based on regionalism and provincialism that reflect ethnic and sectarian divides than citizen needs and programs' merit. What was once introduced as an Iraq identity is now replaced by regional affiliations based on quota-infused ethnicity and sectarianism. For example, the Kurdish region stresses a quota-based demand for the region's share of public revenue when negotiating with the central government. So do the Shi'a provinces in the south and the Sunni Arabs in mid-Iraq (Springborg, 2011). At the end of the process, quota becomes the formula for engaging in what is perceived to be an Iraqi affair while at the same time driving Iraq toward fragmented regions based on a legalized and Constitutional quota system.

## Public Administration

The U.S. occupation of Iraq in 2003 brought with it a group of exiled Iraqi politicians that lacked political base inside Iraq and were cut off from the socio-political dynamics in the country. These politicians were installed to power by the American administrators of Iraq, emphasizing a quota-driven type of governance in all spheres of public affairs (International Crisis Group, 2011). Militia forces belonging to these exiled leaders, especially those who were trained in Iran, quickly filled the gap left by the disbanded Iraqi army and formed the state's new police force and army (Mingus, 2012). These groups used their position in power to settle old scores with the Sunni Arab tribes and to push toward their marginalizing through systemic disempowering measures that often used violence to achieve their ends (International Crisis Group, 2011). With the Sunnis out of the political and administrative process, the "de-Baa'thification" process, and the near destruction of most state apparatus, the leadership of inept and inexperienced exiled political groups suddenly found themselves in a position of power. Public administration fell victim to these groups and was severely decapitated. Because of the paralysis of public administration, the effective and efficient delivery of public good collapsed and public services were severely damaged and paralyzed (Dawoody, 2007; International Crisis Group, 2011).

Despite Iraq's massive oil wealth, funding public programs remains minuscule. Governmental leaders periodically announce massive funding of public projects, only to realize that the contracts that they have signed are fictional entities, and the allocated funds for these contracted have been siphoned off. This process creates a new breed of bureaucratic parasites that use government to enrich their own pockets and advance their own interests at the expense of what has been left of the country and the people trapped within it (International Crisis Group, 2011; Springborg, 2011).

Iraqis today, with the exception of those living in the autonomous Kurdish region in the north, lack basic necessities in life. Public service is virtually non-existent. There is a shortage of food, electricity, clean water, medications, professional staff, jobs, postal services, adequate education system, adequate public health system, effective security system, domestic products, and economic development projects in all of Iraq, excluding the Kurdish region. Roads, irrigation, and public facilities are in poor condition. Fraud, theft, and corruption are rampant (International Crisis Group, 2011). Academic degrees are openly sold to the highest bidder without the need for the recipient to attend or complete an academic program. Many officials in the Iraqi government have designated Ph.D. initials after their names, while most did not complete high school.

There is also no system of accountability in today's Iraq. While there are stipulations in the Iraqi Constitution for transparency enforced by the American occupation, the transparent process in public affairs reveals that services and programs exist on paper only. Since the governmental system is locked between trading partners of exiled politicians who are now governing Iraq, any measures for accountability in examining these transparent processes to assure accuracy and expose theft of public funds and frauds are missing (International Crisis Group, 2011; Mingus, 2012).

## The Influence of Iran

One of the biggest beneficiaries of the U.S. occupation of Iraq is Iran. Not only did the U.S. occupation of Iraq rid Iran of its arch nemesis Saddam Hussein, but it also enabled Iran through its ties with the Iraqi Shi'a political groups to influence the political dynamics in Iraq and dictate Iraq's domestic and foreign policy in the direction of Iranian political and economic interests.

One of the fatal characteristics of the Shi'a political groups in Iraq is their unwavering loyalty to Iran. This is partly because of sharing the same sectarian identity with Iran and partly because of the Islamic Republic's long history of supporting these groups in fighting the Baa'th regime. Such a loyalty is often exercised at the expense of the nation-state and the Iraqi people as a whole, making Iraq a mere satellite state under Iranian political influence.

With President Obama ending the Iraq War and pulling most American combat troops out of Iraq in 2011, Iran quickly filled the void left by the Americans. Such a vacuum is furthering Iran's grip on the political process in Iraq and expanding an influence that ranges from trade, intelligence sharing, training of security forces, to dictating foreign policy (Eisenstadt, Kinghts, & Ali, 2011). Today's Iraq is a bridge between Iran and Syria to support the embattled regime of Bashar Al-Assad against the Syrian revolution (Zumwalt, 2013).

## The Kurds

After their failed uprising in 1991 in the aftermath of Desert Storm, the Kurds benefited from the U.S.' policy of boxing in the regime of Saddam Hussein in Iraq through the enforcement of a No-Fly-Zone over northern Iraq from 1991 to 2003. The zone enabled the two main Kurdish political parties, the Kurdistan Democratic Party and Kurdistan Patriotic Union to form a de facto region in the Kurdish area of northern Iraq. Internal strife and periodic skirmishes between the two Kurdish parties, however, threatened the newly emerging autonomous region, until the establishment of a cease-fire and power-sharing as of 1996. The resulting Kurdish Regional Government (KRG) experienced a relatively stable situation in Kurdistan and the region gradually begun distancing itself from the Iraqi nation-state while emphasizing its ethnic-infused autonomy (Charountaki, 2010). After 2003, the new Iraqi Constitution recognized the Kurdish region as a legal autonomous region within a federated Iraq. Public funds from Iraqi national revenues are allocated to KRG based on a quota system and the size of the Kurdish population in the region. Kurdish militias, known as the Peshmargah, are reorganized and retrained to form the region's new security forces (Hegener, 2010). KRG diplomatic missions are open in a number of countries, including the United States.

During the Baa'th regime the oil producing city of Kirkuk in northern Iraq was forcefully depopulated of its Kurdish residents in order to prevent it from joining the autonomous Kurdish region in northern Iraq, and to provide economic means for the region to secede from Iraq and declare full independence (Anderson & Stansfield, 2009). KRG maintains that the ethnic identity of the city is Kurdish, a notion disputed by the city's other large ethnic residents—the Turkomans (Hegener, 2010). On their part, the Turkomans are pushing toward regionalizing Kirkuk under their influence and as a standalone autonomous region in Iraq (Springborg, 2011). A future census is planned in order to determine the ethnic identity and future affiliation of the city, which may further complicate the political situation in Iraq.

The prospect of KRG remaining part of Iraq is weak with or without Kirkuk joining the region. Already there are numerous oil explorations taking place in Kurdistan, led by Chevron and Exxon corporations, and despite objections by Iraq's central government who sees such matters as permitted for the federal government alone (Cutler, 2013; Hegener, 2010; *IKJ News*, 2013). KRG's relations with neighboring Turkey and Iran are also improving both economically and politically, reducing concerns and sensitivity by these countries on the plight of their own Kurdish populations and their political aspirations.

Although the Kurdish region in Iraq is much more stable and secure from the rest of Iraq, and economically, is witnessing sizable growth in investments and development, it is, nevertheless, exhibiting numerous sets of complex political, administrative, and social problems. Corruption, for example, is plaguing the region and defusing progress in the region's development. Control of the political process by the two main Kurdish parties is undermining opportunities for democracy and civic institutions to take hold. This is in addition to countless cases of human rights abuses against political dissidents (Enders, 2013; Hassanpour, 2013) as well as crimes against women in the forms of honor killings (Begikhani, Hague, & Ibraheem, 2012). Tribalism is also a concern because of its continuation to influence the political process (Rubin, 2013).

## Terrorism

Prior to 2003, Al-Qaeda membership inside Iraq was virtually non-existent. The main terror inflicted on the Iraqi people was by the Baa'th regime and its security apparatus (Makiya, 1998). After 2003, however, the Syrian and Iranian borders were opened in order for Jihadists to pour into Iraq, bleed the invading American army, and prevent it from continuing its campaign toward Iran and Syria (International Crisis Group, 2011). The administration of George W. Bush sought an opportunity to engage these foreign Jihadists inside Iraq and use Iraq as a magnet to attract them. Iraqi citizens, however, were caught in the middle and became causalities of the war (Naylor, 2009). Remnants of the former regime, along with disgruntled Sunni Arab tribes who were pushed out of power in 2003 also joined the fray in fighting U.S. troops.

Insecurity and daily suicide bombings as such became daily occurrences in Iraq. This continued until 2006 when U.S. Commander, General David Petraeus engaged local Sunni Iraqi tribes to fight the foreign Jihadists in exchange for sharing the political process in Iraq (Mingus, 2012). Such a tactic reduced, but did not completely eliminate, the number of terrorist activities in Iraq. After President Obama's order to pull major U.S. combat troops out of Iraq in 2011, car bombings started once again to rise, ignited by the government of Nuri al-Maliki's sectarian policies and his tendencies to "Saddamize" Iraq (Zumwalt, 2013). Many Iraqis suspect al-Malki for politicizing terrorism and failing to provide security in order to keep the public frightened and shift attention from his failed policies (International Crisis Group, 2011).

## Conclusion

Iraq is a failed state by all measures, especially in administrative functions. It started as a failed state in 1921 and today, appears even more so. The governmental coercive policies have only masked the failure. This flawed model was further exposed when its political formula was revised in 2003 by the U.S. occupation of Iraq. Today's Shi'a -dominated government of Nouri al-Maliki is making the failed model even more apparent than before because of its sectarian policies, corruption, and incompetence. Iraqi political leaders are more focused on bickering among themselves for advancing their own narrow interests than paying attention to the country's massive problems (Zumwalt, 2013).

Inefficiency, waste, corruption, theft, nepotism, sectarianism, ineffectiveness, dysfunction, manipulation, political prisoning and torture, politicizing the judiciary system, and surrendering sovereignty to Iran are all symptoms of a failed nation-state model in its decaying and final stage. Many Iraqi cities, including Baghdad are still suffering from lack of basic services, such as electricity, clean water, sanitation, adequate public health system, adequate education system, postal services, and security. Adding to this is a growing army of the unemployed—nearly two million internally dispersed refugees and more than two million refugees abroad (Mingus, 2012).

Car and suicide bombings, especially during religious holidays, are a daily occurrence in Iraq (International Crisis Group, 2011). Since 2003, more than 122,000 Iraqi civilians have been killed (*Iraq Body Count*, 2013). This is in addition to kidnapping. Government officials, including Prime Minister al-Maliki, are accused by Amnesty International of rape, torture, abuse of prisoners, and creating secret detention centers. Iraqi police have been infiltrated by sectarian militias and are continually engaged in assassinations, political intimidation, and torture (Jamil, 2013; Yan, 2013).

The ethnic Kurds are living in a de facto state and increasingly distancing themselves from the nation-state. Most Kurds prefer to live in their independent state than to continue to be part of Iraq (Charountaki, 2010).

Oil has always being the glue that forcing conflicting ethnic and religious groups in Iraq to live together under the umbrella of the nation-state (Alnasrawi, 2002). Without oil, none of these groups can live independently. Thus, strife among these groups for control of oil revenue has always been the mantra for political action in Iraq. The group with most access to petro-money, the more opportunity it has to improve its political and socio-economic condition in Iraq. Conflicts over access to oil revenue has always marred the Iraqi political map and dictated its schisms.

Although Iraq began as a failed state, it was able to sustain itself through brutality and aggressive coercive measures aimed at reconstructing Iraqi society through artificial engineering. Because of the nation-state's non-organic nature, failure became a hallmark of its operations, especially after 2003 as a result of decentralizing state structure. The natural progression for this failed state is to collapse. A collapse dynamic will reshuffle the internal order of Iraq's societal groups and randomly lead toward the emergence of a new organic formula. Without its collapse, the sustaining the nation-state will only prolong the inevitable and will result in catastrophe.

What we are witnessing today in Iraq is a process of self-organization where components of the failed and outdated model are rearranging themselves in order to come up with a new model better fit to survive in the new environment. Self-organization is the idea that systems are capable of self-organizing themselves to live autonomously and adapt to changes in their environments (Vesterby, 2008). This concept is also known as autopoiesis (Maturana & Varela, 1980). A key notion of this concept is self-referentiality (Sandri, 2008). The idea of self-reference designates the unity that a dynamic system is for itself, and that unity can be produced through relational operations (Little, 1999).

If we look at autopoiesis and self-referentiality in Iraq, we must understand them within the processes of change in Iraqi political formula that are multi-layered, multi-directional, and continually morphing in a state of flux within an irreversible trajectory of time and motion. If the internal order is incapable of change, then the Iraqi system's entire structural order must collapse in order to allow for a new structural order to emerge and deal with the new environmental changes. Sustaining Iraq's older structures through artificial engineering may buy the failed nation-state some time, but it will not prevent its ultimate collapse, at which point it may be accompanied with catastrophe.

The relationship between the Iraqi nation-state formula and its environment operates on feedback loops that are either positive or negative. Feedback as stimuli is retransmitted by the environment and causes random changes in the agent's internal processes (Wheatley, 2006). This behavior contains the formula's morphology from static equilibrium to a state of chaos and disorder. Disorder, as the current situation dictates now in Iraq, will lead to new structures and political forms that will be different from the current model. The phase-shifts within this process in Iraqi political trajectory from equilibrium to disequilibrium to equilibrium within this context will continue to exhibit self-organizing, irreducible, and unpredictable processes of change.

# Building Capacities in Public Financial Management in a Post-Conflict Country: A practice from the Ministry of Finance and the Institute of Finance of Lebanon

*Ibrahim El Ghandour*
*Sabine Hatem*
*Lamia Moubayed Bissat*
*Carl Rihan*

## Abstract

This paper highlights the potential role that a leading training institution can play in post-conflict reconstruction, drawing on the experience of the Institut des Finances Basil Fuleihan, in supporting and complementing the Lebanese Ministry of Finance's policies and reform goals with capacity development. The paper shortly introduces the importance of Public Financial Reform in the Middle East and North Africa (MENA) region and emphasizes the positive role that training and capacity development can have on such reforms. It then seeks to address the importance of such reforms and capacity development in post-conflict Lebanon, presenting the experience of the Institut des Finances Basil Fuleihan and assessing it against four main criteria that define a suitable framework for sustainable capacity development, namely the Action Environment, the Public Sector Institutional

Context, the Task Network, and the Organizational Structure. It tries to provide elements of response to the following set of questions:

- What is the most suitable administrative and financial set-up, and recommended organizational culture required to effectively run a capacity-building institution?

- What is the role of political leadership?

- Is the successful reform of core governance institutions of a country both a necessary and sufficient condition for overall governance improvement?

- What is the role of donors? How can the country make its homegrown agenda prevail?

## Introduction

The universal trend is moving towards demanding more performance and accountability from the public sector. In answer to various social and economic pressures, governments around the world have initiated sets of public finance reforms, often adopting different scopes and approaches.

In Lebanon, more than 15 years of wars and invasions (1975–1990) have damaged the country's economic, social, and institutional capabilities. In 1993, taking the lead on the reform and modernization agenda, the Ministry of Finance of Lebanon embarked on a comprehensive reform program that targeted public finance as an entry point to the modernization of civil service and the state as a whole. It engineered the groundwork for a comprehensive reform program under three broad categories:

1. Fiscal and economic policy formulation and implementation;

2. Public financial management; and

3. Service delivery to both the public and to other government agencies.

To streamline reform initiatives and ensure their sustainability, the Lebanese Ministry of Finance (MOF) established the Institut des Finances Basil Fuleihan (IOF) in 1996, in order for it to become a source of sustainable, high-quality, and specialized training and communication services as well as for it to properly coach and prepare the new generation of leaders. Since its inception, the Institute has become the main provider of financial management training to public sector agencies in Lebanon, and a specialized resource center for the public at large. It has, in fact, become the school of finance of the government.

This study presents an in-depth look at the institution. It attempts to reflect upon the Institute's experience to date, to narrow down key factors of success or failure, and to identify lessons that will be of value to other institutions, countries, and the donor community.

**172**

# The Importance of Public Financial Management Reform in the MENA Region

The World Bank (2013b) report on "Public Financial Management in the Middle East and North Africa" stated that:

> According to the most recent World Bank data, governments throughout the Middle East and North Africa (MENA) region spent approximately $407 billion dollars in 2007 in delivering their policy, regulatory and service functions. The way in which this money is spent has huge implications for their broader development trajectory. (p. 1)

A well-functioning Public Financial Management (PFM) system is a prerequisite for the implementation of sustainable government policies aimed at promoting economic growth and social development. Sound PFM policies and practices respond to the challenges of greater economic openness and globalization and act as a lever for equity in development, fair access to public service, and poverty reduction. Moreover, efficient public expenditure performance entails that government choices be consistent with national monetary and fiscal policies, and achieve sustainability over time.

In recent years, countries all over the world have experimented with public finance reforms. Generally, these reforms have included the move towards performance-focused policies; multi-year programming frameworks in budgeting through fiscal and revenues projections; the shift from cash to accrual accounting; and the enhancement of oversight and scrutiny frameworks. For the past 10 years, countries in the MENA region have made strong commitments to modernize fiscal performance, public finance operations, and governance (World Bank, 2013b, pp. ii–xiv).

The driving forces behind these reforms were many; they included: supporting economic growth; improving social welfare; rebuilding state apparatus; and benefiting from international assistance. Moreover, the financial crisis of 2007–2008, which has blown through the MENA region's economic landscape, and the increasing popular desire for good governance, integrity and rule of law—which were reflected by demands for a more inclusive, efficient, and transparent public sector—reiterated the need for proper and sustainable PFM reform. As a matter of fact, deficiencies in PFM systems that hindered the provision of public services and social policies were among the main catalysts of the Arab revolutions (Alami & Karshenas, 2012).

Moreover, the governments of countries that have not witnessed mass-scale uprisings are similarly expected to meet popular demands and promote better efficiency, performance and value-for-money in their delivery of public services. But the question remains—how to best address the rising PFM-related challenges in order to pave the way for a sustainable economic and social development model?

Drawing on his long experience in Africa, Stephen Peterson (2011) delineated a strategy for stakeholders to adopt prior to embarking on reforms. He identified four tasks in successfully initiating public sector reforms: "recognize, improve, change and sustain" (Peterson, 2011, p. 209). According to Peterson (2011), stakeholders and policymakers are encouraged to act carefully to recognize the contextual environment of the reforms. The author points out that "All too often, governments in developing countries do not understand the strengths of their systems and are too quick to change them, often on the advice of others," while improving current practices can sometimes prove to be more effective than change (Peterson, 2011, pp. 210–211). A key component that could allow for the improvement of current practices is capacity development.

## Capacity Development: The Missing Factor

Within the context of the efforts invested by local and regional stakeholders, as well as by the donor community for the purpose of successfully implementing PFM reform lies a key challenge in supporting the development of adequate country capacities. Country capacities and their potential for development have come to be considered among the most critical factors for strengthening governance and improving development performance. According to the Organisation for Economic and Co-operation and Development (OECD, 2013), development efforts can fail—even if supported with funding—should the development of sustainable capacity not be given greater and more careful attention. This matter has become increasingly recognized by stakeholders (p. 7). Creating sustainable sources of quality training and capacity-building has the power to stimulate change and modernization. Capacity development facilitates the transfer of technical and managerial knowledge and skills, but also influences attitudes, provokes organizational reviews, and creates an enabling environment conducive of change. As such, capacity development becomes a powerful catalyst for reform and modernization programmes by allowing for the development of an efficient, competent, and responsible civil service that reflects the aspirations of the public.

However, implementing reform and accompanying it with capacity development has proven to be challenging and arduous. Training institutions have been pressured to overhaul their regulatory frameworks, internal structures, scope of work, and institutional networks in order to keep abreast with the challenge of supporting reform policies. Of equal importance is the fact that many countries in the region are now experiencing political instability and armed conflicts, a matter which further renders capacity development and cooperation initiatives as difficult as they are necessary. In that respect, training institutions—whether local, regional or international—are expected to play a central role in such transitional settings. They are expected to foresee, trigger, and accompany change.

# Rebuilding Public Financial Management Systems in a Post-Conflict Era: The Case of Lebanon

Lebanon has witnessed more than 15 years of civil war (1975–1990) and invasions that have led to across-the-country destruction amounting to a loss equivalent to well over US$25 billion in physical assets (Republic of Lebanon, 2007, p. 1). The country's infrastructures and institutions were hampered by years of neglect, and more significantly, the country's social canvas was greatly shattered. While the Taef Agreement of 1989 might have ended the physical conflict, the true challenge, in fact, lay ahead. Financing Lebanon's reconstruction and rebuilding its human and physical capacities following the end of the war brought the Lebanese government to launch a comprehensive Public Finance reform plan.

However, while such a program was rooted in the conviction "that economic recovery and growth can act as the single most important unifying force in restoring Lebanon's battered national fabric" (Saidi, 1999, p. 249), it was also understood that without a well-planned and equitable distribution of public resources, regional disparities would surface and stability would inevitably relapse. It was, therefore, imperative to acknowledge that for any peace to be sustained, it had to outweigh any prospect for resurgence of conflict.

The aftermath of the prolonged war brought a pressing need to reduce the growing fiscal deficit. The country had witnessed substantially increasing debt charges, absorbing a high percentage share of total revenues. This resulted in a chronic budget deficit that required borrowing to finance it, which led to an ever-growing public debt.

| Table 1. Economic growth rates for the period 1993–2012 (Annual Percentages) | | | | | | | | | |
|---|---|---|---|---|---|---|---|---|---|
| **Year** | **1993** | **1994** | **1995** | **1996** | **1997** | **1998** | **1999** | **2000** | **2001** | **2002** |
| GDP growth | 7% | 8% | 6.5% | 5.1% | -2.3% | 3.6% | -0.5% | 1.3% | 4% | 3.4% |
| **Year** | **2003** | **2004** | **2005** | **2006** | **2007** | **2008** | **2009** | **2010** | **2011** | **2012** |
| GDP growth | 3.2% | 7.5% | 1.0% | 0.6% | 7.5% | 9.3% | 8.5% | 7.0% | 3.0% | - |

*Source*: GDP Growth (%) for Lebanon for 1993–2012, World Databank, The World Bank, 2013c.

| Table 2. Gross and net public debt for the periods from the end of 1993 until end-December 2010, as a percentage of GDP | | | | | | | | |
|---|---|---|---|---|---|---|---|---|
| | Dec-93 | Dec-94 | Dec-95 | Dec-96 | Dec-97 | Dec-98 | Dec-99 | De-00 | Dec-01 |
| Gross public debt | 50% | 71% | 78% | 99% | 98% | 109% | 132% | 151% | 166% |
| Net public debt | 39% | 53% | 63% | 80% | 92% | 101% | 116% | 141% | 158% |
| | Dec-02 | Dec-03 | Dec-04 | Dec-05 | Dec-06 | Dec-07 | Dec-08 | Dec-09 | Dec-10 |
| Gross public debt | 164% | 166% | 165% | 176% | 179% | 167% | 156% | 146% | 137% |
| Net public debt | 153% | 156% | 152% | 159% | 166% | 155% | 138% | 126% | 117% |

*Source*: General debt overview, Lebanese Ministry of Finance, 2013c.

The war period had been an obstacle for the Ministry of Finance in what relates to its ability to efficiently perform its functions. The advent of peace in 1990 marked a new era in which the Ministry would seek to reclaim its lost role as the public sector's leader of governance and central PFM institution. Setting the recovery course on track was sternly undermined by war damages in infrastructure, physical assets, and human resources. By the early 1990s, the Lebanese MOF premises were scattered over 11 buildings across the country. The average age of the Ministry's staff reached a high of 56 years (for a retirement age set at 64 for civil servants); its skilled personnel had emigrated, retired, or passed away. Recruitment had been stalled since 1975 and there had been no capacity-building initiatives taking place since then. The compensation framework was inadequate, the administrative system was outdated and administrative procedures were perceived as over-centralized and complicated.

In 1992, the Ministry of Finance embarked on a comprehensive reform program that targeted public financial management through three components:

1. Fiscal and economic policy formulation and implementation;
2. Public financial management; and
3. Service delivery to the general public and to other government agencies.

Having set a clear vision and well defined priorities, the Lebanese MOF opted for a reform implementation plan based on a project approach of "Islands of Excellence" that was coordinated by a central unit reporting to the Minister. The unit was in charge of policy formulation, project management, and technical assistance coordination. The aim of the Ministry was to re-establish an efficient and accountable organization supported by modern fiscal, monetary, trade, and market structural reforms. The main characteristics of these modernization initiatives included policy reform, institutional capacity-building (organizational, technical and administrative), transparency, easy access to information, and data dissemination. In establishing an efficient PFM system, the government hoped to effectively establish a peace course and reboot the economy to pre-war growth levels at the least. The action framework took into account six key functions of effective PFM systems, delineated by Andersson and Isaksen (2012) as part of the conceptual framework of PFM reform, namely: Governance, Planning and Budgeting, Accounting, Payments, Audit, and Revenues.

| Table 3. Conceptual framework | |
|---|---|
| **Functions** | **Components** |
| Governance | Parliamentary and Cabinet role in planning, budgeting, accounting, audit |
| Planning & Budgeting | Work plans, multi-year plans (national medium-term plans as well as PRSPs), one-year plans, annual budgets, multiyear budgets, poverty strategy, MTFF/MTEF, sector programme, project planning, recurrent budget, capital/investment budget, statistics, policy analysis |
| Accounting | Bookkeeping, statistic, operational accounting, quarterly reports, mid-annual reports, annual final accounts, result reports, chart of accounts, classification, tracking studies |
| Payments | Tranches, periodicity, payment system, treasury account, bank statement, liquidity, reconciliation, disbursement audit, disbursement, payment authorisation, bank account, procurement |
| Audit | Internal audit, independent audit, own/external audit, financial/management audit, performance/value-of-money audit |
| Revenues | Customs/taxes, fees, donations, loans, direct/indirect taxes, revenue ratio, collection of taxes/fees |

*Source*: Best practice in capacity building in public finance management in Africa: Experiences of NORAD and Sida, p. 8 by G. Andersson & J. Isaksen, 2012, Bergen, Norway: Chr. Michelsen Institute, Development Studies and Human Rights.

# Institutionalizing Capacity Development

The capacity of the public service to implement and manage state functions, including public finance, remained a critical factor for the successful implementation of the Lebanese home-grown reform agenda. In this respect, capacity-building emerged as a key component in the reform projects: the successful outcome of reforms planned by the Lebanese government depended to a large extent on proper application. Proper application itself depended on the extent to which the government would recognize the need for the development of training programs bent on instilling professional working practices and training a new generation of highly skilled staff. It was therefore essential to recognize the centrality of professional training, continuous learning, information systems, and modern human resources management systems, which would in turn re-establish an efficient delivery of public services.

Human resources development therefore became a priority at the MOF. The Ministry also acknowledged that governance in post-war reconstruction entailed significant concentration on restoring institutional legitimacy by widening the Ministry's outreach and increasing its credibility. This comprehensive reform program also entailed widening the participation and involvement of the public, and more specifically the private sector and civil society organizations.

For this purpose, the Lebanese Ministry of Finance established the Institute of Finance in 1996. It was maintained that the Institute would become a sustainable source of high quality specialized training, a space for dialogue with partners and a specialized resource center for the public at large.

In the section to follow the authors discuss the experience the Institute has so far accumulated in building capacities in PFM-related issues in an attempt to document lessons learnt. It includes four levels of analysis identified by Mary E. Hilderbrand and Merilee S. Grindle (2013) as concomitant to capacity-building interventions: the Action Environment, the Public Sector Institutional Context, the Task Network, and the Organizational Structure (pp. 8-17).

## The Action Environment

The Action Environment, identified as the first level of analysis, studies the social, political, and economic conditions in which an organization (in this case, the MOF of Lebanon and more specifically the IOF) attempts to operate (Hilderbrand & Grindle, 2013).

## Socio-Political Conditions

Although the post-conflict constitution, the Taef Accord, provided Lebanon with a sound framework for proper recovery, peace, and social cohesion remained fragile. Politically and socially, Lebanon was fresh out of a civil war that has shaken its very foundations, and was lacking political stability and leadership. In the immediate years after the civil war, the MOF was still suffering from heavy financial restrictions that adversely affected its ability to support reform programs and capacity-building programs. Practices and skills had become obsolete due to the stalemate state of training initiatives. Moreover, the period of post-war peace was often marred by tremendous security threats such as the intermittent Israeli attacks in 1996, 1999, leading to the full-fledged 2006 assault. These violent episodes often forced the government and the MOF to shift their efforts to reconstructing damaged areas and assisting conflict-stricken citizens. Furthermore, since 2005, Lebanon witnessed a series of internal and external shocks that overshadowed any near future hopes for a full-fledged recovery and further deepened the division between the communities of Lebanon:

- Prime Minister Rafic Hariri was assassinated in 2005 along with Member of Parliament, Basil Fuleihan; wide protests broke out and led to the eventual withdrawal of Syrian troops and the resignation of the government;

- A series of assassinations and explosions ravaged Lebanon through the next three years, killing many promising new leaders;

- Israel launched, in 2006, a rampaging attack that imposed heavy costs on Lebanon, estimated at around $2.8 billion (U.S.) in total direct cost of early recovery and reconstruction (Republic of Lebanon, 2007, p. 5);

- In May 2007, a three-month war broke out between the Lebanese army and Islamic militants in the Palestinian refugee camp of Nahr-el-Barid in Tripoli;

- Sectarian clashes broke out in 2008 culminating in human losses and increased social fragmentation; and

- The Syrian crisis spilled over to Lebanon, increasing political divisions among the two main political camps and pouring more than 400,000 refugees into the country (Dockery, 2013).

## Economic Conditions

Due to political circumstances, no budget law has been passed in Lebanon since 2005, a matter which weighs heavily upon the PFM system and upon the reform agenda. Despite the political and social turmoil, Lebanon was still able to record high-quality economic indicators. For instance, in 2004, real growth hit 7. 4% and budget deficit declined to less than 8% (UNDP, 2013, p. 41). In the aftermath of the 2006 Israeli attack on Lebanon, the Lebanese Government embarked on an ambitious reform program and committed to pursuing economic, social, and financial reforms in-line with a comprehensive strategy presented at the Paris III conference (Republic of Lebanon, 2007). The Government and the MOF centered their priorities on:

- undertaking revenue management and administrative reform, towards a function-based structure;

- undertaking budget and financial management reform through reducing the fiscal deficit, rationalizing public expenditure, and reforming the public pension system;

- strengthening debt management;

- creating sustainable growth by reviving the economy, establishing a liberal economic environment, and encouraging the private sector to act as the engine of growth; and

- Improving the business environment through improved dialogue with the private sector, trade unions, and professional syndicates (Lebanese Ministry of Finance, 2013a, pp. 80–81).

Over time, the MOF had come to play a key role in the impressive growth and resilience that the Lebanese economy manifested since the signing of the Taef Agreement. The Ministry initiated revenue management and administration reforms that reaped impressive results in favor of the Lebanese economy.

## Enabling Conditions

## Political Support

In the direct post-war era, the role of the state had become further indispensable in regulating inefficiencies and adjusting social discrepancies. New political leaders had to work towards regaining their legitimacy to implement and even initiate reform plans. The Lebanese Government recognized early on the need of a source that would introduce training programs, and hence, a highly skilled personnel, to the MOF. With the close support and collaboration of the French government, the Institute of Finance was established in 1996, under a French–Lebanese bilateral protocol of administrative cooperation.

Table 4. Fiscal performance by economic classification (1992-2011)

| (in LL billion) | Total revenue | Tax revenue | Non-tax revenue | Treasury revenues | Total expenditures | Wages and salaries | Interest payments and foreign debt principal repayment | Other current expenditures | Capital expenditures | Other treasury expenditures, EDL, budget advances, unclassified expenditures and customs cashiers |
|---|---|---|---|---|---|---|---|---|---|---|
| 2011 | 14,070 | 9,885 | 3,468 | 718 | 17,600 | 5,533 | 6,034 | 1,648 | 676 | 3,709 |
| 2010 | 12,684 | 9,976 | 2,043 | 666 | 17,047 | 5,066 | 6,218 | 1,653 | 701 | 3,409 |
| 2009 | 12,705 | 8,967 | 3,069 | 669 | 17,167 | 4,936 | 6,087 | 1,594 | 550 | 4,000 |
| 2008 | 10,553 | 7,182 | 2,613 | 758 | 14,957 | 3,970 | 5,304 | 1,364 | 514 | 3,804 |
| 2007 | 8,749 | 5,583 | 2,511 | 655 | 12,587 | 3,583 | 4,940 | 1,138 | 558 | 2,367 |
| 2006 | 7,316 | 4,943 | 1,945 | 428 | 11,879 | 3,307 | 4,557 | 1,063 | 551 | 2,401 |
| 2005 | 7,405 | 4,867 | 2,117 | 421 | 10,203 | 3,193 | 3,534 | 1,197 | 534 | 1,745 |
| 2004 | 7,515 | 5,169 | 1,907 | 439 | 10,541 | 3,094 | 4,021 | 937 | 817 | 1,672 |
| 2003 | 6,655 | 4,502 | 1,717 | 436 | 10,593 | 3,087 | 4,874 | 871 | 714 | 1,047 |
| 2002 | 5,830 | 3,995 | 1,390 | 445 | 10,139 | 3,008 | 4,622 | 691 | 610 | 1,208 |
| 2001 | 4,646 | 2,961 | 1,299 | 386 | 8,875 | 2,992 | 4,312 | 626 | 325 | 620 |
| 2000 | 4,684 | 2,934 | 1,238 | 512 | 10,621 | 2,908 | 4,197 | 863 | 900 | 1,754 |
| 1999 | 4,873 | 3,350 | 1,109 | 414 | 8,453 | 2,760 | 3,624 | 709 | 1,097 | 265 |
| 1998 | 4,449 | 3,097 | 882 | 470 | 7,906 | 2,352 | 3,352 | 798 | 1,061 | 343 |
| 1997 | 4,010 | 2,684 | 579 | 747 | 9,162 | 2,466 | 3,378 | 1,851 | 1,467 | n.a |
| 1996 | 3,534 | 2,869 | 665 | n.a | 7,225 | 2,261 | 2,653 | 1,088 | 1,223 | n.a |
| 1995 | 3,033 | 2,100 | 933 | n.a | 5,856 | 1,869 | 1,875 | 896 | 1,216 | n.a |
| 1994 | 2,241 | 1,656 | 585 | n.a | 5,204 | 1,710 | 1,488 | 756 | 1,250 | n.a |
| 1993 | 1,855 | 1,208 | 647 | n.a | 3,017 | 1,295 | 784 | 545 | 393 | n.a |
| 1992 | 1,138 | n.a | n.a | n.a | 2,219 | 660 | 518 | 895 | 146 | n.a |

Source: Public finance statistics 1992–2011, Lebanese Ministry of Finance, 2013b.

## Technical and Financial Assistance

Given the support provided by the French Government, the IOF was offered a healthy and enabling financial and functional environment, a platform the Government of Lebanon could not have secured in these early stages of reconstruction. Securing this sound operational framework was a prerequisite to the success of its early mission: enhancing the technical and operational skills and competencies of the MOF staff and developing their sense of adherence to a professional community. During many of the difficult periods that followed, and which required a strong commitment from the Ministry's side, the MOF was rather incapacitated to pilot the mission of the Institute. French sponsorship was proven crucial yet again, especially before the year 2000.

## The Institute within its Action Environment

The IOF played, and is still playing, an integral part in implementing and supporting reform initiatives on several fronts through capacity-building programs, sustained dialogue with all stakeholders, and citizen-awareness initiatives. It has actively worked towards creating and disseminating a "PFM culture" among the civil service. Indeed, its technical trainings in the various areas of PFM have improved the capacities of the MOF and public sector staff that benefited from these training programs. In fact, the World Bank Country Financial Accountability Assessment had recognized the key role the IOF had assumed in carrying capacity development for fiscal reform and management for the Lebanese MOF (World Bank, 2013a). It described the Institute as "a valuable resource that can be developed in order to mitigate serious staffing shortages that will soon impair the Government's ability to manage and reform its PFM system" (World Bank, 2013a, p. xii).

### Figure 1. Respondents' satisfaction with how management training improved their work.

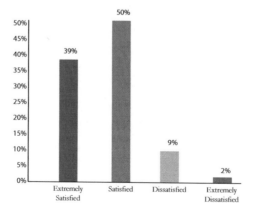

*Source*: 15 years in review: Results of the beneficiaries' satisfaction survey p. 15, Institut des Finances Basil Fuleihan, 2012a.

The support of public procurement reform provides a concrete example of the central role played by the IOF in PFM reform. In order to meet the reform objectives of public procurement, for example, the MOF and the IOF synchronized their actions towards the following fields:

1. The standardization of public procurement procedures into a national procurement guide and the five national bidding documents and their dissemination to achieve an efficient procurement cycle and enhance transparency and integrity;

2. Professionalizing training delivery on a competency-based framework and building the capacities and operational skills of civil servants working in public procurement;

3. The transfer of knowledge and the introduction and adaptation of international good practices and trends such as sustainable public procurement (Institut des Finances Basil Fuleihan, 2012d); and

4. Building of a community of practice in public procurement at the central, sub-central and local levels.

In the period 2008–2010 alone, a total of 351 trainees attended 11 different training courses on public procurement. In what amounts to customs reforms, the IOF has closely accompanied the continuous modernization process launched in 1993, which was aimed at reorienting the culture and role of customs towards one that emphasizes trade facilitation, and contributes to the improvement of Lebanon's trade competitiveness as well as its potential accession to the World Trade Organization. Since 1996, the IOF has trained more than 7,000 agents of the Customs Administration, thus helping to promote the image of a new, modern, responsive and professional public administration. As for the introduction of the new Tax Procedure Code in 2009, more than 1,000 staff from the MOF and concerned syndicates took part to the training programs organized at the IOF.

## The Public Sector Institutional Context

A second level of analysis that affects capacity-building intervention is the Public Sector Institutional Context. This dimension revolves around the laws and regulations affecting civil service and Government operations of which the operations of public institutions. Administrative rules and regulations can have different effects on the public's sector ability to carry out its function and further initiate reforms and enhancements (Hilderbrand & Grindle, 2013). In Lebanon, the Civil Service Board (CSB) handles the public sector organizational sphere. It is a central agency operating under the tutelage of the Presidency of the Council of Ministers. The CSB is responsible for organizing civil service operations, recruiting civil servants, setting the entrance and qualification exams, and managing personnel issues such as compensation schemes, promotion patterns, etc.

However, ever since the start of the civil war in 1975, the Lebanese civil service has been suffering from employment and recruiting irregularities that has cast a dim outlook on the sector's performance and future. Public sector recruitment was further restricted by Decision No. 14 of the Council of Ministers dated 9 December, 1999, in an attempt to resolve a surplus problem the sector was undergoing. This measure continues to undermine the human capacity of the civil service, in addition to any effort for effective staff planning and career path development.

Furthermore, the absence of a national strategy that institutionalizes training for civil servants has further burdened the capacity of the Lebanese administrations. Training that would service the public sector was weak until 1975, when it was nearly halted. The Institute of Finance was created in 1996 to fill part of this gap; and has since been operating as the main provider of capacity-building and training agency in the Lebanese public sector. In the past years, the picture has slightly changed and a number of institutions operating on various scopes were created:

- The National School for Administration (ENA) was created in 2002 and situated the responsibility for public administration training at a national level. Unfortunately, it was not provided with the most efficient operating framework;

- The Office of State Minister for Administrative Reform also organizes training programs for civil servants, mainly on topics related to information and communication technologies and management; and

- Other training institutes targeting specific administrations such as the Ministry of Justice, Internal Security Forces, and the Rafic Hariri International Airport were also recently either created or refurbished. However, these institutions provide technical services to specific target audiences and their contribution on the wider public sector scope remains limited.

In such a context, the MOF provided the IOF with a strong ground to act as a modernization tool to its outdated practices. The year 2003 was a turning point, as the Institute was granted the legal status of a public autonomous agency operating under the tutelage the Minister of Finance. Since then, it has benefited from a yearly budget allocation from the MOF, and enjoys independent management as well as financial and administrative autonomy (Lebanese Ministry of Finance, 2013a). Also in 2003, the IOF was appointed by the Council of Ministers as the main provider of training in PFM to the Lebanese public sector. This decision has steered the IOF towards becoming the School of Finance of the Lebanese Government. The IOF was one of the very few projects whose sustainability was ensured.

## Figure 2. The Institute supports the Ministry of Finance in improving financial management in all public administrations and institutions.

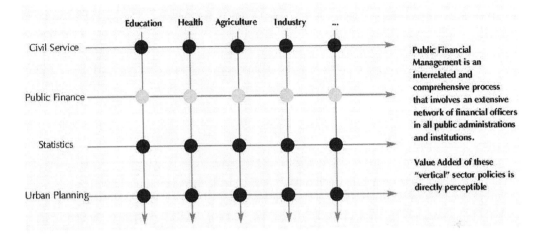

*Source*: Training catalogue 2012–2014. p. 4, Institut des Finances Basil Fuleihan, 2012d.

## The Task Network

The Ministry of Finance acts as the head of the Public Financial Management system. It is the guarantor of budget preparation, proper execution, and reliable accounting systems, as well as the enabler of sound monitoring and controlling mechanisms. Reforms at the Ministry of Finance's level thus affect the entire public sector's PFM.

Therefore, the role of leadership at the managerial level, combined with the competencies at the staff level is considered to be the enabling factor that puts these reforms into practice. However, sound PFM reform should not take into consideration reforms solely at the MOF level. As a matter of fact, the horizontal nature of public finance and the execution of the budget, which affects all of the administrations and institutions operating in the public sphere, imply that all the public sector is involved and responsible for the proper implementation of sound PFM practices.

As such, sound capacity development that would enable and accompany such practices and reforms at the MOF level should also be directed to the entire civil service. Capacity development, as previously mentioned, would affect the performance of the entire public sector in terms of public financial management, leading to support and proper implementation of the reforms implemented by the Ministry of Finance. As such, the Institute had to envisage interacting with a wide set of players, stakeholders, and service recipients. The IOF focused its strategy on promoting a culture of value-for-money and accountability, while presenting contemporary best practices in the field of PFM. Its action focused on two intertwined aspects:

catering for the betterment of overall institutional capacities through improved procedures, and awareness-raising and fostering the improvement of individual competencies.

In its effort to sustain and expand its task network as well as to create sustainable synergies with its direct and indirect stakeholders, the Institute operated on the following levels:

## Training and HR Development

Training programs provided by the Institute were addressed to the four main directorates of the MOF: the Directorate General of Finance (DGF), the Directorate General of Customs (DGC), the Directorate General of Cadastre and Land Registry (DGCLR), and the Directorate General of National Lottery (DGNL). Staff training and development have been precursors to, and concomitants of, the main categories of reform and of the introduction of new technologies.

The IOF embraced four types of programs:

- preparatory programs for entry and promotion exams;
- induction training for new recruits;
- specialized job-related trainings; and
- continuous trainings.

| Table 5. Number of beneficiaries from IOF training programs (1996–2010) | | | | | | | | |
|---|---|---|---|---|---|---|---|---|
| **Year** | **1996** | **1997** | **1998** | **1999** | **2000** | **2001** | **2002** | **2003** |
| No. of Trainees | 270 | 428 | 1315 | 1135 | 1137 | 1453 | 2263 | 2741 |
| **Year** | **2004** | **2005** | **2006** | **2007** | **2008** | **2009** | **2010** | **TOTAL** |
| No. of Trainees | 2977 | 4068 | 4391 | 3302 | 2742 | 4192 | 3159 | 35673 |

## Developing Training Modules

In 15 years, the IOF developed for its clientele 120 training modules ranging from public finance, to economy, taxation, accounting, law, management and leadership, financial education, training engineering, foreign languages, information technologies, customs and cadastre (Institut des Finances Basil Fuleihan, 2012d).

## Expanding the Beneficiaries List

Since 2003, beneficiaries expanded to include new categories such as public institutions (public hospitals, water authorities, etc.), Parliament, municipalities, other ministries and the public sector at large (Institut des Finances Basil Fuleihan, 2012c).

## Establishing Specialized Communities of Practice

The wider audience targeted by the training programs has helped creating national communities of practices specialized in various areas of PFM such as procurement, budget, accounting, financial education, and training. Training programs at the IOF have also been characterized by:

- a standardized training engineering and management system monitored through a "Training Protocol" for quality management;
- interactive training methods;
- the expertise of a wide network of qualified and competent trainers;
- reference material put at the disposition of the trainers, trainees and the public; and
- the know-how of a training team specialized in multiple fields of intervention.

## Supporting Human Resources Management

On the other hand, the IOF was involved in the various aspects of human resources management. More specifically, the IOF assisted and supported the recruitment and training new MOF employees by designing and conducting the three-month induction training for more than 1,600 new recruits at MOF. This initial training aimed to ensure the harmonious and smooth integration of new recruits within the administration.

From the results of the survey conducted by Infopro which measured, for a representative sample of 1,547 individuals who attended IOF training programs from 2005 until 2009, satisfaction levels with various IOF training activities.

### Figure 3. Training courses attended per type since 2005.

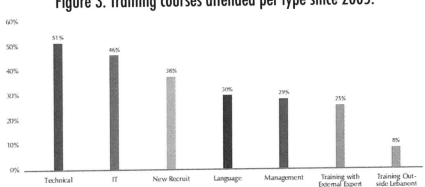

*Source*: 15 years in review: Results of the beneficiaries satisfaction
survey p. 9, Institut des Finances Basil Fuleihan, 2012a.

**Figure 4. Respondents' satisfaction with understanding their rights and duties as civil servants-**

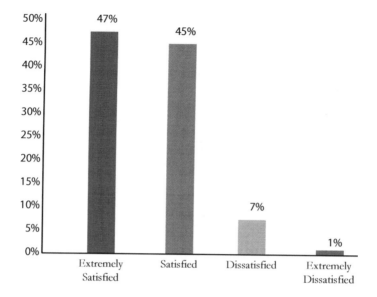

*Source*: 15 years in review: Results of the beneficiaries satisfaction survey p. 10, Institut des Finances Basil Fuleihan, 2012b.

**Figure 4. Respondents' satisfaction with acquiring the needed knowledge to start working at the Ministry of Finance.**

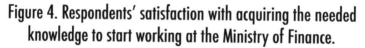

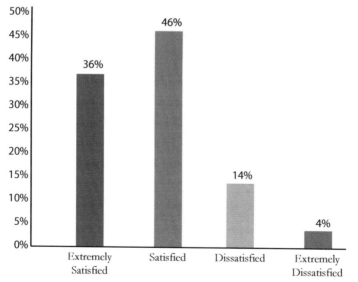

*Source:* 15 years in review: Results of the beneficiaries satisfaction survey p. 10, Institut des Finances Basil Fuleihan, 2012a.

Finally, at a national level, the IOF has assisted the Directorate General of Finance in improving the quality of the recruitment process by redesigning the content of the entry examination by the CSB to the third and fourth categories, in parallel to conducting a communication campaign for the 2006/2007 recruitment session, in an effort to attract the most qualified staff to the MOF.

## Advisory Role

The IOF has also played an advisory role upon the establishment of new units within the MOF, accompanying the Ministry throughout the establishment of new units that the development of the capacities of these units.

The introduction of the Value Added Tax (VAT) provides an example of the accompanying role played by the Institute in the process of supporting the implementation of fiscal reform: The 18 mid-managers and 300 MOF staff selected to establish the new VAT unit in 2002 received up to 140 days of specialized training on systems and procedures before commencing their jobs, in addition to good practices study visits to Tunis, Morocco, Egypt, Singapore, France, Canada, and Ireland, in an effort to expose concerned staff to interesting international practices. Also prior to the introduction of the new tax, extensive public awareness-raising and education campaigns targeting different client groups were conducted. As a result, instead of having to personally collect and manually fill long and complicated forms, the taxpayer receives by post easy-to-complete forms including standard taxpayer information incorporated in advance by the system. A stamped addressed envelope is included for postal returns. Payments processes have also been speeded-up. The above has helped to achieve a high level of compliance in a very short period. In fact, the courteous and efficient service provided to customers won the Lebanese Ministry of Finance the 2007 United Nations Public Service Award (Lebanese Ministry of Finance, 2013a, p. 10).

## Communicating within the Task Network

The IOF underwent an active internal and external communication campaign through several initiatives and a set of scholarly publications. The internal campaign was aimed at defining a professional community (the Ministry of Finance) and developing a sense of belonging within it. This was mainly effectuated through the publication of a quarterly newsletter—*Hadith el-Malia*.

The external campaign was specifically aimed at reinforcing the national vision of the ministry, promoting transparency, facilitating easy and equal access to information, and bridging the gap between the private and public sectors.

Over the years, the Institute has:

- published the Citizens' Guides series, a set of guides aiming at raising citizen awareness on the most important tax procedures;

- designed and coordinated the implementation of communication strategies for specific projects such as the UN Public Service Award (Lebanese Ministry of Finance, 2008, p. 10);

- organized programs and events dedicated to the Lebanese youth such as the participation in job fairs and the organization of one-day orientation programs to introduce university students to the MOF;

- supported the work of the Joint Consultative Committees between public and private sectors aimed at improving the relationship between taxpayers and the financial and customs administrations and expediting administrative procedures;

- produced booklets, pamphlets and flyers directed to the citizens on major tax procedures;

- set-up a public documentation center, the Library of Finance, specialized in PFM publications; and

- organized several awareness events, conferences and workshops and participated in major book fairs to promote the reform program undertaken by the MOF.

More recently, the IOF decided to contribute more actively to the policy dialogue arena in Lebanon and the Arab World. As such, it launched a biannual journal, *Assadissa*, which tackles public financial management and state modernization in Lebanon and the Arab world. It is an "ambitious attempt to bring together some of the foremost thinkers and practitioners concerned in state modernization and public finance reform in Lebanon and the Arab region and to foster dialogue between researchers, practitioners, and policy-makers" (Bissat and Abi Saab, 2011, pp. 102-103).

The communication activities of the IOF were thought and designed to promote and reinforce good governance through consensus building, enhanced inclusiveness, reponsiveness and transparency as well as improved awareness of laws and regulations by the citizens.

## Partnership Building

Since 2004, the IOF worked towards becoming a regional center of excellence in the Middle East and North Africa. It sought, and was able to build strong partnerships with regional and international organizations and launch a series of regional services aiming at positioning itself as a regional training hub. A major highlight and moreover, a precedence in the MENA region was that the IOF's working language is Arabic. The technical assistance and support in capacity-building expertise was being provided in Arabic; this advantage made the regional cooperation efforts much more in-line with needs of the targeted partners.

## Figure 6. The Institute's local, regional, and international partners.

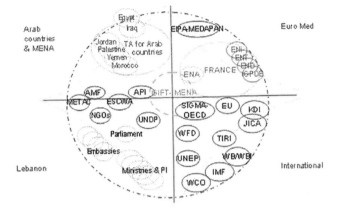

## Bilateral Initiatives

The IOF worked on reinforcing bilateral cooperation with Arab governmental institutions through the organization of technical study tours that would allow the Arab counterparts to get acquainted with the reforms undertaken by the Lebanese Ministry of Finance and the IOF. It offered diversified tailor-made training programs in response to pressing training needs of civil servants in the region.

## The Governance Institutes Forum for Training in the Middle East and North Africa (GIFT-MENA) Network

Still, the biggest leap was the creation in 2006 of a network of civil service training schools and institutes in the MENA region—known as the GIFT-MENA network. The network works towards increasing regional cooperation and exchange and focuses on following pillars:

- Capacity-building and training, exchange of expertise and good practices;
- Easy access to knowledge information and material curriculum development; and
- Institutional set-up and networking.

The network provided an innovative platform for civil service training operators in the region to get together and exchange their experiences, best practices, and knowledge with peers. GIFT-MENA serves as a global hub for networking among MENA centers of excellence, in a collective effort to document successful regional experiences, knowledge, and solutions to specific reform implementation constraints in areas mainly related to taxation, public financial management, and public sector performance. The network marked the launch of the first South–South cooperation initiative in the MENA region from Beirut (*GIFT MENA Learning Network*, 2013). It also stimulated the development of new training modules in the Arabic language (*Regional Programs*, 2013). The added value of the network remained that it was born out of the will of its members who took a determined step towards the establishment of a collaborative regional environment to disseminate knowledge and share expertise, resources and know-how.

## Regional and International Organizations

The IOF has consolidated its relations with regional and international organizations operating in MENA through the signature of several Memoranda of Understanding. Such agreements played a major role in placing the Institute of Finance at the heart of the learning and training panorama in the region. Main agreements were signed with:

- the World Bank Institute, in April 2004—the agreement envisages building on Lebanon's human capital advantage and fostering knowledge-sharing activities in the MENA region;

- the World Customs Organization (WCO), in January 2006: The agreement designates the IOF as the WCO regional training center for the Gulf countries;

- the Arab Planning Institute, in January 2009, for the joint organization of yearly events; and

- the ADETEF (Agency for International Cooperation of the French Ministries of Economy and Finance), in January 2010, for the development of the GIFT-MENA network.

The IOF also maintains close collaborative ties with other regional and international organizations such as the Middle East Technical Assistance Center, the Islamic Development Bank, the Economic and Social Commission for Western Asia, UN agencies, and other organizations in addition to embassies and international representations based in Lebanon. The regional and international exposure it enjoys granted the IOF access to a wide pool of Arab and international experts, trainers, consultants that have a solid academic background and practical expertise in addition to their knowledge of the regional context.

## Cooperation with France

The Institute was established on a basis of a French–Lebanese bilateral protocol. As such, the IOF has maintained a close and distinguished cooperation with France, and in particular with the ADETEF. The Institute acts as the local link for ADETEF, ensuring the coordination and follow-up of bilateral cooperation initiatives with the Lebanese administration. In partnership with ADETEF, the IOF started in 2007 to provide technical assistance services to the development of training centers at the Ministries of Finance of Jordan and Palestine. It has also been coordinating demands from Morocco, Yemen, Iraq, and Egypt. These types of institutional cooperation efforts were set in accordance to the respective countries development agendas in order to secure the proper advantages. The "ADETEF-IOF for MENA" consortium offered a platform to tackle common and cross-boundary issues at a regional and multi-country level, to disseminate the French expertise and good international practices at a larger scale, and most of all, to implement capacity development programs that enjoy strong local ownership.

## Organizational Structure

An undeniable factor contributing to the success of capacity building interventions is the organizational framework in which stakeholders attempt to carry out their efforts (Hilderbrand and Grindle, 2013). Since its inception, the IOF defined a roadmap for its organizational goals and sought to instill a sense of mission and commitment to these goals among its staff. Such an effort was vital as for providing the IOF with an identity that would strengthen its legitimacy as a public institution. However, compared to other public institutions in Lebanon, the IOF enjoys a singular organizational structure and management scheme.

### Human Resources

Four departments, Training, Administration, Information and Communication, Institutional Building and Outreach, make up the organizational structure of the IOF. They draw their efficiency on the IOF's ability to tap on polyvalent and highly qualified staff recruited based on a competitive selection process.

### Trainers

The IOF does not employ any in-house trainers. It draws on the expertise of a wide network of more than 220 professionals, practitioners, and experts carefully selected from the Ministry of Finance, other public institutions, the private sector, and the academia. The IOF also works on continuously enhancing the skills and competencies of its network of trainers by sending them to trainings abroad, exposing them to best international practices and organizing yearly train the trainer programs. In fact, a satisfaction survey carried out in 2009 by an external consultancy firm indicates that the majority of trainees were satisfied with the high abilities of the trainers (Institut des Finances Basil Fuleihan, 2012d, pp. 18-19).

## Figure 6. Average level of satisfaction for trainer characteristics.

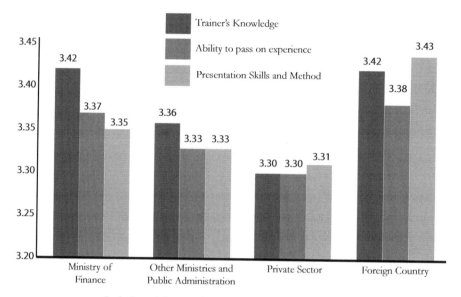

Scale from 1 (extremely dissatisfied) to 4 (extremely satisfied)

*Source*: 15 years in review: Results of the beneficiaries' satisfaction survey p. 18, Institut des Finances Basil Fuleihan, 2012a.

## Resources

The legal status of public institution granted in 2003 (Financial and Administrative Autonomy, 2013) provided the IOF with a yearly budget allocation drawn from the MOF overall budget to run operations. It also allows the IOF to receive donations/grants/aids that may be made available by local, regional and international organizations. In this context, the IOF has, on several occasions tapped into external funding provided by the donor community. External funding was granted to advance on the capacity-building and reform agenda of the MOF. The funds were used to answer growing training demands for training in PFM by stakeholders outside the MOF, develop new training modules and tools, build the institutional capacities of the IOF, and provide it with the means to develop into an evolving learning institution.

| Year | Contribution of the MOF | | Donor Funding |
| --- | --- | --- | --- |
| | in LBP | equiv. in USD | in USD |
| 1996 | | | 361,442.48 |
| 1997 | | | 361,442.48 |
| 1998 | | | 361,442.48 |
| 1999 | | | 557,965.65 |
| 2000 | 44,780,000 | 29,853.33 | 417,446.38 |
| 2001 | 400,000,000 | 266,666.67 | 472,684.49 |
| 2002 | 500,000,000 | 333,333.33 | 183,371.56 |
| 2003 | 490,000,000 | 326,666.67 | 288,444.31 |
| 2004 | 660,000,000 | 440,000.00 | 177,800.80 |
| 2005 | 600,000,000 | 4,00,000.00 | 160,263.24 |
| 2006 | 600,000,000 | 400,000.00 | 170,263.24 |
| 2007 | 900,000,000 | 6,00,000.00 | 259,763.24 |
| 2008 | 1,200,000,000 | 666,666.67 | 202,079.14 |
| 2009 | 1,200,000,000 | 800,000.00 | 148,517.37 |
| 2010 | 1,400,000,000 | 933,333.33 | 820,272.03 |
| TOTAL | 7,794,780,000 | 5,196,520.00 | 4,943,198.89 |

Table 6. The IOF Financial resources (1996–2010)

# Lessons Learned and Findings

## Achievements at the MOF

Fifteen years later, there is a wide acknowledgement that the effort started in 1993, and continuing, transformed the MOF, the main "client" of the IOF from antiquated turn-of-century operation, atrophied by years of neglect during the civil war, to state-of-the-art process benchmarked by other countries. In spite of the difficult political and security situation that still prevailed in Lebanon, programs were successfully implemented and capacities built in a sustainable fashion. Visible, tangible, desirable results were achieved since macroeconomic stability was sustained and showed incredible resilience in face of internal and external shocks such as multiple Israeli attacks on Lebanon, internal confessional and political conflicts, and the international financial crisis. The main service improvements for citizens, the private sector, and civil society have been realized in terms of speeding-up the delivery of services provided by the MOF (such has post clearance controls in customs, e-declaration, and payments in private banks, etc.); increasing the validity, accuracy, and consistency of assessments and records; improving the availability and accessibility of valid, comprehensive and up-to-date financial, fiscal, and trade data; and improving the delivery of services to other government entities. The staff of the MOF is considered to be among the most qualified of the Lebanese administration. Indeed, specialized technical capability was built in fiscal and PFM policy development and management; high quality staff was recruited, well prepared, and coached.

At the IOF, adapted and enhanced training material was provided in the Arabic language; networks of partners and contacts with local, regional, and international stakeholders were established and their expertise was put at the disposition al of all stakeholders. Demands for replication from other countries in MENA were channeled. And most of all, Lebanon was able to set a status of a post-conflict developing country that has a record of success in critical areas of governance reform: capacity-building in financial governance.

First delegated to upgrade the technical skills of the MOF staff, the IOF assumes today a much wider mission:

- Building the skills and knowledge of the Ministry of Finance staff;
- Enhancing the capacity in financial management of Government agencies;
- Improving financial education of citizens, internal and external communication, and information to the public;
- Networking with local, regional and international institutions; and
- Acting as a regional hub for training in PFM.

## Main Challenges

A set of challenges were identified as critically restraining to the work of IOF:

- A limited budget to run operations and respond to all training demands, in the context of an unsteady economic situation characterized by a high level of insecurity and an increasing public debt;
- The absence of a national strategy regulating training within the public sector as well as the absence of legislation instating the right of civil servants to benefit from training;
- The absence of linkages between training received and career path development;
- Difficulties to recruit and retain professional qualified staff at the IOF prior to the institutionalization of the Institute in 2003 (when it was granted the status of public autonomous agency);

- Little awareness by the Lebanese public of the IOF initiatives. This challenge was addressed with a more proactive press coverage and external relations strategy including representation of the IOF at major local, regional, and international events; and

- A certain resistance to change and to moving from traditional work practices to improved and modern procedures from the "old" generation at the MOF.

## Ingredients of Success

It is important to have an in-depth look at the ingredients of success and lessons learnt from 15 years of service to the Lebanese Ministry of Finance, the public sector and the MENA region. The main factors identified as drivers of performance may be the following:

1. A strong political endorsement by the Minister of Finance: all consecutive ministers of finance provided their support to the IOF and were committed to its mission. This was a necessary and sufficient condition for success, particularly in cultures like Lebanon where there is strong respect for authority, position, and status within the governance hierarchy, and where political and sectarian affiliations can still outweigh professional qualifications in the public sector.

2. Government and local ownership: the story of the IOF cannot be isolated from other reform initiatives taken by the GOL. Experience has made it clear that sustainability of efforts was the function of having visionary leaders at a policymaking level and qualified civil servants at the technical level. Also, the involvement and co-ownership of the staff at MOF in training initiatives facilitated the achievement of a performance record by the IOF.

3. Institutional location: The institutional location of the IOF at the heart of the MOF, being the trend setter and key institution driving the national reform agenda, imparted the Institute with considerable internal (within the public sector) and external (among donors, the private sector, and civil society) legitimacy.

4. Quality and commitment of staff: the staff of the IOF, qualified in relevant fields and multilingual, was enabled to speak the same "languages," not only as the administration but also as donors, and to be sufficiently credible technically to make reasonably informed judgments about problem identification and channeling—and sometimes giving and interpolating—advice concerning the development and implementation of appropriate reform and capacity-building solutions. It is also significant that all staff members were Lebanese nationals. This has facilitated to a great extent the relationship and communication with the local administration and promoted an approach of peer-to-peer learning.

5. Administrative and financial flexibility: the administrative and financial autonomy that the IOF enjoys from its status of public institution provides the staff, beneficiaries, and all partners with a flexible and adaptable work environment to cater to their needs and requests. A different administrative set-up might have constituted an additional challenge to the performance of the IOF.

6. Approach to reform—no single recipe for success: the IOF has always put forward a pragmatic, progressive, and participatory approach to reform. It has promoted national consultations and the involvement of all concerned stakeholders such as the Court of Audit, the Parliament and others in any major reform initiative. It has looked at reform as a continuous and long-lasting process, not limited to a particular time schedule. Finally, the IOF continuously worked toward being an actor of reform and having a voice in the adoption and adaptation of knowledge and practices made available by the international community and foreign experts.

7. Benefiting from the experience sharing: taking the time to study and learn from other/peer experiences before engaging into reform was key to design effective solutions, mainly in the capacity-building area.

8. Performance record of accomplishment: the record of accomplishment and sustained evolution within the MOF and the IOF is securing the continuing strong support of the public, the business community, and the donor community.

9. Demand for replication: the recognition by regional and international actors of the performance and success of the IOF and their request for the provision of technical assistance increased the sense of responsibility of the staff at the IOF and provided additional incentive to strengthen their approach and continuously improve their practices.

10. The role of the donor community: the donor community provided substantive technical and financial support to PFM reform in Lebanon. Lessons from experience encourage the donor community to rethink approaches and rhythm, suggesting greater use of country systems, better coordination, and heavier investment in the country institutions over longer periods of time to leave out linear models to the benefit of flexibility and longer term follow-up. The donor community in Lebanon recognizes the role of the IOF and provides it with its support.

# Conclusion

The MOF and IOF experience in the field of Public Financial Management in post-Taef Lebanon overcame—and continues to overcome—a plethora of security, political, social, and economic challenges. Is this enough to call it a "best practice"? It should be understood that best practices in governance are relevant to the conditions, circumstances, legal environment, and needs of each country. What is important is to acknowledge with objectivity the success of an institution within its institutional and operational framework.

In 15 years, the services of the IOF are largely satisfactory to their users, and in many cases exceeded expectations. Beneficiaries expressed their great appreciation of capacity-building activities as it helped them acquire new skills, improve their knowledge and work practices. Satisfaction was also derived from the professionalism and performance of trainers. In respect to communication activities, the role of the IOF improved citizen-awareness of PFM issues and led to better participation of all concerned stakeholders in the process of devising policies and understanding new procedures at the MOF.

The action of the IOF for better financial governance has instilled a culture of good governance based on four pillars:

1. Strategic vision: civil servants are equipped with perspective on what is considered good practice in their job and what is needed to reach this goal;

2. Efficiency: civil servants are encouraged to achieve results making the best use of available resources;

3. Responsiveness: people—civil servants—are trained to better serve other people—the citizens; and

4. Accountability and public service ethics.


The IOF is looked at from within and outside Lebanon as an efficient institution inspired by a philosophy of continuous improvement and development, performance and client-service delivery. It is a good prototype of a performing organization in a post-conflict environment that has undoubtedly contributed to set one governance record for Lebanon and the MENA region.

# Abandoning Predictions and Control: Lessons for the Middle East

## Alexander Dawoody
## Peter Marks

## Abstract

We live in a complex world that forces us to abandon what we inherited from linear observation of events and phenomena. The linear applications of control, prediction, objectivity, rationalism, singular causality, and breaking the whole into parts then observing each part separately are no longer capable of understanding the complex nature of reality. This paper addresses the need for adapting complexity paradigms—such as forecast, subjectivity, phase shift, collapse dynamics, interconnectedness, mutual causality, and chaos—in observing the complex nature of the world, especially in the Middle East. By learning from complexity, avoiding arguments for prediction, control, and stability, we can offer realistic solutions to Middle Eastern problems, learn from models such as the BRICS (Brazil, Russia, India, China, and South Africa) cooperative experience, and help the movement toward sound governance that became vocal after the Arab Spring makes study progress forward.

# Introduction

Events in life, whether in politics or the economy, are not predictable (Barabasi, 2003). One can assess a change through forecast, but not accurately predict the exact nature of change. Predictability is an inherent trait we continue using from the linear observation of the world (Miller & Page, 2007). Yet, life is complex. We live in a world of participatory collusion among particles where entities are separated by space and possess no mechanism for communicating with one another or exhibit correlations in their behavior (Overman & Loraine, 1996).

Structures collapse and evolve because of consistently small reasons that grow larger and become more nonlinear (Brem, 1999; Dawoody, 2011; Guastello, 2002). We are devoid of visible causal links between elements and rely, instead, on interdependence and extremely low predictability (Kauffman, 1993). Hence, we exhibit a fatal tendency and a propensity to predict (Brown, 1995). With prediction we aim to prevent systemic volatility and persist on the illusion of maintaining "stability" through artificial engineering (Goldstein, 2007). This type of error, often adapted by policymakers, is a recipe for disaster and often results in catastrophe (Brown, 1995). Another error is control (Capra, Juarrero, & Uden, 2007). We do this in our daily routine interactions, or in public and economic policies (Harrison, 2006). Although all indicators point to the contrary and results demonstrate the fatality of such behavior, we, nevertheless, persist in maintaining this trait (Buchanan, 2003).

After the global financial crisis and its impact on Middle Eastern economies, notably in countries such as Dubai and Egypt, governmental responses in the Middle East were mainly focused on predicting future trends in the global economy in order to avoid repeated consequences. Prediction, however, would not help because the transpired crisis was only an underling symptom, not the causal element in economic changes. Hence, this paper attempts to illustrate that prediction and a subsequent public policy bent on control are mere errors and not real solutions.

Since the Middle East involves many countries with varying systems of government, attempting to analyze issues of governance on a regional level and as one coherent set is difficult. Yet, and because of the interconnectedness of the region and its shared interests, values, and history, the ripple-effects of events in one part of the region may have consequences extending to the entire region. Governmental policies in each particular country in the region will then respond to that event based on its own calculus. While we cannot treat the region as a whole, we can, nevertheless, appreciate its interconnectedness and the impact of events on its social, economic, and political trajectory (Dawoody, 2013).

We are no longer constrained by a single ontological model. Truth can now be seen not as an attribute inherent in a system or event, but as the meaning we attribute to that system (Buchanan, 2003). This kind of ontological liberation is evident in the paradigm shift to the world of nonlinear sciences (Wheatley, 2006). These types of shifts include moving from structure to process, from objective to epistemic science, and from building block to network (Evans, 1999). Nonlinearity and its model free us from the burden that comes from needing to control rather than to evoke process and relationship (Overman & Loraine, 1996). This understanding forces us to examine public policy in the Middle East and its role in the economy not through the isolated observation of its building-blocks, but in relationship of these particles with themselves and the environment of the system as a whole (Dawoody, 2011; Johnson, 2002).

## Learning from Complexity

Complexity sciences teach us many things that we can apply to public policy and economic development in the Middle East. An important lens that we can learn and adapt from complexity sciences is the notion of self-organization. Self-organization is the idea that living systems are capable of self-organizing themselves in ways that all their components and processes can jointly produce the same components and processes as autonomous agents (Vesterby, 2008). This concept is also known as autopoiesis (Maturana & Varela, 1991). A key notion of this concept is self-referentiality (Sandri, 2009). The idea of self-reference designates the unity that a dynamic system is for itself, and that unity can be produced through relational operations (Little, 1999).

Autopoiesis and self-referentiality must be understood within processes of change that are multi-layered, multi-directional, and continually morphing in a state of flux within an irreversible trajectory of time and motion. Public policy interaction with the economy follows this multi-directional trajectory of irreversible movement in time in order to remedy the inadequacy and trappings of linearity. Emphases here are on synergy as the real future, in-the-moment, relationships, patterns of similarities and differences across time and space, mutual causality, awareness, and transformation through emergence (Juarrero & Rubino, 2008; Nicolis & Prigogine, 1989). Instead of a line, there are loops, networks and webs that are interconnected and interplaying with each other and with their environments (Brown, 1995; Dawoody, 2011).

The interplay between a dynamic system and its environment is an on-going enterprise of continuous relationships of interplaying and interconnected networks (Johnson, 2002). Changes that take place in the system's environment act as "kicks" to generate changes within the system's internal structure (Dawoody, 2011). Communications between the system and its environment is based on positive and negative feedback (Morgan, 2006). Environmental kicks are received by the system through its sensory receptors which act as strange attractors in order to prepare the system internally to reshuffle its internal structure and change its older order to correspond to changes in the environment. If the internal order is incapable of change, then the system's entire structural order must collapse in order to allow for new structural order to emerge and deal with the new environmental changes (Prigogine & Stengers, 1984). Sustaining the older structures through artificial engineering may buy the system some time, but it will not prevent its ultimate collapse, at which point it may be accompanied with catastrophe (Brown, 1995; Dawoody, 2011).

Without the collapse of the older structure there will be no birth of a new order. This concept is also referred to as bifurcation (Kuznetsov, 2010), and is translated in phase shifts in the order of the system's dynamics (Wheatley, 2006). As the self-organizing order emerges out of the interaction of elements within the system, the system's own parameters become unstable and the older order starts to collapse (Brem, 1999). Public policy in the Middle East, regardless of the type of government, must be understood according to this perspective in order to safeguard it from costly errors of resisting change or attempting artificial engineering (Dawoody, 2011; Richardson & Goldstein, 2007).

The relationship between the system and its environment operates on feedback that is either positive or negative (Morgan, 2006). Feedback as stimuli is retransmitted by the environment and causes random changes in the agent's internal processes (Wheatley, 2006). This behavior contains the agent's morphology from static equilibrium to a state of chaos and disorder; disorder then leads to new structures and practices (Prigogine, 1996). The phase-shifts from equilibrium to disequilibrium to equilibrium are self-organizing and irreducible, and unpredictable (Nicolis & Prigogine, 1989). Understanding public policy's role in the economy of the Middle East through a complexity lens enables us to capsulate the bigger picture in change dynamics and have a better appreciation of the multilayered dynamics that interplay during their display (Richardson & Goldstein, 2007).

## Arguments against Stability

A market economy is sometimes said to be self-organizing (Krugman, 1996; Redmond, 2010). Self-organization is related to the question of how (labor) markets come into being by consumptive and productive activities by actors. The notion of the invisible hand (Smith, 2010) is a predecessor of the self-organization notion and holds that interactions lead to coordination as an unintended consequence of the self-interested behavior. Or as Hayek (1967) coins his catallaxy that states the spontaneous order of the free market as a "self-organizing system of voluntary cooperation" (p. 108).

Traditionally, the self-regulating properties of the price mechanism are emphasized (negative feedback) which stabilizes the equilibrium. However, stable equilibria cannot explain the driving forces of economic development, and in a changing environment, markets hardly ever reach a state of perfect coordination due to problems in information processing (Witt, 1997). New profit opportunities are opened when individuals successfully innovate; this opening of new knowledge diffuses through the economy and creates new products, technologies and/or markets. These self-augmenting features of the market process create positive feedback away from the stable equilibrium and have a de-coordinating effect. Due to the self-regulating and self-augmenting features production, trading, and division of labor are taking place, but there are surprises, misallocations, backlashes and losses (Witt, 1997).

According to Marx, capitalism is the combination of capital and industrial (later the service sector was added) operations that monopolizes labor in turning raw materials into products and generating surplus (profit) in the process (Marx, 2012). The market used for the introduction (sale) of goods is national, hence creating a national bourgeoisie, antagonistic within itself because of the competition for market niche, but united in safeguarding its interests against labor (Marx & Engels, 2011).

Democracies emerged to protect these means of production through enacted laws and public institutions (Przeworski, 1986). With the rise in labor demand and unity, the national boundaries of a capitalism market gradually started to blur and fuse with each other (Ricardo, 2010). The national bourgeois and the socio-political and economic system that it had represented at one point morphed into global capitalism (Frieden, 2007). Public entities also morphed to either restrict or support this growth under the guise of providing stability (Gilpin, 2001). Global organizations, such as the World Trade Organization, the World Monetary funds, and the World Bank emerged in order to support these new developments (Eichengreen, 2008).

While many economists hold that planning disturbs the self-organizing system, from a socialist economic perspective, the state should direct production and pricing due to considerable market failures—for instance, to protect against severe deprivation. However, this leads to distortions of the pricing mechanism. The public restraint on competition has a lasting hindering effect on the process of self-control of the catallaxy (Streit, 1993). The problems created by the interference are not recognized as related, which triggers even more interventions to neutralize the ill side-effects. Hence, the intervening institutions become locked-in (North, 1990; Pierson, 2000; Olson, 1982).

It is here that classic capitalism as professed and its dynamics of booms and busts explained by Adam Smith (2010) evolved to predatory capitalism. The public sector's constant interference in the affairs of predatory capitalism—either supporting it through subsidies, tax cut, tariff regulations, and anti-labor measures, or preventing its collapse through bailouts—are exercises of suppressing volatility in the name of stability (Acharya & Richardson, 2009). In doing so, the public sector had tied its fate with the fate of predatory capitalism, choking in the process, windows for natural evolution and for the complex system to self-organize and adapt to changes in the environment (Ott, 2003).

Companies that survive in the competitive market do so by luck or design, coming close to maximizing profits (Alchian, 1950). The magic of the market is that, through individual consumptive and productive self-interest, the actors enforce self-regulating features (Witt, 1997). A system is resilient in the sense that it can absorb a certain amount of disturbances without changing state. There are two ways of looking at this. From a linear perspective (engineering), resilience is how far the system has moved and how much time was necessary for the system to return to its single equilibrium steady-state after a perturbation. From a complexity perspective (ecological), resilience is the amount of disturbances that can be absorbed before flipping over into another regime of behavior, i.e. to another stability domain (Gunderson, 2000). In the latter multiple stable states exist. Adam Smith (2010) called for the market to heal itself without government interference and artificial engineering, arguing against price control and calling instead for the market's invisible hand to work the fluctuations.

Today, however, and because of the morphing of classic nation-state capitalism (bourgeoisie oriented market) to global predatory capitalism, price controls by government are designed to limit volatility on the basis that stable prices are better for the consumer/citizen (Stiglitz, 2010). The behavior of the economy is thus heavily influenced by events of the past and the inherited institutional structure. These institutional structures will determine the overall economic performance. The evolutionary pattern of institutions will select out inefficient institutional forms that are not capable in surviving within the perpetuated suboptimal institutions (Poirot, 2001). These suboptimal institutions reinforce the pattern of institutional evolution undermining the efforts to transform it. Changes will then likely be discontinuous, because they need to cross a certain threshold. The long-term consequence of price controls by governments is a costly explosion that exceeds the benefits gained (Taleb & Blyth, 2011).

## Departing from Booms and Busts

In the development of market economies, institutions were designed to regulate the relationship between capital and labor, or to protect vital interests of economic agents. These institutions tune economic fluctuations to a certain socially acceptable range (Matutinovic, 2006). On the other hand, the continuous drive of profit making, growth preference and cost cutting and diffusion of knowledge drive an economic system to instability (Witt, 1997). Hence, we have both goal-oriented tuning and dynamic drivers balancing in the capitalist market (Matutinovic, 2006). This makes the evolutionary path of the economic system unpredictable and nonlinear. Nonlinearity gives rise to uncertainty about the future behavior of economic variables and the rules that govern behavior (Poirot, 2001).

The morphing of national capitalism to predatory global capitalism is grounded in the rise of complexity, interdependence, and unpredictability. There are three general responses to shifting stability and crises. A first is to test the resilience of a system by doing nothing, but wait to see if the system will return to an acceptable state. The second is actively trying to get the system back to the desired stability, and third is to accept that the system will irreversibly change and adapt to this new altered state (Gunderson, 2000). These complex systems, according to Taleb and Blyth (2011), if experiencing artificially suppressed volatility by the public sector, become extremely fragile (even if they do not exhibit visible risks at the beginning or appear to be calm while silent risks are accumulating under that calm). It is, therefore, dangerous not to examine low probability risks and remove them from observation (Taleb & Blyth, 2011).

Yet, the public sector seems bent on adapting policies to eliminate fluctuation and prevent booms and busts in the market in order to sustain the illusion of stability (Stiglitz, 2010). This is particularly true in the Middle East. During most of the 20th century, this command and control approach focused on controlling a certain target variable of interest (replacing uncertainty of nature with certainty of control), but then slowly changed other parts of the system and lost the resilience of the system (Gunderson, 2000). These policies can weaken both the market and the public sector. Examples of these policies can be illustrated in measures such as over-regulation, reducing velocity through lowering interest rates, providing government loans, enforcing price control, and sustaining stability.

These measures often come in two types: conforming to the market mechanism or regulating it to ease-up its side-effects (Krugman, Obstfeld, & Melitz, 2011). Both types, however, are suppressive of volatility and have unintended and unforeseen consequences (Nowak, 2008). It is better to tolerate these systems' fluctuations and allow them to absorb their bumps in order for true organic change to take place from within these systems, including their collapse (Guastello, 2002). Suppressing volatility not only fails to avoid these bumps, but it also increases the probability of leading these systems toward major explosions (Juarrero & Rubino, 2008). That is, instead of applying a linear perspective to prevent the system from moving toward unintended system configurations, one should nurture and preserve the elements that enable the system to renew and reorganize itself, i.e. complexity perspective (Allison & Hobbs, 2004). The public sector, as such, must allow market failures in order to allow for new and more salient orders to emerge (Miller & Page, 2007).

These systems, regardless of public sector interventions (Gruber, 2009), will eventually experience explosions, undoing years of illusionary government-desired stability (Elliot & Kiel, 1996). Often, they will end up far worse than they were in their initially volatile state. The longer it takes for these systems to explode and collapse, the worse the outcome will be for both the public and private sectors (Sandri, 2009). These crises typically end in default and restructuring with high levels of debt that take years to work off, and have a lasting effect on housing, output and employment as businesses and consumers rebuild their balance sheets (Reinhart & Rogoff, 2011). Though sector reform will not by itself overcome chaotic hysteresis, such a reform will not be possible without effective regulatory design in the sector (Poirot, 2001).

# Implications for Middle Eastern Economies

Should Middle Eastern economy not be in the realm of linear disciplines? Is the public sector's role in the Middle East to observe how the private sector is operating and understand when not to intervene? Complexity sciences do not specify where a specific discipline ought to operate in any region or country. The specifics of each discipline are the subject and responsibility of its agents. Complexity, however, gives us good recommendations on what to avoid in order to better understand our world and the complex, interconnected and interweaving dynamics of our function regardless of the discipline with which we are involved.

Complexity, for example, advises us to avoid control, prediction, long-term planning, and artificial engineering. It encourages minimizing uncertainties without necessarily presenting it as a formula for staring at a crisis. Limiting control over policies does not produce 'wise' and self-regulating systems. However, allowing the system to collapse when it reaches atrophy and dissipation in its natural cycle, and avoiding the prolonging of outdated order through interjected public policies can be beneficial in sustaining a healthy interaction between any system and its environment; bypassing catastrophes, and allowing for the nature of things to exist, mature, go through changes, collapse, and emerge in newer structures naturally and without artificial engineering.

If the United Arab Emirates (UAE) did not interfere in bailing out Dubai during its financial crisis, for example, the financial system in Dubai would have exhibited its natural cycle of decay, collapse, and the rebirth of a new structure that better fits in responding to changes in the environment. However, by interjecting itself in the economy to prevent the natural cycle of progression in the financial industry, UAE had only delayed the inevitable through the artificial engineering of the bailout. In doing so, it had invited a catastrophe that is much more harmful when it takes place at the eventual collapse of this decaying system than if it had been allowed to collapse and self-organize naturally. The case of the European Union's interjection in Greece, the IMF (International Monetary Fund) interjection in Egypt, and the U.S. government's interjection to save Wall Street are other examples.

According to Dawoody (2013), the Middle East is a rich region. It has the world's largest oil reserves located in countries such as Saudi Arabia, Iraq, Iran, Algeria, Libya, Kuwait, UAE, Qatar, and Oman (Black, 2011). A large segment of the population in the Middle East is also skilled and highly educated, with the youth constituting a large portion (Djerejian, 2009). The region's wealth is also complemented by richness in history, culture, and past scientific achievements (Goldschmidt, 2005). The region's diversity in languages, social and ethnic groups, folklore, and deeply rooted societal values also contribute to its resiliency against internal and external threats (Lust, 2013). This is in addition to the region's capacity to adapt and learn from other models (Bradfer, 2011). Another opportunity is networking with expatriates from many countries in the Middle East who have migrated abroad and gained sufficient expertise, wealth, and knowledge that can be beneficial for the region. Some of these expatriates are Nobel laureates, scientists, artists, economists, journalists, and political leaders. Networking between the region and these expatriates can promote venues for openness, and increase technological, academic, artistic, social, economic, and scientific developments. Networking can also involve cooperation with global organizations in the fields of arts, sciences, and technologies to foster progress through innovation and change.

There are many challenges facing the Middle East as a region. According to Dawoody (2013), the most important are the following:

- Economic Disparity: Although the region includes some of the wealthiest oil-producing countries, and the per-capita in these countries is among the highest in the world, the majority of people in the Middle East are among the poorest in the world (Aydin, 2005). This economic disparity, coupled with increasingly alarming over-populated poor communities is becoming a recipe for discontent, upheaval, and unrest. The Arab Spring is an example for such malcontent (Gelvin, 2012).

- Political Tyranny: The Middle East is, to a large extent, nondemocratic, authoritarian, elitist, and governed through police-states (Heydemann, 2000)—both before and after the Arab Spring. Basic forms of individual rights and freedom are missing. Accountability, transparency, ethics, and citizen participation in governance are virtually non-existent. On the other hand, nepotism, censorship, political oppression, unlawful detention, torture, kidnapping, and summary execution are rampant (Habeed, 2012). Such a challenge can lead to social upheaval and unrest. The current revolution in Syria against the despotic al-Assad regime is an example.

- Ineffective Public Administration: Many countries in the Middle East suffer from a heavily politicized, inept, incompetent, and corrupt public administration (Long, Reich, & Gasiorowski, 2010). In effect, public administration in the Middle East reflects the decadent nature of the region's political reality by emphasizing the deficiency of transparent and accountable civic institutions, lack of merit-based professional cadre, and the absence of apolitical civil service systems (Dabashi, 2012). Ineffective public administration in the Middle East also contributes to the institutionalization of corruption, incompetence, low-productivity rate, lack of sound planning and evaluation, and a paralysis in public service.

- Reactionary Cultural Traditions: Some reactionary cultural traditions and their residuals are decapitating the Middle East and holding it from living up to its fullest potentials (Djerejian, 2009; Heydemann, 2000). Examples of these reactionary traditions are disempowering women, suppressing voices of dissent, oppressing minorities, and favoring collectivism over individual freedom (Moghadam & Karshenas, 2006). Instead, outdated norms are enforced and justified as traditions, such as tribalism, chauvinism, bigotry, honor killing, female genital mutilation, and misogynist behaviors (Joseph & Slyomovics, 2000).

- Lack of Accountability: Most governments in the Middle East are notorious for avoiding accountability, shifting blames outward, and enforcing the sense of victimhood (Dabashi, 2012). The result is the avoidance of self-criticism and the inability to arrive at realistic solutions for social, political, and economic problems. Moving through a crisis without any meaningful solution while blaming outsiders for the crisis becomes a justification for maintaining the status quo and avoiding any obligation to accomplish real services for the public (Lynch, 2013).

- Mistrust: There is an old saying in the Middle East that states "we agree to disagree." This notion is based on centuries of mistrust in the Middle East between governmental apparatus and the public. This, in return, has contributed to the lack of transparency and accountability in governance, the institutionalization of corruption, and the prevalence of unethical conducts and abuse of power (Moghadam & Karshenas, 2006).

- The Curse of Oil: The reliance on oil as the source of public revenue in the Middle East has eliminated the need for a system of taxation to support governmental functions. As a consequence, governmental accountability to the taxpayers has been eliminated (Chaudhry, 1997). The reliance on oil revenue, as such, is enabling governments in the Middle East to be unaccountable for the public while benefiting the very few who reside at the helms of political power (Heydemann, 2000).

- Israeli–Palestinian Conflict: The unresolved Israeli–Palestinian issue has enabled governments in the Middle East to manipulate the issue in order to shift attention away from them (Dabashi, 2012). The false slogan of "resisting Israel in support of the Palestinian people" by Iran and Syria, for example, has been a clever disguise to camouflage these regimes' despotism and an excuse to justify their lack of democratic reforms (Heydemann & Leenders, 2013).

## Learning from BRICS

There are more commonalities within the countries of the Middle East than between Brazil, Russia, India, China, and South Africa. Yet, and despite the few commonalities between Brazil, Russia, India, China, and South Africa, these five countries were successful in creating an economic block that is beneficial to their economy in particular and to the global economy as a whole. Even though political differences between these four countries are vast, these differences did not become barriers for the creation of their "cooperative" block. The Middle East can learn from such a model, especially when it has more opportunities for success than the BRIC model because of the region's shared attributes (Dawoody, 2013).

According to Dawoody (2013), all members of the model, with South Africa currently joining the block to make the model hence known as BRICS (*Economist*, 2013) are developing Third World nations. They share many characteristics with the Middle East in this regard. The innovative approach in the BRICS model and its unique use of human capital can also be another learning element for the Middle East. Thus, the BRICS model can provide a useful blueprint for identifying strengths, weaknesses, opportunities, and threats (SWOT) facing the Middle East and devise strategies for planning an environment suitable for the emergence of a regional cooperative that may lead the Middle East toward prosperity and force governance to be more responsive to citizens' needs. Learning from the BRICS model can also provide an environment for the training and development of a credible, transparent, accountable, and competent administrative cadre that can become instrumental in moving the region forward through coordination and collective planning and decision-making processes (Jones, 2012).

In order to learn from the BRICS model, establish a credible public administration, and devise a formula for offsetting challenges through the correct use of opportunities, several measures are needed without having to resort to prediction, control, or sustaining outdated systems through artificial engineering. These measures, according to Dawoody (2013), include creating transparent and accountable civic institutions, providing partnerships between the public and civic institutions through continuous dialogues, openness, evaluations, and assessments, improving the standards of public service through a merit-based system and direct accountability to the public, supporting freedom of expression and gathering in order to eliminate past practices of censorship, respecting voices of dissent, and establishing clear and strict ethical codes in public service. It also includes divorcing public administration from the political process, eliminating corruption, fraud, abuse, nepotism, cronyism, and misuse of public funds, eradicating outdated reactionary cultural norms and empowering women and minority groups, establishing an ongoing network between academia and practitioners to help build a credible cadre of apolitical and professional public administration, and providing a medium for experts in public policy and administration to share experiences and examine successful models for governance in the world, such as the BRICS model (Dawoody, 2013).

Learning measures, according to Dawoody (2013), can also include creating public forums as watch guards for the public interest, increasing the role of professional public administrators in capacity-building, building relationships between international and regional professional organizations devoted to the public interest and democratization, providing legal safeguards for investments and economic developments in the region, and promoting innovation in technology and scientific research devoted to improving the quality of life in the Middle East. Learning from the BRICS model may also include measures such as encouraging investments and capital ventures in the Middle East, establishing sound trade policies that will encourage economic growth and employment, increasing the quality of teaching and education in public policy and administration in the Middle East, increasing the representation of women, ethnic, and minority groups in governance, shifting public discourse from personality cult and hero worshipping toward the building of competent and democratic civic institutions, promoting peace and prosperity in the Middle East and ending all forms of violence, promoting globalization and shifting the status quo toward new possibilities, conducting workshops and training for practitioners in public policy and administration, and contributing to ongoing researches on public policy and administration in the Middle East (Dawoody, 2013).

## Conclusion

We need to accept and get comfortable with the absence of visible causal links between elements masking a high degree of interdependence and extremely low predictability. No matter how much time we spend on devising models and instruments for predictability, we will never be able to trace chance (Capra, 2004). So policymakers and public administrators should be trained to avoid control, predictability, the use of catalyst as cause, or explaining systems through events (especially last events).

Once we accept that predictability is fraught with difficulties, we need to overcome the fear of chance and randomness (Juarrero & Rubino, 2008). When accepting that stability is an illusion that we should not constantly try to maintain, randomness and variation are not feared, but rather welcomed since they are the source of variation and innovation. That is, when we allow for complexity to govern our analyses and observations, we can rescue ourselves from control and prediction. This, of course, means that low probability risks are no longer neglected or pushed away into end tails statistical probabilities. In fact, they need to be visible to allow for volatility. This volatility is necessary in order for the complex system to self-organize.

This understanding will shift the emphasis from control to enhanced flexibility, in which systems are allowed their natural booms and busts, where collapse is a natural consequence in system morphology, instead of massive blowups. Systems would be able to absorb our imperfection rather than that we seek to change them.

As such, a typical dynamic system can exhibit a variety of temporal behavior. When the behavioral history of a system is examined, the nature of change becomes the core of its inquiry (Brown, 1995). If a system becomes unstable, it will move first into a period of oscillation, swinging back and forth between two different states. After this oscillation stage, the next state is chaos, and it is then the wild gyrations begin (Dawoody, 2011; Wheatley, 2006).

If we look at public policy in the Middle East as a dynamic system and examine the nature of changes within it, especially in relation to the economy, we can see these changes requiring oscillation, chaos, and the birth of new order. However, often these changes are artificially engineered in the shape of reforms in order to stop the systemic collapse and prolong its decaying structure beyond its natural time.

We need to realize that fluctuations can take place (Kendall, Schaffer, Tidd, & Olsen, 1997). Fluctuations are initiated by changes in the environment and lead to corresponding changes within the system through positive and negative feedback. Positive feedback translates changes in the environment to more changes in the system's internal dynamics, and fewer changes in the environment will lead to fewer changes within the system. Negative feedback, on the other hand, is when more changes in the environment lead to fewer changes within the system, while fewer changes in the environment lead to more changes within the system (Morgan, 2006). This environmental stochasticity increases the probability of some policies of program extinction. The policies and programs that evolve are those that are selected against (Dawoody, 2011; Kendall, Schaffer, Tidd, & Olsen, 1997).

The resulting configuration within the system's internal order is emergent, allowing for new structures, patterns and processes to emerge through self-organization in order to fit best with the changing dynamics in the environment (Vesterby, 2008). The relationship between the system and its environment is an active relationship that benefits from feedback and translates into systemic morphology (Ruelle, 1993). Stimuli from the environment and the system's response are based on short or long-term transitions and corresponding changes in the system's internal dynamics are irreducible, unpredictable, and nonlinear (Dawoody, 2011).

Newton's laws in physics and the subsequent linear interpretation that came out of it was a tremendous step in human progress that unveiled new frontiers, including in public policy. These perspectives helped shaping modern decision-making processes, analytical thinking, and interpretations of the world (Kauffman, 1993). However, nonlinearity has uncovered an entire new frontier (Kiel, 1999) that transcends singular causality, certainty, predictability, hierarchy, centralization, and control (Wheatley, 2006). It presents another way into looking to the world (Dawoody, 2011; Kaplan & Glass, 1997).

The linear approach to public policy reduces process to the simplistic notions of accountability versus non-accountability. Citizenry interests are simplified into public opinion, which triggers the political system to irritate the administrative system, reducing responsiveness and causing the alienation of citizenry itself (Little, 1999). It is this drive toward nonlinearity that places demands on public policy to develop new perspectives for dealing with challenges (Kiel, 1999).

In order for public policy to live within a continually changing environment of the economy, it must act as a dynamically adapting system. This nonlinear system must be composed of many interacting and autonomous agents on global, national, state, and local levels. Each agent has to be associating with the other as partners. In such a scheme, no single agent can be poised in a controlling position. Instead, the autonomy and network nature of the associations among the agents must enable continuous transformation of the economy by meshing more suitably with changes in the external structures of the economic system than to trap it within an outdated mode or order (Dawoody, 2011).

According to Dawoody (2010), in transforming the public's economic "needs" from a hierarchal structural order into a nexus, governmental self-actualization can be transformed from a final stage in a hierarchical setting into an element within a complex and interconnected process that is integral to the process itself. Self-actualization will then not be regarded as a separate part of progression and there would not be duality between process and goal. Instead, goal and process will be interconnected within a web of holistic treatment, observation, and morphology. In essence, the process will be transformed into self-actualization through phase-shift toward emergence. In discovering and rediscovering needs within this process of self-actualization, governance will be self-organizing itself to deal better with the global market and geopolitics through an interconnected series of interplay based on autonomously emerging dynamic capacities. Within the morphology of this process, integrated needs will either mature, collapse, or morph to other needs and contribute to the systemic self-actualization in governance.

By restructuring public needs/demands in governance from a hierarchical order into a loop of association, old structural procedures both in political dialogue and administrative systems will have to identify societal and national needs not according to hierarchal order, influence of special interests, or as a response to events. Rather, these needs have to be connected together as integral parts of one nexus that requires collaboration among various players for the purpose of resource allocation, programming, and strategic planning based on coordination. Policymakers and public administrators in the Middle East must allow for internal changes to take place within governance in the region in response to changes in the region's environment (Dawoody, 2010).

We need to shift our focus from control to influence and from prediction to anticipation. We need to deemphasize prediction and long-term planning. Instead, we need to acknowledge the uncertain outcome of deterministic systems, accept the unexpected and random consequences, and engage in processes and pattern observation. This orbital decomposition will enable us be part of self-transcendency constructs, appreciate patterns of similarities and differences, welcome change, and better prepare for emergence of the new (Dawoody, 2010). One of the most important lessons learned from the Arab Spring is that predictability and control are fruitless. If the Mubarak regime in Egypt, the Bin Ali regime in Tunisia, the al-Qaddafi regime in Libya, the Salih regime in Yemen, and the al-Assad regime in Syria were able to predict the Arab Spring before it took hold, or if they were capable of controlling their populous under the continuous yoke of tyranny, they would not be in where they are now - the trash bin of history.

The future of the Middle East, without a need for prediction and linear analysis, is hopeful. The Arab Spring is an ongoing process in a continuous cycle of change. This is why learning from other models in the world, such as the BRICS model, can be useful.

# REFERENCES

## PART 5

## Israeli Elections and the Middle East Peace Process

## References

Aronoff, M. J. (1993). *Power and ritual in the Israel Labor Party: A study in political anthropology.* Armonk, NY: M. E. Sharpe.

Golan, A., & Nakdimon, S. (1978). *Begin* (in Hebrew). Tel Aviv, Israel: Yedioth Aharonot.

Hurwitz, H., & Medad, Y. (Eds.). (2011). *Peace in the making: The Menachem Begin-Anwar Sadat personal correspondence.* New York, NY: Gefen.

Olmert, J. (2011). Israel–Syria: The elusive peace. *Digest of Middle East Studies, 20*(2), 202–211.

Oren, M. B. (2002). *Six days of war, June 1967 and the making of the modern Middle East.* Oxford, UK: Oxford University Press.

Peled, Y. (2001). *Shas: Etgar Ha –Yisraeliyut* (in Hebrew). Tel Aviv, IL: Yedioth Aharonot.

Shapira, Y. (1991). *The road to power: Herut Party in Israel.* Albany, NY: SUNY Press.

Yanai, N. (1981). *Party leadership in Israel: Maintenance and change.* Philadelphia, PA: Turtledove.

# The Palestinian Reconciliation Process and its Impact on the Political System: A Post-Arab Spring View

## References

Abbas, M. (2011, 23 September). Full transcript of Abbas speech at UN General Assembly: Palestinian President Mahmoud Abbas addresses UN General Assembly after submitting application for recognition to UN Chief Ban Ki-moon. *Haaretz.* Retrieved from http://www.haaretz.com/news/diplomacy-defense/full-transcript-of-abbas-speech-at-un-general-assembly-1.386385

Abbas to head unity government as factions signed agreement. (2012, 6 February). *Ma'an News Agency.* Retrieved from http://maannews.net/eng/ViewDetails.aspx?ID=458196

al-Rabi' al-'Arabi wara' ziadat wazn qiadat al-dakhil 'ala hisab qiadat al-kharij. (2012, 29 January). *Al-Sharq al-Awsat.* Retrieved from http://aawsat.com/details.asp?section=4&issueno=12115&article=661034&feature=

Ben-Yishai, R. (2011, 24 August). IDF investigation: Egyptians took part in the attack near Eilat. *Ynet.* Retrieved from http://www.ynetnews.com/articles/0,7340,L-4113302,00.html

Brand, L. (1988). *Palestinians in the Arab world: Institution building and the search for state.* New York, NY: Columbia University Press.

Cobban, H. (1985). *The Palestinian Liberation Organization: People, power, and politics.* Cambridge, UK: Cambridge University Press.

Cole, J. (2006). Anti-Americanism: It's the policies. *The American Historical Review, 111*(4), 1120–1129.

Frisch, H. (1998). *Countdown to statehood Palestinian state formation in the West Bank and Gaza.* Albany, NY: SUNY Press.

Gaza leader promises 'difficult days' for Israel. (2012, 9 January). *Al-Ahram Online.* Retrieved from http://english.ahram.org.eg/NewsContentPrint/2/0/31269/World/0/Gaza-leader-promises-difficult-days-for-Israel.aspx

Hamas' Meshaal urges West to back Palestinian deal. (2011, 8 May). *Jerusalem Post.* Retrieved from http://english.ahram.org.eg/NewsContentPrint/2/0/31269/World/0/Gaza-leader-promises-difficult-days-for-Israel.aspx

Hass, A. (2012, 23 December). Two years of Arab Spring: Tunis, Cairo ... Ramallah? *Haaretz.* Retrieved from http://www.haaretz.com/news/features/two-years-of-arab-spring-tunis-cairo-ramallah.premium-1.489289

International Monetary Fund. (2011, 13 April). *Macroeconomics and fiscal framework for the West Bank and Gaza. Seventh review of progress.* Staff report for the meeting of the ad hoc liaison committee. Retrieved from http://www.imf.org/external/country/ WBG/RR/2011/041311.pdf

Ismail Haniya says Jihad is only strategic option for Islamic ummah. (2012, 11 February). *Teharen Times.* Retrieved from  http://www.tehrantimes.com/politics/95345-ismail-haniya-says-jihad-is-only-strategic-option-for-islamic-ummah-

Levi, E. (2011, 21 December). Abbas meets freed prisoners in Ankara. *Ynet.* Retrieved from http://www.ynetnews.com/articles/0,7340,L-4165039,00.html

Masadir lil-al-Quds: Nasa'ih khalijia li-Haniyah bi-'adm ziarat Iran. (2012, 7 February). *al-Quds.* Retrieved from http://www.alquds.com/news/article/view/id/331958

Parsons, N. (2005). *The politics of the Palestinian Authority: From Oslo to Al-Aqsa.* New York, NY: Routledge.

Rabbani, M. (2008). Khalid Mishal: The making of a Palestinian Islamic leader [Interview by Mouin Rabbani]. *Journal of Palestine Studies, 37*(1), 59–73.

Sayigh, Y. (1997). *Armed struggle and the search for state: The Palestinian national movement 1949–1993.* Oxford, UK: Clarendon Press.

Turkey says want host Hamas office. (2012, 30 January). *Today's Zaman,* Retrieved from http://www.todayszaman.com/news-270062-turkey-says-wont-host-hamas-office.html

# The Basis of China's Pro-Palestine Stance and the Current Status of its Implementation*

*The author wishes to express his gratitude to "Sino-Israel Global Network & Academic Leadership", the Israel Embassy and Shanghai Consulate in China, the Palestine Embassy in China, the Palestine Investment Fund, H. H. Ambassador Ramadan, China's Middle East Special Envoy H. H. Ambassador Wu Sike, and my colleague, Professor Liu Kang for their support for the idea and the execution of the trip.

## References

Chen, Y. (2012). China's relationship with Israel, opportunities and challenges: Perspectives from China. *Israel Studies, 17*(3), 1–21.

Daniel, B. (2013). Democracy at the bottom, meritocracy at the top, experimentation in between. *China–United States Exchange Foundation.* Retrieved from http://www.chinausfocus.com/political-social-development/democracy-at-the-bottom-meritocracy-at-the-top-experimentation-in-between/

Fan, H. (2012). Observations of the current conditions of Palestinians in Hebron H2 Sector. *World Ethno-National Studies, 4,* 71–79.

Sun, B. (2010). The historical dilemma of the Middle East problem and China's Middle East Policy. *Journal of China Executive Leadership Academy Pudong, 4,* 5–8.

Xu, J. (2012). Causes and lessons of the failure of Israel's public diplomacy. *West Asia and Africa, 4,* 43–55. Retrieved from http://www.cssn.cn/news/556962.htm

# PART 6

# ICT, Social Media, and the Arab Transition to Democracy: From Venting to Action

## References

*Agence France Presse.* (2006, June 14). Weblogs soar in Gulf States. Retrieved from http://www.aljazeera.com/archive/2006/06/2008410121639969113.html

*Al Arabiya.* (2013, June 12). Kuwait MPs pave way for setting up telecoms regulator. Retrieved from http://english.alarabiya.net/en/2013/06/12/Kuwait-MPs-pave-way-for-setting-up-telecoms-regulator-.html

Al-Hakeem, M. (2008, September 8). Islamists call on Saudi leaders to act against 'dangerous' liberal ideology. *Gulfnews.com.* Retrieved from http://m.gulfnews.com/islamists-call-on-saudi-leaders-to-act-against-dangerous-liberal-ideology-1.130379?utm_referrer=

*Al Jazeera.* (2011, February 14). Timeline: Egypt's revolution. Retrieved from http://www.aljazeera.com/news/middleeast/2011/01/201112515334871490.html

Almadhoun, S. (2010). Status of freedom of information legislation in the Arab world. *Right2Info.org* Retrieved from http://goo.gl/XsQYWz

Al-Mukhtar, R. (2013, March 25). Saudi Arabia to ban Skype. *Arab News*. Retrieved from http://www.arabnews.com/news/446001

Alterman, J. B. (1998). *New media, new politics? From satellite television to the Internet in the Arab world*. Washington, DC: Washington Institute for Near East Policy.

*Arabian Gazette*. (2013, May 31). MENA Internet users. Retrieved from http://arabiangazette.com/mena-internet-users-infographic-20130531/

Arab Network for Human Rights Information. (n.d.). Implacable adversaries: Arab governments and the Internet. Retrieved from http://www.anhri.net/en/wp-content/uploads/2012/02/Implacable-Adversaries.pdf

*Associated Press*. (2007, February 9). Bloggers in Mideast transforming dialogue but face clampdowns by authorities. Retrieved from http://usatoday30.usatoday.com/news/world/2007-02-09-mideast-blogs_x.htm?csp=34

*Associated Press*. (2013, June 10). Kuwait woman gets 11-year prison sentence for Twitter posts against emir. Retrieved from http://www.foxnews.com/world/2013/06/10/reports-kuwait-woman-gets-11-year-prison-sentence-for-twitter-posts-against/

*Associated Press in Doha*. (2012, November 29). Qatari poet jailed for life after writing verse inspired by Arab spring. *The Guardian*. Retrieved from http://www.guardian.co.uk/world/2012/nov/29/qatari-poet-jailed-arab-spring

Barrett, R. (2012, August 9). New trends in Arab defense spending. *Al-Akhbar*. Retrieved from http://english.al-akhbar.com/node/10936

BBC. (2010, June 19). The virtual revolution programme 2: Enemy of the state? Retrieved from http://www.bbc.co.uk/virtualrevolution/makingofprog2.shtml

*BostInno*. (2011, August 22). The Libyan revolution through social media. Retrieved from http://bostinno.streetwise.co/2011/08/22/the-libyan-revolution-through-social-media/

Boustany, N. (2004, April 30). Al-Jazeera's learning curve. *Washington Post*. Retrieved from http://www.highbeam.com/doc/1P2-173900.html

Bradshaw, T., & Blitz, J. (2011, June 15). Anti-Gaddafi forces add Twitter to armoury. *Financial Times* (London). Retrieved from http://www.ft.com/intl/cms/s/73b8b1c4-9770-11e0-af13-00144feab49a,Authorised=false.html?_i_location=http%3A%2F%2Fwww.ft.com%2Fcms%2Fs%2F0%2F73b8b1c4-9770-11e0-af13-00144feab49a.html&_i_referer=#axzz1ZoY9xO4P

Bulos, N. (2013, August 2). Syria opens new front in social media war: Instagram. *Los Angeles Times* Retrieved from http://www.latimes.com/news/world/worldnow/la-fg-wn-syria-president-bashar-assad-instagram-20130801,0,4908939.story

Burkhart, G. E., & Older, S. (2003). *The information revolution in the Middle East and North Africa: Mr-1653, Issue 1653*. Santa Monica, CA: Rand Corporation. Retrieved from http://www.rand.org/content/dam/rand/pubs/monograph_reports/2005/MR1653.pdf.

Carnegie Endowment for International Peace. (2010, September 22). Kifaya (The Egyptian movement for change). Retrieved from http://egyptelections.carnegieendowment.org/2010/09/22/the-egyptian-movement-for-change-kifaya

Central Intelligence Agency. (2011, September 27). Libya. *CIA World Fact Book*. Retrieved from https://www.cia.gov/library/publications/the-world-factbook/geos/ly.html

Central Intelligence Agency. (2013a, July 10). Tunisia. *CIA World Fact Book*. Retrieved from https://www.cia.gov/library/publications/the-world-factbook/geos/ts.html

Central Intelligence Agency. (2013b, July 10). Egypt. *CIA World Fact Book*. Retrieved from https://www.cia.gov/library/publications/the-world-factbook/geos/eg.html

Chomsky, N. (2011, March 29). Egypt, Tunisia, Mideast, India, and Class . . . [Interview with S. Pattanayak]. *Znet*. Retrieved from http://www.zcommunications.org/egypt-tunisia-mideast-india-and-class-by-noam-chomsky

Chozick, A. (2012, November 29). Official Syrian Web sites hosted in U.S. *New York Times*. Retrieved from http://www.nytimes.com/2012/11/30/world/middleeast/official-syrian-web-sites-hosted-in-us.html?_r=0

CNN. (2013, May 7). Khalfan abandons Twitter in celebration of the disqualification of the Brotherhood in Egypt]. Retrieved from http://arabic.cnn.com/2013/middle_east/7/5/khalfan.brotherhood/index.html

CPJ (Committee to Protect Journalists). (2004, December 1). CPJ concerned about government censorship. Retrieved from http://cpj.org/2004/12/cpj-concerned-about-government-censorship.php

CPJ (Committee to Protect Journalists). (2007, February 2). Egyptian blogger jailed for insulting Islam, Mubarak. Retrieved from http://cpj.org/2007/02/egyptian-blogger-jailed-for-insulting-islam-mubara.php

CPJ (Committee to Protect Journalists). (2012, May 2). 10 most censored countries [Special Report]. Retrieved from http://www.cpj.org/reports/2012/05/10-most-censored-countries.php#runners-up

Deen, T. (2004, October 13). Is Al-Jazeera the new symbol of Arab nationalism? *Antiwar.com*. Retrieved from http://www.antiwar.com/ips/deen.php?articleid=3772

Dettmer, J. (2013, April 4). Syria's Media War. *The Daily Beast*. Retrieved from http://www.thedailybeast.com/articles/2013/04/04/syria-s-media-war.html

*Economist*. (2008, February 7). How governments handle the news. Retrieved from http://www.economist.com/node/10666436

El-Amrani, I. (2010, January 24). Taming Arab satellite television. *The Arabist*. Retrieved from https://arabist.net/?tag=satellite

Elkin, M. (2011, February 2). New video: Cairo geeks survive Tahrir Square assault. Retrieved from http://www.wired.com/dangerroom/2011/02/cairos-band-of-geeks-survives-tahrir-square-assault

*Emirates24/7*. (2011, October 30). Arab population hits 367 million. http://www.emirates247.com/news/region/arab-population-hits-367-million-2011-10-30-1.425959

*Eurasia Review*. (2012, November 10). US blasts Iran over torture and death of blogger, extends state of emergency order. Retrieved from http://www.eurasiareview.com/10112012-us-blasts-iran-over-torture-and-death-of-blogger-extends-state-of-emergency-order/

Fisher, W. (2004). Arab Internet users are caught in a terrible web. *Arab Info Guide.* Retrieved from http://arabinfo.blogspot.com/2004/12/arab-internet-users-are-caught-in.html

Freedom House. (2012a). Freedom of the press: Oman. Retrieved from http://www.freedomhouse.org/report/freedom-press/2012/oman

Free speech in the media during the Libyan civil war. (2013, August 5). *Wikipedia.* Retrieved from http://en.wikipedia.org/wiki/Free_speech_in_the_media_during_the_Libyan_civil_war

Howard, P. N., Duffy, A., Freelon, D., Mari, W., & Mazaid, M. (2011). Opening closed regimes: What was the role of social media during the Arab Spring? *Project on Information Technology & Political Islam-Working Paper 2011.1.* University of Washington, Dept. of Communication. Retrieved from http://www.scribd.com/doc/66443833/Opening-Closed-Regimes-What-Was-the-Role-of-Social-Media-During-the-Arab-Spring

Human Rights Watch. (2005, November). *False freedom: Online censorship in the Middle East and North Africa, 17*(10). Retrieved from http://www.hrw.org/node/11563/section/3

Human Rights Watch. (2013, June 30). *Saudi Arabia: 7 convicted for Facebook postings about protests: EU should publicly condemn prison terms for peaceful dissent.* Retrieved from http://www.hrw.org/news/2013/06/29/saudi-arabia-7-convicted-facebook-postings-about-protests

Internet Censorship by Country. (2013, August 4). *Wikipedia.* Retrieved from http://en.wikipedia.org/wiki/Internet_censorship_by_country

Internet World Stats. (2011, December 31). Arab speaking Internet users' stats. Retrieved from http://www.internetworldstats.com/stats19.htm

Internet World Stats. (2012a, June 30). Internet usage statistics for Africa. Retrieved from http://www.internetworldstats.com/stats1.htm

Internet World Stats. (2012b, December 31). Middle East: Iraq. Retrieved from http://www.internetworldstats.com/middle.htm

Internet World Stats. (2012c, June 30). Yemen: Internet usage, broadband and telecommunications reports. Retrieved http://www.internetworldstats.com/me/ye.htm

Internet World Stats. (2012d, June). Kuwait Internet usage and telecommunications. Retrieved from http://www.internetworldstats.com/me/kw.htm

Internet World Stats. (2012e, June 30). United Arab Emirates Internet usage, broadband and telecommunications reports. Retrieved from http://www.internetworldstats.com/me/ae.htm

Iraq Body Count. (2013). Documented civilian deaths from violence. Retrieved from http://www.iraqbodycount.org/database/Janardhan, N. (2011). New media: In search of equilibrium. In M. A. Tétreault, G. Okruhlik & A. Kapiszewski (Eds.), *Political change in the Arab Gulf States: Stuck in transition* (pp. 225-245). Boulder, CO: Lynne Rienner Publishers.

Karam, Z. (2013, July 31). Latest platform for Syria's president: Instagram. *cnsnews.com.* Retrieved from http://cnsnews.com/news/article/latest-platform-syrias-president-instagram

*Khaleej Times.* (2013, July 11). Survey reveals high levels of adoption of social media in Iraq. Retrieved from http://www.khaleejtimes.com/displayarticle.asp?xfile=data/middleeast/2013/July/middleeast_July117.xml&section=middleeast&col=

Khalifa, M. (2012, October 5). The role of information technology in defeating the Arab regimes: Facebook 2-0 Arab presidents. *International Federation of Library Associations and Institutions.* Retrieved from http://www.ifla.org/publications/the-role-of-information-technology-in-defeating-the-arab-regimes-facebook-2-0-arab-pres

List of countries by number Internet users. (2013, July 15). *Wikipedia.* Retrieved from http://en.wikipedia.org/wiki/List_of_countries_by_number_of_Internet_users

Lotan, G., Graeff, E., Ananny, M., Gaffney, D., Pearce, I., & Boyd, D. (2011). The revolutions were tweeted: Information flow during the 2011 Tunisian and Egyptian revolutions. *International Journal of Communication, 5,* 1375-1405. Retrieved from http://www.aish.es/files/laura/Revoluciones%20tuiteadas(1).pdf

Lubin, G. (2011, March 2). These are the controversial satellite photos that set off protests in Bahrain. *Business Insider.* Retrieved from http://www.businessinsider.com/bahrain-google-earth-2011-3?op=1

Maynard, A. (2013, April 28). 12 key statistics on how Tunisians use social media. *Wamda.* Retrieved from http://www.wamda.com/2013/04/12-key-statistics-on-how-tunisians-use-social-media-infographic

McEvers, K. (2013, July 24). Iraq's sectarian divide deepens amid Syrian conflict. *National Public Radio.* Retrieved from http://www.npr.org/templates/story/story.php?storyId=205058162&sc=17&f=

*Middle East Online.* (2005, March 15). Bahrainonline editor released. Retrieved from http://www.middle-east-online.com/english/?id=12986

MobiThinking. (2010). Using mobile Web-based research to deliver insights into the mobile-only generation: Interview with On Device Research. Retrieved from http://mobithinking.com/mobile-research-casestudy

*National.* (2009, March 9). UAE leads most gulf region with most Twitter users. Retrieved from http://www.thenational.ae/lifestyle/uae-leads-gulf-region-with-the-most-twitter-users

Neon Tommy. (2011). Egypt blacks out Web, texting and Twitter. *USCAnnenburg.* Retrieved from http://www.neontommy.com/news/2011/01/egypt-blacks-out-web-texting-and-twitter

News24.com. (2013, April 11). Kuwait seeks tough media penalties. Retrieved from http://www.news24.com/World/News/Kuwait-seeks-tough-media-penalties-20130411

Opennet.net. (2007). Yemen. Retrieved from https://opennet.net/sites/opennet.net/files/ONI_Yemen_2007.pdf

Preston, J. (2011, May 22). Seeking to disrupt protesters, Syria cracks down on social media. Retrieved from http://www.nytimes.com/2011/05/23/world/middleeast/23facebook.html?_r=0

Radsch, C. (2012, December 10). Revolutionaries unveiled: Cyberactivism & women's role in the Arab Uprisings. *Mufta.* Retrieved from http://muftah.org/revolutionaries-unveiled-cyberactivism-womens-role-in-the-arab-uprisings/

Rebhy, A. (2012, November 29). Lawyer: Qatari poet gets life for 'insulting' emir. *Associated Press.* Retrieved from http://bigstory.ap.org/article/lawyer-qatari-poet-gets-life-insulting-emir

Refugee Review Tribunal. (2009). RRT Research Response: IRN34845. *Research & Information Services Section.* Retrieved from http://www.refworld.org/pdfid/4b6fe2510.pdf

Reporters Without Borders. (2006, November 7). List of 13 Internet enemies. Retrieved from http://en.rsf.org/list-of-the-13-internet-enemies-07-11-2006,19603

Reporters Without Borders. (2010, March 18). Countries under surveillance 2010 - United Arab Emirates. Retrieved from http://www.refworld.org/docid/4c21f6661a.html

Reporters Without Borders (2011, March 11). Countries under surveillance: Libya. Retrieved from http://en.rsf.org/surveillance-libya,39717.html

*Reuters*. (2013a, March 31). Saudi Arabia may try to end anonymity for Twitter users. Retrieved from http://www.financialexpress.com/news/saudi-arabia-may-try-to-end-anonymity-for-twitter-users/1095377 and http://www.stateofsearch.com/the-arabic-web/

*Reuters*. (2013b, June 5). Saudi Arabia bans Viber Web communication tool. *Al Arabiya*. Retrieved from http://english.alarabiya.net/en/business/technology/2013/06/05/Saudi-Arabia-bans-Viber-web-communication-tool-.html

Ross, M. L. (2011, September/October). Will Oil Drown the Arab Spring? Democracy and the Resource Curse. *Foreign Affairs*. Retrieved from http://www.relooney.info/SI_Milken-Arabia/0-Important_32.pdf

RT. (2013, March 30). Social media crackdown: Saudi Arabia may spy on Twitter users. Retrieved from http://rt.com/news/saudi-arabia-twitter-control-084/

Sajbl, C. (2012). The Arabic Web: Numbers and facts. *The State of Search*. Retrieved from http://www.stateofsearch.com/the-arabic-web/

Sakr, N. (2007). *Arab media and political renewal: Community, legitimacy and public life*. London, UK: I.B. Tauris.

Salama, V. (2013a, March 29). Saudi Arabia: The Internet's enemy cracks down on Skype, Whatsapp, and Viber. Retrieved from http://www.thedailybeast.com/articles/2013/03/29/saudi-arabia-the-internet-s-enemy-cracks-down-on-skype-whatsapp-and-viber.html

Salama, V. (2013b, April 4) Middle East activists muzzled and arrested in Arab Gulf States. *The Daily Beast*. Retrieved from http://www.thedailybeast.com/articles/2013/04/04/middle-east-activists-muzzled-and-arrested-in-arab-gulf-states.html

Sanad, M. N. (2011, March 7). The people and army were never together. Retrieved from www.maikelnabil.com/2011/03/blog-post_07.html

Sankowska, H. (2007, May 2). Egypt's bloggers do it better. *Cafebabel.com*. Retrieved from http://www.cafebabel.co.uk/article/egypts-bloggers-do-it-better.html

Smith, G. (2012, August 24). How social media users are helping NATO fight Gadhafi in Libya. *Globe and Mail*. Retrieved from http://www.theglobeandmail.com/news/world/how-social-media-users-are-helping-nato-fight-gadhafi-in-libya/article583325/

Stepanova, E. (2011). The role if information communication technologies in the "Arab Spring": Implications beyond the region. Retrieved from http://www.gwu.edu/~ieresgwu/assets/docs/ponars/pepm_159.pdf

Tait, R. (2007, February 19). Iran shuts down website critical of president. *The Guardian*. Retrieved from http://www.guardian.co.uk/technology/2007/feb/19/news.newmedia

Tétreault, M. A., Okruhlik, G., & Kapiszewski, A. (Eds.) (2011). *Political change in the Arab Gulf states: Stuck in transition.* Boulder, CO: Lynne Rienner Publishers

TheAge.com. (2007, April 18). Bahraini blogger libel trial begins. Retrieved from http://news.theage.com.au/technology/bahraini-blogger-libel-trial-begins-20070418-82c.html

US Department of State. (2004, February 25). Saudi Arabia: Country reports on human rights practices. Retrieved from http://www.state.gov/j/drl/rls/hrrpt/2003/27937.htm

US Department of State. (2010). Internet in Libya (2010–2011). Retrieved from http://www.state.gov/j/drl/rls/hrrpt/2010/nea/154467.htm

US Department of State. (2011, April 8). 2010 human rights report: Libya. Retrieved from http://www.state.gov/j/drl/rls/hrrpt/2010/nea/154467.htm

US Department of State. (2012). Libya 2012 human rights report. *Bureau of Democracy, Human Rights and Labor.* Retrieved from http://www.state.gov/documents/organization/204585.pdf

Wali, S. O., & Sami, D. A. (2011, Janurary 28). Egyptian police using U.S.-made tear gas against demonstrators. ABC News. Retrieved from http://abcnews.go.com/Blotter/egypt-protest-police-us-made-tear-gas-demonstrators/story?id=12785598

Walters, T. J. (2012, November 14). Social media and the Arab Spring. Retrieved from http://smallwarsjournal.com/jrnl/art/social-media-and-the-arab-spring

Westall, S., & Lyon, A. (2013, July 31). Kuwait's ruler pardons people convicted of insulting him. *Firstpost.World* Retrieved from http://www.firstpost.com/world/kuwaits-ruler-pardons-people-convicted-of-insulting-him-998673.html

Wikipedia. (2013a, July 15). List of Countries by Number Internet Users." Retrieved from http://en.wikipedia.org/wiki/List_of_countries_by_number_of_Internet_users

Wikipedia. 2013b. Internet Censorship by Country. Retrieved August 4 from http://en.wikipedia.org/wiki/Internet_censorship_by_country

Wikipedia. 2013c. Free Speech in the Media During the Libyan Civil War. Retrieved August 5 from http://en.wikipedia.org/wiki/Free_speech_in_the_media_during_the_Libyan_civil war

Worth, R.F. 2010. Web Tastes Freedom Inside Syria, and It's Bitter. *New York Times*, Retrieved September 29. Retrieved from http://www.nytimes.com/2010/09/30/world/middleeast/30syria.html?_r=0

# Challenges of State-Controlled Media in Egypt

# References

*Africa Research Bulletin*. (2011a). All three indices show a return of confidence, *48*(7), 19202.

*Africa Research Bulletin*. (2011b). Fragile transition. *48*(10), 19297–19298.

*Africa Research Bulletin*. (2012a). Transition plans. *49*(2), 19191.

*Africa Research Bulletin*. (2012b). Filling the deficit. 49(3), 19489.

Ahram Online (2012, 11 March). Egypt parliament to consider rejecting US aid. Retrieved from http://english.ahram.org.eg/NewsContent/3/12/36526/Business/Economy/Egypt-parliament-to-consider-rejecting-US-aid.aspx

*Al Ahram* (2011a, 31 January). Mubarak yaltaki bi kadat 'al gaish [Mubarak meets his military commanders]. Retrieved from http://ar.wikipedia.org/wiki/

*Al Ahram* (2011b, 12 February). Al shaab 'askat 'al nizam [The people have toppled the regime]. Retrieved from http://ar.wikipedia.org/wiki

*Al Ahram* (2011c, 3 August). Al pharoon fi qafas 'al itiham [The pharaoh locked in a cage]. Retrieved from http://ar.wikipedia.org/wiki/

Al Ahram Center for Political & Strategic Studies. (2011). *January 25 revolution*. Cairo, EG: Rabei, O.

Bassiouni, A. (2012). *Egypt's revolution*. Cairo, EG: National Association for Culture.

Building a Better Egypt. (2011, 16 September). *School of Global Affairs and Public Policy, American University Cairo*. Retrieved from http://www.aucegypt.edu/GAPP/Pages/BuildingaBetterEgypt.aspx

Campbell, D. (2011). *Egypt unshackled: Using social media to attack the system*. Oxford, UK: Cambria.

Dubai School of Government. (2011, 11 December). *Arab social media report*. Retrieved from www.arabsocialmediareport.com

*Egypt Independent* (2013, 11 March). Maspero nearly LE20 bn in debt, says State TV official. Retrieved from http://www.egyptindependent.com/news/maspero-nearly-le20-bn-debt-says-state-tv-official

Feifer, G. (2011, 16 December). Looking for opportunity in the Egyptian crises, *Radio Free Europe*. Retrieved from http://www.rferl.org/content/egypt_united_states_commentary_mubarak_obama/2296838.html

GAPP Execed. (2010, 20 July). *GAPP executive education, American University Cairo*. Retrieved from http://www.aucegypt.edu/GAPP/execed/Pages/default.aspx

Khalil, A. (2012). *Liberation square*. Cairo, EG: AUC Press.

Khamis, S. & K. Vaughn. (2011, 6 November). Cyberactivism in the Egyptian revolution: How civic engagement and citizen journalism tilted the balance. *Arab Media and Society, 13*. Retrieved from http://www.arabmediasociety.com/?article=769

Radsch, C. C. (2011). Blogosphere and social media. In E. Laipson (Ed.), *Seismic shift: Understanding change in the Middle East,* (pp. 67–82). Washington, DC: Henry L. Stimson Center.

Shenker, J. & Siddique, H. (2010, 15 July). Hosni Mubarak left red faced over doctored red carpet photo. *The Guardian.* Retrieved from http://www.guardian.co.uk/world/2010/sep/16/mubarak-doctored-red-carpet-picture

Taylor, M. (2010). *Crises on campus: A bold plan for reforming our colleges and universities.* New York, NY: Alfred A. Knopf.

Trofimov, Y. (2011, 14 June). Egypt opposes U.S.'s democracy funding. *Wall Street Journal.* Retrieved from http://online.wsj.com/article/SB10001424052702304665904576383123301579668.html

Tucker, V. (2012, 25 January). Assessing Egypt in 'freedom in the world.' *Freedom House.* Retrieved from http://www.freedomhouse.org/blog/assessing-egypt-%E2%80%98freedom-world%E2%80%99

# Challenging a Terrorist Tag in the Media: Framing, the Politics of Resistance, and an Iranian Opposition Group

## References

AFP. (2009, 28 February). Iran urges Iraq to expel opposition group. Retrieved from http://www.google.com/hostednews/afp/article ALeqM5iQnDOb4ldCk74Y7ToO7UPjKtPqSA

Allen, K. (2011, 14 April). Camp Ashraf is a barometer of Iraq's human rights. *The Guardian.* Retrieved from http://www.guardian.co.uk/commentisfree/2011/apr/14/camp-ashraf-iraq-human-rights

Associated Press. (2012, 1 March). US offers the MEK a way off terror list. *Washington Post.* p. A10.

BBC News. (2007). PMOI. Retrieved July 17 from http://news.bbc.co.uk/2/hi/programmes/newsnight/6272661.stm. See also BBC News (2007, July 18).

BBC News. (2007, 18 July). *Washington snubbed Iran offer.* Retrieved July 18 from http://news.bbc.co.uk/2/hi/middle_east/6274147.stm

Benford, R. D., & Snow, D. A. (2000). Framing processes and social movements: An overview and assessment. *Annual Review of Sociology, 26*(1), 611–639.

Bennett, W. L. (1990). Toward a theory of press state relations in the United States. *Journal of Communication, 40*(2), 103–125

Birkland, T. A. (1998). Focusing events, mobilization, and agenda setting. *Journal of Public Policy, 18*(1), 53–74.

Bramlet-Solomon, S. (2001). Newspaper editorials show few regional differences. *Newspaper Research Journal, 22*(4), 28–43.

Callaghan, K., & Schnell, F. (2000). Media frames, public attitudes, and elite response: An analysis of the gun control issue. *Public Integrity, 1*(4), 47–74.

Callaghan, K., & Schnell, F. (2001). Assessing the democratic debate: How the news media frame elite policy discourse. *Political Communication, 18*(2), 183–212.

Chilton, P. (1987). Metaphor, Euphemism and the Militarization of Language. *Current Research on Peace and Violence, 10*(1), 7–19.

Chong, D., & Druckman, J. N. (2007). Framing public opinion in competitive democracies. *American Political Science Review, 101*(4), 637–655.

Cobb, R. W., & Elder, C. D. (1983). *Participation in American politics: The dynamics of agenda-building.* Baltimore, MD: Johns Hopkins University Press.

Cronin, A. K. (2003). The 'FTO List' and Congress: Sanctioning designated foreign terrorist organizations (Congressional Research Service Report RL32120). Washington, DC: US Government Printing Office, October 21.

Dalton, R. J., Beck, P. A., & Huckfeldt, R. (1998). Partisan cues and the media: Information flows in the 1992 presidential election. *American Political Science Review, 92*(1), 111–126.

Dicke, C., Hosenball, M., & Hirsh, M. (2005, 14 February). Looking for a few good spies. *Newsweek.* p. 30.

Druckman, J. N. (2001). On the limits of framing: Who can frame? *Journal of Politics, 63* (4), 1041–1066.

Dryfuss, R. (2002, March 25). Colin Powell's list: The targeting of 'terrorist' groups harks back to earlier repression of dissent, *The Nation Magazine.* Retrieved from http://www.thirdworldtraveler. com/Dissent/Colin_Powells_List.html

Dudouet, V. (2011). *Anti-terrorism legislation: Impediments to conflict transformation.* Berghof Policy Brief No. 2, 11/2011. Berghof Conflict Research. Retrieved from http://www.berghof-conflictresearch.org/en/publications/policy-briefs/

Edwards, S. (2008, 28 November). Disaster in the making: Call for UN to act. Iranian dissidents interned in Iraq. *The Gazette (Montreal).* p. A16.

Entman, R. (1993). Framing: toward clarification of a fractured paradigm. *Journal of Communication, 43*(4), 51–58.

Eurlex. (2012, 25 June). Council Decision 2012/333/CFSP of 25 June 2012 updating the list of persons, groups and entities subject to Articles 2, 3 and 4 of Common Position 2001/931/CFSP on the application of specific measures to combat terrorism and repealing Decision 2011/872/ CFSP. *Official Journal L, 165,* 72–74. Retrieved from http://eurlex.europa.eu/LexUriServ/ LexUriServ.do?uri=OJ:L:2012:165:0072:01:EN:HTML

Fender, B. J. (2007, 25 June). Britain's Foreign and Commonwealth Office. Second Witness Statement to Proscribed Organisations Appeal Commission, POAC. p. 4.

Foucault, M. (1980). *Power/knowledge: Selected interviews and other writings, 1972–1977.* Brighton, Sussex, UK: Harvester Press.

Freedom fighter or foe? (2003, 5 June). *The Australian.* p. 9.

Friedland, R., & Alford, R. R. (1991). Bringing society back in: Symbols, practices, and institutional contradictions. In W.W. Powell & P. J. DiMaggio (Eds.), *The new institutionalism in organizational analysis* (pp. 232–266). Chicago, IL: University of Chicago Press.

Gamson, W., & Wolfsfeld, G. (1993). Movement and media as interacting systems. *Annals of the American Academy of Political and Social Science, 528*, 104-125.

Gamson, W. A., & Lasch, K. E. (1983). The political culture of social welfare policy. In S. E. Spiro & E. Yuchtman-Yaar (Eds.), *Evaluating the welfare state* (pp. 397–415). New York, NY: Academic Press.

Gamson, W. A., & Modigliani, A. (1989). Media discourse and public opinion on nuclear power: A constructionist approach. *American Journal of Sociology, 95*(1), 1-37.

Gans, H. J. (1979). *Deciding what's news: A study of CBS evening news, NBC nightly news, Newsweek and Time.* New York, NY: Pantheon.

Goffman, E. (1974). *Frame analysis: An essay on the organization of experience.* New York, NY: Harper & Row.

Golan, G. J. (2010). Editorials, op-ed columns frame medical marijuana debate. *Newspaper Research Journal, 31*(3), 5–61.

Gross, J. (2011). Proscription problems: The practical implications of terrorist lists on diplomacy and peacebuilding in Nepal. *Praxis, 26*, 38–59.

Habermas, J. (1993). On the pragmatic, the ethical, and the moral employments of practical reason (C. P. Cronin, Trans.). In J. Habermas and C. P. Cronin (Eds.), *Justification and application: Remarks on discourse ethics* (pp. 1–17). Cambridge, MA: MIT Press.

Hamilton, G. (2012, 28 February). Help Iran's MEK: Chair of rights group; On terrorist list; Rights and democracy board members defend anti-regime force. *National Post.* p. A1.

Hamilton, J. T. (2004). *All the news that's fit to sell: How the market transforms information into news.* Princeton, NJ: Princeton University Press.

Helbling, M., Hoeglinger, D., & Wuest, B. (2010). How political parties frame European integration. *European Journal of Political Research, 49*(4), 496–521.

Herman, E. S., & Chomsky, N. (1988). *Manufacturing consent: The political economy of the mass media.* New York, NY: Pantheon.

Hooks, B. (1992). *Black looks: Race and representation.* Boston, MA: South End Press.

Hynds, E. C., & Martin, C. H. (1979). How non-daily editors describe status and function of editorial pages. *Journalism Quarterly, 56*(2), 318–323.

Isikoff, M. (2002, 26 September). Ashcroft's Baghdad connection. *Newsweek.* Retrieved from http://www.thedailybeast.com/newsweek/2002/09/25/ashcroft-s-baghdad-connection.html

Jehl, D. (2003, April). U.S. bombs Iranian guerrilla forces based in Iraq. *The New York Times,* 17, B1.

Keddie, N. R., & Richard, Y. (1981). *Roots of revolution: An interpretive history of modern Iran.* New Haven, CT: Yale University Press.

Kempster, N. (1997). US designates 30 groups as terrorists. *The Los Angeles Times.* Retrieved from http://articles.latimes.com/1997/oct/09/news/mn-40874

Kinder, D. R., & Sanders, L. M. (1996). *Divided by color: Racial politics and democratic ideals.* Chicago, IL: University of Chicago Press.

Kingdon, J. W. (1984). *Agendas, alternatives, and public policies*. New York, NY: HarperCollins.

Kingdon, J. W. (1995). *Agendas, alternatives and public policies* (2nd ed.). New York, NY: Longman.

LaFranchi, H. (2009, 31 July). US to investigate Iraqi raid on Iranian camp. *Christian Science Monitor*, p. 2.

Lazarsfeld, P. F., & Merton, R. K. (1948). Mass communication, popular taste and organized social action. In L. Bryson (Ed.), *The communication of ideas* (pp. 95–118). New York, NY: Harper & Row.

Leigh, D. (2005, 31 May). 'Tank girl' army accused of torture: Guardian and Human Rights Watch find evidence of abuse by Iranian revolutionaries under US protection. *The Guardian*, p. 9.

Mariner, J. (2003). Trivializing terror. *Counterpunch*. Retrieved from http:// www.counterpunch. org/2003/05/29/trivializing-terrorism /

Matesan, I. E. (2012). What makes a frame resonant? Hamas and the appeal of opposition to the peace process. *Terrorism and Political Violence, 24*(5), 671–705.

McAdam, D., & Scott, W. R. (2005). Organizations and movements. In G. F. Davis, D. McAdam, W. R. Scott, & M. N. Zald (Eds.), *Social movements and organization theory* (pp. 4–40). Cambridge, UK: Cambridge University Press.

McCarthy, J., & Zald, M. N. (1994). Resource mobilization and social movements: a partial theory. In M. N. Zald & J. McCarthy (Eds.), *Social movements in an organizational society: Collected essays* (pp. 15–48). New Brunswick, NJ: Transaction Books.

McCombs, M. E., & Shaw, D. L. (1972). The agenda-setting function of mass media. *Public Opinion Quarterly, 36*(2), 176–187.

Moin, B. (2001). *Khomeini: Life of the Ayatollah*. New York, NY: Thomas Dunne.

Morrison, J. (2010, August 9). European alert. *Washington Times*, World, p. A8.

Muller, M. (2008). Terrorism, proscription and the right to resist in the age of conflict. *Denning Law Journal, 20*, 111–131.

Nisbet, M. C., & Huge, M. (2006). Attention cycles and frames in the plant biotechnology debate: Managing power and participation through the press/policy connection. *Press/Politics, 11*(2), 3-40.

Norris, T. (2006). *Framing of gay rights in mass media outlets: A content analysis of newspaper editorial pages*. Paper presented at American Sociological Association, Montreal, Quebec, August 11–14. Retrieved from http://citation.allacademic.com/meta/p_mla_apa_research_citation/0/9/6/8/8/ p96880_index.html

Peterson, S. (2008, 11 February). Iran sees less threat in exiled MKO militants. *The Christian Science Monitor*, World, p. 6.

Peterson, S. (2011, 8 August). Iranian group's big-money push to get off US terrorist list. *The Christian Science Monitor*, p. 3.

Pfetsch, B., & Silke, A. (2011). *Media agenda building in online and offline media – Comparing issues and countries*. Paper presented at the 6th ECPR General Conference, University of Iceland, Reykjavik, August 25–27.

Pickett, B. L. (1996). Foucault and the politics of resistance. *Polity, 28*(4), 445–466.

Pillar, P. R. (2001). *Terrorism and US foreign policy*. Washington, DC: Brookings Institution Press.

Rabinowitz, A. (2010). Media framing and political advertising in the Patients' Bill of Rights debate. *Journal of Health Politics, Policy and Law, 35*(5), 771–795.

Reese, S. D. (1991). Setting the media's agenda: A power balance perspective. In J. A. Anderson (Ed.), *Communication yearbook* (pp. 309–340). Newbury Park, CA: Sage.

Richardson, J. D., & Lancendorfer, K. M. (2004). Framing affirmative action: The influence of race on newspaper editorial responses to the University of Michigan cases. *The International Journal of Press/Politics, 9*(4), 74–94.

Rochefort, D. A., & Cobb, R. W. (1994). Problem definition: An emerging perspective. In D.A. Rochefort, & R. W. Cobb (Eds.), *The politics of problem definition: Shaping the political agenda* (pp.1–31). Lawrence, KS: University Press of Kansas.

Rohlinger, D. A. (2002). Framing the abortion debate: organizational resources, media strategies, and movement-countermovement dynamics. *Sociological Quarterly, 43*(4), 479–507.

Ryan, C., Anastario, M., & Jeffreys, K. (2005). Start small, build big: negotiation opportunities in media markets. *Mobilization: An International Journal, 10*(1), 111–128.

Ryan, M. R. (2004). Framing the war against terrorism. *Gazette: The International Journal for Communication Studies, 66*(5), 363–382.

Safavi, A. (2009, 27 July). Freedom fighters labeled as terrorists. *Global Politician*. Retrieved from http://www.globalpolitician.com/default.asp?25756-ncri-mek-pmoi-iran/

Safavi, A. (2010, 2 March). Reality check: Understanding the Mujahedin-e Khalq (PMOI/MEK). *Huffington Post*. Retrieved from http://www.huffingtonpost.com/ali-safavi/mujahedin-e-khalq-pmoimek_b_482770.html

Schneider, B. (2012). Sourcing homelessness: How journalists uses sources to frame homelessness. *Journalism, 13*(1), 71–86.

Shapiro, J. (2008). The politicization of the designation of foreign terrorist organizations: The effect on the separation of powers. *Cardozo Public Law, Policy & Ethics Journal, 6*(3), 547–600.

Snow, D. A., & Benford, R. D. (1992). Master frames and cycles of protest. In A. D. Morris and C. M. Mueller (Eds.), *Frontiers in social movement theory* (pp. 133–155). New Haven, CT: Yale University Press.

Stock, N. (2012, 1 June). The wisdom of reforming terrorist designations. *Middle East Channel, Foreign Policy*. Retrieved from: http://mideast.foreignpolicy.com/posts/2012/06/01/the_wisdom_of_terrorist_designation_reform

Sullivan, G., & Hayes, B. (2011). Blacklisted: Targeted sanctions, preemptive security and fundamental rights. *European Center for Constitutional and Human Rights*. Retrieved from http://www.statewatch.org/news/2010/dec/eu-ecchr-blacklisted-report.pdf

Terkildson, N., Schnell, F. I., & Ling, C. (1998). Interest groups, the media and policy debate formation: An analysis of message structure, rhetoric and source cues. *Political Communication, 15*(1), 45–61.

Themner, L., & Wallensteen, P. (2011). Armed conflicts, 1946–2010. *Journal of Peace Research, 48*(4), 525–536.

Thomas, R. (2005). Theorizing the micro-politics of resistance: New public management and managerial identities in the UK public services. *Organization Studies, 26*(5), 683–706.

Tilly, C. (2004). Terror, terrorism, terrorists. *Sociological Theory, 22*(1), 5–13.

Tversky, A., & Kahneman, D. (1981). The framing of decisions and the psychology of choice. *Science, 211*(4481), 453–458.

Ungar, S. (2007). Public scares: changing the issue culture. In Moser, & L. Dilling (Eds.), *Creating a climate for change: Communicating climate change and facilitating social change* (pp. 81-88). Cambridge, UK: Cambridge University Press.

UN Security Council. (2013, March). *Al-Qaida sanctions list.* Retrieved from http://www.un.org/sc/committees/1267/aq_sanctions_list.shtml

US Department of State. (2012, 28 September). *Foreign terrorist organizations.* Retrieved from http://www.treasury.gov/resource-center/sanctions/SDN-List/Pages/default.aspx

US Department of State. (2012, 17 December). Individuals and Entities Designated by the State Department Under E.O. 13224. *Bureau of Counterterrorism.* Retrieved from http://www.state.gov/j/ct/rls/other/des/143210.htm

US Department of Treasury. (2013, 11 March). Specially designated nationals and blocked persons list. *Office of Foreign Assets Control.* Retrieved from http://www.treasury.gov/ofac/downloads/t11sdn.pdf

Van Dijk, T. A. (1996). Power and the news media. In D. Paletz (Ed.), *Political communication in action* (pp. 9–36). New York, NY: Hampton Press.

Wiktorowicz, Q. (2004). Framing jihad: Intramovement framing contests and Al-Qaeda's struggle for sacred authority. *International Review of Social History, 49*(S12), 159–177.

Zaller, J., & Chiu, D. (1996). Government's little helper: US press coverage of foreign policy crises, 1945–1991. Political Communication, 13, 385–405.

# PART 7

# Under New Management: What the Arab Spring Tells us about Leadership Needs in the Middle East and North Africa

## References

Abdallah, I. A., & al-Homoud, M. A. (2001). Exploring the implicit leadership theory in the Arabian Gulf States. *Applied Psychology: An International Review, 50*(4), 506–531.

Abdulla, F. (2010, February 15). Stereotypes can stymie the UAE's development. *The National.* Retrieved from http://www.thenational.ae/news/stereotypes-can-stymie-the-uaes-development

Abrahart, A., Kaur, I., & Tzannatos, Z. (2000). *Government employment and active labor market policies in MENA in a comparative international context.* Paper presented at MDF3, Cairo. Retrieved from http://info.worldbank.org/etools/docs/library/206519/almps%20in%20mena%202000.pdf

Akhtar, S. (2011, 26 February). MENA: Emerging developments and challenges. *AfricaBusiness.com.* Retrieved from http://africabusiness.com/2011/02/26/mena-emerging-developments-and-challenges/

al-Dabbagh, M., & Assaad, C. (2010a). Beyond leader development: Advancing new leadership development models in GCC. *Dubai School of Government Policy Brief,* Policy Brief No. 21, September.

al-Dabbagh, M., & Assaad, C. (2010b). Taking stock and looking forward: Leadership development in the Arab World. *Dubai School of Government Working Paper Series,* Working Paper No. 10-09, November.

al-Yahya, K. (2008). The over-educated, under-utilized Arab professional: Why doesn't human capital development bring desired outcomes? Evidence from Oman and Saudi Arabia, *Dubai School of Government Working Paper Series,* Working Paper No. 08-01, January.

al-Yahya, K. (2009, 2 July). *The Gulf paradox: Skilled people, in the wrong jobs.* Dubai, UAE: Dubai School of Government.

al-Yahya, K., Lubatkin, M., & Vengroff, R. (2009). The impact of culture on management and development: A comparative review. *Dubai School of Government Working Paper Series,* Working Paper No. 09-01.

Andersen, R. R., Seibert, R.F., & Wagner, J. G. (2012). *Politics and change in the Middle East* (10th ed.). Boston, MA: Longman Publishers.

Bell, A. H., & Smith, D. M. (2010). *Developing leadership abilities.* (2nd ed.). Upper Saddle River, NJ: Pearson.

Beschel, Jr., R. P. (2010). A note from the publisher. *Middle East and North Africa Governance News & Notes, 4*(1), 1-2.

Biygautane, M. (2011, May 15). Nation-building is about creating human capital. *Gulf News.* Retrieved from http://gulfnews.com/business/opinion/nation-building-is-about-creating-human-capital-1.807692

Boumarafi, B. (2009). Knowledge management approach to performance: A United Arab Emirates experience. *Digest of Middle East Studies, 18*(2), 17–26.

Carroll, W. K., & Carson, C. (2003). The network of global corporations and elite policy groups: A structure for transnational capitalist class formation? *Global Networks, 3*(1), 29–57.

Chaaban, J. (2010). Job creation in the Arab economies: Navigating through difficult waters. *Arab Human Development Report Research Paper Series*. United Nations Development Program.

Chene, M. (2007). Overview of corruption in MENA countries. *U4 Expert Answer; U4 Anti-Corruption Resource Centre.*

Cochran, A., & Pain, K. (2000). A globalizing society? In D. Held (Ed.), *A globalizing world? Culture, economics, politics* (pp. 5–46). New York, NY: Routledge.

Common, R. K. (2011). Barriers to developing leadership in the sultanate of Oman. *International Journal of Leadership Studies, 6*(2), 215–228.

Coleman, M. (2011). Transnational civic education inquiry in the lands of contention. *Digest of Middle East Studies, 20*(2), 277–290.

Crotty, S. (2010, September). Poor management is too pervasive not to be addressed. *Dubai School of Government.* Retrieved from http://www.dsg.ae/en/publication/Description.aspx?PubID=196&PrimenuID=11&mnu=Pri

Daft, R. L. (2008). *The leadership experience* (4th ed.). Mason, OH: Thomson South-Western.

Dastmalchian, A., Javidan, M., & Alam, K. (2001). Effective leadership and culture in Iran: An empirical study. *Applied Psychology: An International Review, 50*(4), 532–558.

Department of Economic and Social Affairs. (2007). *Innovations in governance in the Middle East, North Africa, and Western Balkans: Making governments work better in the Mediterranean region.* New York, NY: United Nations.

Dubai School of Government. (2007, September). *Executive summary - Women and leadership development: perspectives, policies and pedagogies workshop.* Dubai, UAE.

Dubai School of Government. (2008, 14 April). State of the region forum: Leveraging opportunity, managing risk. *State of the Region Forum.* Dubai, UAE.

el-Massnaoui, K. & Biygautane, M. (2011) Downsizing Morocco's public sector: Lessons from the voluntary retirement program: Case studies in governance and public management in the Middle East and North Africa, no. 3. Dubai, UAE: Dubai School of Government.

Fukuyama, F. (2008, 20 February). Challenges to democracy in the twenty-first century. [Distinguished speaker series] (pp.1-20). Johns Hopkins University.

George, B. (2003). *Authentic leadership: Rediscovering the secrets of creating lasting value.* San Francisco, CA: Jossey-Bass.

Giddens, A. (2002). *Runaway world: How globalization is reshaping our lives.* London, UK: Profile.

GIFT-MENA (n.d.). The directory of public service training institutes in MENA. *World Bank Institute.* Retrieved from http://www.ioflebanon.com/ResourcesPathDownloadLink/Directory%20of%20Civil%20Service%20Training%20Schools%20in%20MENA-eng-ar-09.pdf

Gurr, T. R. (1970). *Why men rebel.* Princeton, NJ: Princeton University Press.

Harris, R. G. (1993). Globalization, trade and income. *Canadian Journal of Economics, 26*(4), 755–776.

Held, D. (Ed). (2000). *A globalizing world? Culture, economics, politics.* New York, NY: Routledge.

Held, D. & McGrew, A. (1993). Globalization and the liberal democratic state. *Government and Opposition, 28*(3), 261–288.

Held, D. & McGrew, A. (2000). The great globalization debate: An introduction. In D. Held & A. McGrew (Eds.), *The Global transformations reader: An introduction to the globalization debate* (pp. 1–45). Malden, MA: Polity Press.

Hammoud, J. (2011). Consultative authority decision making: On the development and characterization of Arab corporate culture. *International Journal of Business and Social Science* [Special issue], *2*(9), 141–148.

Hofstede, G. (1980). Motivation, leadership and organization: Do American theories apply abroad? *Organizational Dynamics, 9*(1), 42–63.

Hofstede, G. (1984). *Culture's consequences: International differences in work-related values.* Beverley Hills, CA: Sage.

Jreisat, J. E. (2009a). Administration, globalization and the Arab states. *Public Organization Review, 9*(1), 37–50.

Jreisat, J. E. (2009b). Administrative development in the Arab world: Impediments and future reform strategies. *International Conference on Administrative Development: Towards Excellence in Public Sector Performance*, Saudi Arabia, November 1–4. Retrieved from http://www.fifty.ipa.edu.sa/conf/customcontrols/paperworkflash/Content/pdf/m3/en/3.pdf

Kalantari, B. (2005). Middle Eastern public management: A cultural approach to developmental administration. *Public Organization Review, 5*(2), 125–138.

Kennett, P. (2010). Global perspectives on governance. In S. P. Osborne (Ed.), *The new public governance? Emerging perspectives on the theory and practice of public governance* (pp. 19–35). New York, NY: Routledge.

Kettl, D. F. & Fesler, J. W. (2009). *The politics of the administrative process* (4th ed.). Washington, DC: CQ Press.

Khodr, H. (2012). The specialized cities of the Gulf Cooperation Council: A case study of a distinct type of policy innovation. *Digest of Middle East Studies, 21*(1), 149–177.

Khouri, R. G. (2008). Governance newsmaker [Interview: Dr. Tarik M. Yousef, founding Dean of the Dubai School of Government]. *Middle East and North Africa Governance News and Notes, 2*(5). Retrieved from http://web.worldbank.org/WBSITE/EXTERNAL/COUNTRIES/MENAEXT/EXTMNAREGTOPGOVERNANCE/0,,contentMDK:22014980~menuPK:4406842~pagePK:34004173~piPK:34003707~theSitePK:497024~isCURL:Y,00.html

Klingner, D. E. (2004). Globalization, governance, and the future of public administration: Can we make sense out of the fog of rhetoric surrounding the terminology? *Public Administration Review, 64*(6), 737–743.

Lee, M. (2000). Governing the holy land: Public administration in Ottoman Palestine, 1516–1918. *Digest of Middle East Studies, 9*(1), 1–25.

Leung, K. & Bond, M. H. (2004). Social axioms: A model for social beliefs in multicultural perspective. *Advances in experimental social psychology, 36*, 119–197.

Lynn, Jr., L. E. (2010). What endures? Public governance and the cycle of reform. In S. P. Osborne (Ed.), *The new public governance? Emerging perspectives on the theory and practice of public governance* (pp. 105–123). New York, NY: Routledge.

McQuaid, R. W. (2010). Theory of organizational partnership: Partnership advantages, disadvantages and success factors, In S. P. Osborne (Ed.), *The new public governance? Emerging perspectives on the theory and practice of public governance* (pp. 127–148). New York, NY: Routledge.

MacEwan, A. (1994). Globalization and stagnation. *Monthly Review, 44*(11), 1–15.

Mahmoud, N. S. (2003). Towards a strategy to deploy the Internet in developing countries. *Digest of Middle East Studies, 12*(1), 1–12.

Mameli, P. (2011). Achieving effective information privacy: A review of outcome measures used by national data protection authorities. *Proceedings of KAPA/ASPA International Conference, 1*, 105–144.

Mantzikos, I. (2011). Somalia and Yemen: The links between terrorism and state failure. *Digest of Middle East Studies, 20*(2), 242–260.

Meraj, A. (2009, January 1). Efficient government means accountability: We're getting it. *The National.* Retrieved from http://www.ifg.cc/index.php?option=com_content&task=view&id=266 77&Itemid=93&lang=german

Middle East and North Africa Vice Presidency. (2010). *Public financial management reform in the Middle East and North Africa: An overview of regional experience.* Report No. 55061-MNA. The World Bank. Retrieved from http://siteresources.worldbank.org/EXTGOVANTICORR/ Resources/30358631285103022638/MENARegionalPFMOverviewPartIFinal.pdf

Mishrif, A. & Selmanovic, S. (2010). E-government in the Middle East and North Africa: The role of international organizations in the experience of Egypt and Morocco. *2010 International Conference on Public Administration* (pp. 905–926). Retrieved from http://www.kcl.ac.uk/artshums/depts/ mems/people/staff/academic/mishrif/E-governmentintheMiddleEastandNorthAfrica.pdf

Nahavandi, A. (2009). *The art and science of leadership* (5th ed.). Upper Saddle River, NJ: Pearson Prentice Hall.

Newell, T., Reeher, G., & Ronayne, R. (Eds.). (2012). *The trusted leader: Building relationships that make government work* (2nd ed.). Washington, DC: Sage and CQ Press.

Northouse, P. G. (2009). *Introduction to leadership concepts and practice.* Los Angeles, CA: Sage.

Northouse, P. G. (2013). *Leadership: theory and practice* (6th ed.). Los Angeles, CA: Sage.

Osborne, S. P. (2010). Introduction: The (new) public governance: A suitable case for treatment? In S. P. Osborne (Ed.), *The new public governance? Emerging perspectives on the theory and practice of public governance* (pp. 1–18). New York, NY: Routledge.

Perry, G. E. (2000). The Middle East's primitive democratic tradition. *Digest of Middle East Studies, 9*(2), 18–53.

Pestoff, V. & Brandsen, T. (2010). Public governance and the third sector: Opportunities for co-production and innovation? In S. P. Osborne (Ed.), *The new public governance? Emerging perspectives on the theory and practice of public governance* (pp. 223–236). New York, NY: Routledge.

Roddick, A. (2001). *Take it personally: How globalization affects you and powerful ways to challenge it.* London, UK: Thorsons.

Sarayrah, Y. K. (2004). Servant leadership in the Bedouin-Arab culture. *Global Virtue Ethics Review, 5*(3), 58–79.

Saif, I. (2012, May 8). What prevents Arab students from pursuing vocational education? *Al-Hayat.* Retrieved from http://carnegieendowment.org/2012/05/08/what-prevents-arab-students-from-pursuing-vocational-education/aw72

Serrano, M. (2002). Transnational organized crime and international security: Business as usual? In M. Berdal, & M. Serrano (Eds.), *Transnational organized crime and international security: Business as usual?* (pp. 13–36). Boulder, CO: Lynne Rienner.

Smith, P. B., Achoui, M., & Harb, C. (2006). Unity and diversity in Arab managerial styles. *International Journal of Cross Cultural Management, 7*(3), 275–289.

Subotic, S. (2011). Lebanon: Enhancing meritocratic recruitment within the senior civil service. Case studies in governance and public management in the Middle East and North Africa, No. 2. Dubai, UAE: Dubai School of Government, World Bank.

Terry, L. D. (2003). *Leadership of Public Bureaucracies* (2nd ed). Armonk, NY: M.E. Sharpe, Inc.

Terry, R. W. (1993). *Authentic leadership: Courage in action.* San Francisco, CA: Jossey-Bass.

Tompkins, J. R. (2005). *Organization theory and public management.* Belmont, CA: Thomson/Wadsworth.

World Bank. (2012). *Program-for-results operation in support of the national initiative for human development, Phase 2: Technical assessment.* Retrieved from http://www-wds.worldbank.org/external/default/WDSContentServer/WDSP/IB/2012/07/17/000356161_20120717013914/Rendered/PDF/711730WP0P11620disclosed07016020120.pdf

World Economic Forum & Organization for Economic Cooperation and Development. (2011). *Arab World Competitiveness Report 2011–2012.* Retrieved from http://www3.weforum.org/docs/WEF_AWC_Report_2011-12.pdf

# Decentralization Needs Interest Mediation:
## The Moroccan Development Strategy and Partnering with Non-State Actors for the Promotion of Services Offshore

# References

Albrecht, H. (2008). The nature of political participation. In E. Lust-Oskar, & S. Zerhouni (Eds.), *Political participation in the Middle East* (pp. 15–31). London, UK: Lynne Rienner.

Alhamad, L. (2008). Formal and informal venues of engagement. In E. Lust-Oskar, & S. Zerhouni (Eds.), *Political participation in the Middle East* (pp. 33–49). London, UK: Lynne Rienner.

Assens, C., & Abirran, Y. (2010). Networking et pôles de compétitive: Le cas du Technopark de Casablanca, *Innovations, 1*(31), 157–180.

Bellin, E. (2000). Contingent democrats: Industrialists, labor, and democratization in late-developing countries. *World Politics, 52*(2), 175–205.

Bergh, S. I. (2013). 'Inclusive' neoliberalism, local governance reforms and the redeployment of state power: The case of the National Initiative for Human Development (INDH) in Morocco, *Mediterranean Politics, 17*(3), 410–426.

Chabih, J. (2005). *Les finances des collectivités locales au Maroc: Essai d'une approche globale des finances locales.* Paris, FR: L'Harmattam.

Djeflat, A. (1996). Strategies for science and technology-based development and transition: The Maghreb perspective. In G. Zwadie, & A. Djeflat (Eds.), *Technology and transition, the Maghreb at the Crossroads* (pp. 32–46). London, UK: Frank Cass.

Eddelani, O. (2009). Le cluster: Écosystème d'innovation et incubateur d'organisations compétitives, cas de la région de Fès Boulmane. In M. Bousseta, & M. Ezznati (Eds.), *Gouvernance, territoires et pôles des compétitive* (pp. 133–168). Paris, FR: L'Harmattam.

Eisenstadt, S. N., & Roniger, L. (1984). *Patrons, clients and friends: Interpersonal relations and the structure of trust in society.* Cambridge, UK: Cambridge University Press.

Harders, C. (2009). Politik von unten: Perspektiven auf den autoritären Staat in Ägypten. In M. Beck, C. Harders, A. Jünemann, & S. Stetter (Eds.), *Der nahe posten im umbruch: Zwischen transformation und autoritarismus* (pp. 299–323). Wiesbaden, Germany: VS Verlag für Sozialwissenschaften.

Heritier, A. (1993). Policy-analyse: Elemente der Kritik und Perspektiven der

Neuorientierung. In A. Heritier (Ed.), *Policy-analyse, kritik und neuorientierung* (pp. 9–36). Opladen, DE: VS Verlag für Sozialwissenschaften.

Heydemann, S. (2004). Networks of privilege: Rethinking economic reform in the Middle

East. In S. Heydemann (Ed.), *Networks of privilege in the Middle East: the politics of economic reform revisited* (pp. 1–34). Hampshire, UK: Palgrave Macmillan.

Heilmann, M. (1999). Verbände und interessenvermittlung in der VR China: Die marktinduzierte transformation eines leninistischen staates. In W. Merkel & E. Sandschneider (Eds.), *Systemwechsel 4. Die rolle von verbänden im transformationsprozess* (pp. 279–321). Opladen, DE: VS Verlag für Sozialwissenschaften.

Jansen, D., & Schubert, K. (1995). Netzwerkanalyse, netzwerkforschung und politikproduktion: Ansätze der, cross-fertilization. In D. Jansen, & K. Schubert (Eds.), *Netzwerke und politikproduktion: konzepte, methoden, perspektiven* (pp. 9–23). Marburg, DE: Schüren Verlag.

Kennedy, S. (2005). *The business of lobbying in China*. Cambridge, MA: Harvard University Press.

Lust-Oskar, E., & Zerhouni, S. (2008). *Political participation in the Middle East*. London, UK: Lynne Rienner.

Manor, J. (1999). *The Political economy of democratic decentralization*. Washington, DC: World Bank.

Molina, O., & Rhodes, M. (2002). Corporatism: The past, present, and future of a concept. *Annual Review of Political Science, 5*, 305–331.

Polte, W., Steinich, M., & Thomi, W. (2001). Dezentralisierung: wirkungen,gestaltungsprinzipien und handlungsfelder der entwicklungszusammenarbeit. In W. Thomi, M. Steinich, & W. Polte (Eds.), *Dezentralisierung in entwicklungsländern. jüngere ursachen, ergebnisse und perspektiven staatlicher reformpolitik* (pp. 311–344). Baden, DE: Nomos Verlagsgesellschaft.

Rather, W. (2001). Die erfahrungen mit der dezentralisierung in Tunesien unter berücksichtigung der lokalen rahmenbedingungen. In W. Thomi, M. Steinich, & W. Polte (Eds.), *Dezentralisierung in entwicklungsländern. jüngere ursachen, ergebnisse und perspektiven staatlicher reformpolitik* (pp. 107–118). Baden, DE: Nomos Verlagsgesellschaft.

Reddy, P. S. (1999). Local government democratization and decentralization: Theoretical considerations, and recent trends and developments. In P. S. Reddy (Ed.), *Local government, democratization and decentralization: A review of the Southern African region* (pp. 9–29). Cape Town, ZA: Juta & Co..

Rondinelli, D. A., & Nellis, J. (1986). Assessing decentralization policies in developing countries: The case for cautious optimism. *Development Review, 4*(1), 3–23.

Rousset, M. (2010). Le nouveau concept de l'autorité et la modernisation de l'administration Marocain. In Centre d'Etudes Internationales (Ed.), *Une décennie de reformes au Maroc 1999–2009* (pp. 55–71). Paris, FR: Karthala.

Slaoui-Zirpins, S. (2012, 10 October). Anticipation and management of restructuring in Morocco. *European Commission 2011*. Retrieved from: https://ec.europa.eu/employment_social/anticipedia/document/show.do?id=3236

Thomi, W. (2001). Hoffnungsträger dezentralisierung? Zur geschichte, den potentialen und den perspektiven eines instruments. In W. Thomi, M. Steinich, & W. Polte (Eds.), *Dezentralisierung in entwicklungsländern.jüngere ursachen, ergebnisse und perspektiven staatlicher reformpolitik* (pp. 17–41), Baden, DE: Nomos Verlagsgesellschaft.

Vermeren, P. (2006). *Histoire du Maroc depuis l'indépendance*. Paris, FR: Editions La Découverte Repères Histoire.

# Observing the Failed Nation-State of Iraq: A Perspective

# References

Agresto, J. (2007). *Mugged by reality: The liberation of Iraq and the failure of good intentions.* New York, NY: Encounter Books.

Allawi, A. (2007). *The occupation of Iraq: Winning the war, losing the peace.* New Haven, CT: Yale University Press.

Alnasrawi, A. (2002). *Iraq's burdens: Oil, sanctions, and underdevelopment.* New York, NY: Praeger.

Anderson, L., & Stansfield, G. (2009). *Crisis in Kirkuk: The ethnopolitics of conflict and compromise.* Philadelphia, PA: University of Pennsylvania Press.

Arato, A. (2009). *Constitution making under occupation: The politics of imposed revolution in Iraq.* New York, NY: Columbia University Press.

Batatu, H. (2004). *The old social classes and the revolutionary movement in Iraq.* London, UK: Saqi.

Begikhani, N., Hague, G., & Ibraheem, K. (2012, 12 November). Honor-based violence (HBV) and honor-based killings in Iraqi Kurdistan and in the Kurdish diaspora in the UK. *University of Bristol, UK.* Retrieved from http://www.bristol.ac.uk/sps/research/projects/reports/2010/rw9038reportenglish.pdf.

Bennison, A. (2009). *The great caliphs: The golden age of the 'Abbasid Empire.* New Haven, CT: Yale University Press.

Charountaki, M. (2010). *The Kurds and U.S. foreign policy: International relations in the Middle East since 1945.* New York, NY: Routledge.

Cutler, R. (2013, 14 February). Iraq holds back on Exxon's Kurdish deal. *IKJNews.com.* Retrieved from http://ikjnews.com/?p=2743

Dawisha, A. (2009). *Iraq: A political history from independence to occupation.* Princeton, NJ: Princeton University Press.

Dawoody, A. (2006a). The Kurdish quest for autonomy and Iraq's statehood. *Asian and African Studies, 41* (5–6), 483–505.

Dawoody, A. (2006b). Iraqi notes: a personal reflection on issues of governance in Iraq and U.S. involvement. *Journal of Public Voices, VIII* (3), 4–32.

Dawoody, A. (2007). Examining the preemptive war on Iraq: An ethical response to issues of war and nonviolence. *Journal of Public Integrity, 9* (1), 63–77.

Dodge, T. (2005). *Inventing Iraq: The failure of nation building and a history denied.* New York, NY: Columbia University Press.

Eisenstadt, M., Kinghts, M., & Ali, H. (2011). Iran's influence in Iraq: Counting Tehran's whole-of-government approach. *Policy Focus No. 111, Washington Institute for Near East Policy.* Retrieved from http://www.washingtoninstitute.org/uploads/Documents/pubs/PolicyFocus111.pdf

Enders, D. (2013, 20 January). Squelching freedom in Iraqi Kurdistan. *The Progressive*. Retrieved from http://www.progressive.org/mag_enders0606

Haj, S. (1997). *The making of Iraq, 1900-1963: capital, power, and ideology*. Albany, NY: SUNY Press.

Hassanpour, A. (2013, 16 March). The Kurdish experience. *Middle East Research and Information Project*. Retrieved from http://www.merip.org/mer/mer189/kurdish-experience

Hegener, M. (2010). *The Kurds of Iraq*. Amsterdam, NL: Mets & Schilt.

Hiro, D. (2001). Neighbors, not friends: Iraq and Iran after the Gulf Wars. New York, NY: Routlege.

*IKJ News*. (2013, 14 February). Oil giant Chevron enters Kurdistan energy industry. Retrieved from http://ikjnews.com/?p=4571

*Iraq Body Count*. (2013, 13 April). Documented civilian deaths from violence. Retrieved from http://www.iraqbodycount.org/

International Crisis Group. (2011). *Failing oversight: Iraq's unchecked government* (Middle East Report No. 113). Retrieved from http://www.europarl.europa.eu/meetdocs/2009_2014/documents/d-iq/dv/d-iq20111005_06_/d-iq20111005_06_en.pdf

Jamil, D. (2013, 6 April). Mailiki's Iraq: Rape, executions, and torture. *Al Jazeera*. Retrieved from http://www.aljazeera.com/humanrights/2013/03/201331883513244683.html

Kennedy, H. (2006). *When Baghdad ruled the Muslim world: The rise and fall of Islam's greatest dynasty*. Cambridge, MA: Da Capo.

Kent, M. (1976). *Oil and empire: British policy and Mesopotamian oil, 1900–1920*. London, UK: Macmillan.

Little, J. (1999). Governing the government. In G. Morcol & L. Dennard (Eds.), *New sciences for public policy and administration: Connections and reflections* (pp. 151–176). Burke, VA: Chatelaine.

Mahdi, K. (2011). *Oil and oil policy in Iraq: Past and present*. London, UK: Pluto Press.

Makiya, K. (1998). *Republic of fear*. Berkeley, CA: University of California Press.

Marr, P. (2011). *The modern history of Iraq*. New York, NY: Westview.

Maturana, H. R., & F. J. Varela. (1980). *Autopoiesis and cognition: The realization of the living*. Boston, MA: D. Reidel.

Mingus, M. (2012). Progress and challenges with Iraq's multilevel governance. *Public Administration Review, 72* (5), 678–686.

Naylor, D. (2009). *Al-Qaeda in Iraq*. Hauppauge, NY: Nova Science.

Rubin, M. (2013, 11 March). To fight corruption. *Kurdistan Tribune*. Retrieved from http://kurdistantribune.com/2011/fight-corruption-barzani-needs-clean-house/

Sandri, S. (2008). *Reflectivity in economics: An experimental examination on the self-referentiality of economic theories*. Heidelberg, GR: Physica-Verlag HD.

Springborg, R. (2007). *Oil and democracy in Iraq*. London, UK: Saqi.

Tripp, C. (2007). *A history of Iraq*. Cambridge, UK: Cambridge University Press.

Vesterby, V. (2008). *Origins of self-organization, emergence, and cause*. Goodyear, AZ: ISCE.

Yan, H. (2013, 12 April). Report: A decade after Hussein, Iraq still grabbles with human rights abuses. CNN. Retrieved from http://edition.cnn.com/2013/03/11/world/meast/iraq-human-rights

Wheatley, M. (2006). *Leadership and the new sciences*. San Francisco, CA: Berrett-Koehler.

Zumwalt, J. (2013, 12 April). Does Iranian presence mean end of democracy in Iraq? *UPI.com*. Retrieved from http://www.upi.com/Top_News/Analysis/Outside-View/2013/04/09/Outside-View-Does-Iranian-presence-mean-end-of-democracy-in-Iraq/UPI-52801365480420/

# Building Capacities in Public Financial Management in a Post-Conflict Country: A practice from the Ministry of Finance and the Institute of Finance of Lebanon

## References

Alami, R., & Karshenas, M. (2012, 7 February). Deficient social policies have helped spark the Arab Spring. *Centre for Development Policy and Research (CDPR) Development Viewpoint*. Retrieved from http://www.soas.ac.uk/cdpr/publications/dv/deficient-social-policies-have-helped-spark-the-arab-spring.html

Andersson, G., & Isaksen, J. (2012, 17 December). Best practice in capacity building in public finance management in Africa: Experiences of NORAD and Sida. *Bergen, NO: Chr. Michelsen Institute, Development Studies and Human Rights*.Retrieved from http://siteresources.worldbank.org/EXTFINANCIALMGMT/Resources/313217-1196225463975/4440996-1196225852154/NORADSIDA-PFM-CapBuild-Africa.pdf

Bissat, L. M., & Abi Saab, F. (2011, 11 June). Why assadissa? *Assadissa*. Retrieved from http://www.institutdesfinances.gov.lb/english/pdf/ASSADISSA-01.pdf

Dockery, S. (2013, 29 March). U. N. aiding 400, 000 Syrian refugees in Lebanon. *The Daily Star*. Retrieved from http://www.dailystar.com.lb/News/Local-News/2013/Mar-29/211909-un-aiding-400000-syrian-refugees-in-lebanon.ashx

*Financial and Administrative Autonomy*. (2013, April 15). Institut des Finances Basil Fuleihan. Retrieved from http://www.institutdesfinances.gov.lb/english/pdf/Article%2049-ar.pdf

*GIFT-MENA Learning Network*. (2013, 6 April). Institut des Finances Basil Fuleihan. Retrieved from http://www.institutdesfinances.gov.lb/english/Gift_MENA_Learning_Network

Hilderbrand, M. E., & Grindle, M. S. (2013, 11 January). *Building sustainable capacity: Challenges for the public sector*. Cambridge, MA: Harvard Institute for International Development, Harvard University. Retrieved from http://mirror.undp.org/magnet/cdrb/parti.htm

Institut des Finances Basil Fuleihan. (2012a, 11 November). *15 Years in review: Results of the beneficiaries satisfaction survey*. Retrieved from http://www.institutdesfinances.gov.lb/english/loadFile.aspx?pageid=84&phname=FileEN

Institut des Finances Basil Fuleihan. (2012b, 11 November). *Annual report 2011.* Retrieved from http://www.institutdesfinances.gov.lb/english/loadFile.aspx?pageid=71&phname=File1

Institut des Finances Basil Fuleihan. (2012c, 11 November). *Review of the public procurement legal framework in Lebanon.* Retrieved from http://www.institutdesfinances.gov.lb/english/Review-of-the-Public-Procurement-Legal-Framework-in-Lebanon1

Institut des Finances Basil Fuleihan. (2012d, 11 November). *Training catalogue 2012–2014.* Retrieved from http://www.institutdesfinances.gov.lb/english/pdf/Training%20Catalogue%20-%20EN.pdf

Lebanese Ministry of Finance. (2013a, 2 April). *Reforms at the ministry of finance: A clear vision leading the way, 2005–2007 and beyond.* Retrieved from http://www.finance.gov.lb/en-US/finance/Reforms/Documents/Reforms%20at%20MoF/Reforms%20at%20the%20MoF.pdf

Lebanese Ministry of Finance. (2013b, 6 April). *General debt overview.* Retrieved from http://www.finance.gov.lb/en-US/finance/PublicDebt/Pages/PublicDebtTimeSeries.aspx

Lebanese Ministry of Finance. (2013c, 6 April). *Public finance statistics 1993–2011.* Retrieved from http://www.finance.gov.lb/en-US/finance/EconomicDataStatistics/Pages/PublicFinanceStatistic.aspx

OECD. (2013, 6 January). *The challenges of capacity development: Working towards good practice.* Paris: OECD Publishing. Retrieved from http://www.fao.org/fileadmin/templates/capacitybuilding/pdf/DAC_paper_final.pdf

Peterson, S. B. (2011, 27 June). Plateaus not summits: Reforming public financial management in Africa. *Public administration and development, 31*(3), 205–213. Retrieved from http://www.ids.ac.uk/files/dmfile/PlateausnotSummits.pdf

*Regional Programs.* (2013). Institut des Finances Basil Fuleihan. Retrieved from http://www.institutdesfinances.gov.lb/english/Regional_Programs

Republic of Lebanon. (2007, 25 January). Recovery, reconstruction, and reform. *International Conference for Support to Lebanon.* Paris. Retrieved from http://www.pcm.gov.lb/SiteCollectionDocuments/www.pcm.gov.lb/resSecCo/arabic/Paris%20III/english.pdf.

Saidi, N. A. H. (1999). *Growth, destruction and the challenges of reconstruction: Macroeconomic essays on Lebanon.* Beirut, LB: Lebanese Center for Policy Studies.

UNDP. (2013, 10 February). *Lebanon national human development report: Towards a citizen's state.* Retrieved from http://hdr.undp.org/en/reports/national/arabstates/lebanon/name,3303,en.html

World Bank. (2013a, 12 April). *Republic of Lebanon: Country financial accountability assessment.* Washington, DC. Retrieved from https://openknowledge.worldbank.org/bitstream/handle/10986/8774/369691Lebanon1CFAA0white0cover0public.txt?sequence=2

World Bank. (2013b, 12 April). *Public financial management reform in the Middle East and North Africa: An overview of the regional experience.* Middle East and North Africa Vice Presidency. Washington, DC. Retrieved from http://documents.worldbank.org/curated/en/2010/06/13215703/public-financial-management-reform-middle-east-north-africa-overview-regional-experience-vol-1-2-overview-summary

World Bank. (2013c, 12 April). GDP Growth (%) for Lebanon for 1993–2012. Retrieved from http://databank.worldbank.org/data/home.aspx

# References

Acharya, V., & Richardson, M. (2009). *Restoring financial stability: How to repair a failed system.* Indianapolis, IN: Wiley.

Alchian, A. (1950). Uncertainty, evolution and economic theory. *Journal of Political Economy, 58*(3), 211–221.

Allison, H. E., & Hobbs, R. J. (2004). Resilience, adaptive capacity, and the "lock-in trap" of the western Australian agricultural region. *Ecology and Society, 9*(1). Retrieved from http://www.ecologyandsociety.org/vol9/iss1/art3/

Aydin, Z. (2005). *The political economy of Turkey.* London, UK: Pluto Press.

Barabasi, A. (2003). *Linked.* New York, NY: Plume.

Black, E. (2011). *British petroleum and the redline agreement: The West's secret pact to get Mideast oil.* Westport, CT: Dialog Press.

Bradfer, A. (2011).*United Arab Emirates: Facing the future.* Paris, FR: Acr Edition (Acc).

Brem, R. J. (1999). The Cassandra complex. In G. Morcol, & L. Dennard (Eds), *New sciences for public administration and policy: Connections and reflections* (pp. 125–150). Burke, VA: Chatelaine Press.

Brown, C. (1995). *Chaos and catastrophe theories.* Thousand Oaks, CA: Sage.

Buchanan, M. (2003). *Nexus.* New York, NY: W.W. Norton.

Capra, F. (2004). *The hidden connections.* New York, NY: Anchor Books.

Capra, F., Juarrero, A., & Van Uden, J. (2007). *Reframing complexity.* Mansfield, MA: ISCE.

Chaudhry, K. (1997). *The price of wealth: Economies and institutions in the Middle East.* Ithaca, NY: Cornell University Press.

Dabashi, H. (2012). *The Arab Spring: The end of post colonialism.* London, UK: Zed.

Dawoody, A. (2010). Reworking Maslow's hierarchy: A complexity response. *Proceedings of 2010 International Conference on Public Administration, Australia, 1,* 191–196.

Dawoody, A. (2011). Teaching public policy as a nonlinear system. *Journal of US-China Public Administration 8*(4), 372–386.

Dawoody, A. (2013). The Middle East and learning from Brazil, Russia, India, and China (BRIC). *The Innovation Journal, 18*(1), Article 4.

Djerejian, E. (2009). *Danger and opportunity: An American ambassador's journey through the Middle East.* New York, NY: Threshold Editions.

*Economist, The.* (2013, 31 March). Why is South Africa included in the BRICS? *The Economist.* Retrieved from http://www.economist.com/blogs/economist-explains/2013/03/economist-explains-why-south-africa-brics

Eichengreen, B. (2008). *Globalizing capital: a history of the international monetary system.* Princeton, NJ: Princeton University Press.

Elliot, E., & Kiel, D. (1996). *Chaos theory in the social sciences.* Ann Arbor, MI: The University of Michigan Press.

Evans, K. (1999). Imagining anticipatory government. In G. Morcol, & L. Dennard (Eds.), *New sciences for public administration and policy: Connections and reflections* (pp. 195–220). Burke, VA: Chatelaine Press.

Frieden, J. (2007). *Global capitalism: Its fall and rise in the twentieth century.* New York, NY: W. W. Norton.

Gelvin, J. ( 2012). *The Arab uprisings: What everyone needs to know.* Oxford, UK: Oxford University Press.

Gilpin, R. (2010). *Global political economy: Understanding the international economic order.* Princeton, NJ: Princeton University Press.

Goldschmidt, A. (2005). *A concise history of the Middle East.* Boulder, CO: Westview.

Goldstein, J. (2007). A new model for emergence and its leadership implications. In J. K. Hazy, J. Goldstein, & B. B. Lichtenstein (Eds.), *Complex systems leadership theory* (pp. 61–92). Mansfield, MA: ISCE.

Gruber, J. (2009). *Public finance and public policy.* New York, NY: Worth.

Guastello, S. (2002). *Managing emergent phenomena.* Mahwah, NJ: Lawrence Erlbaum Associates.

Gunderson, L. (2000). Ecological resilience–in theory and application. *Annual Review of Ecology and Systematics, 31,* 425–439.

Habeed, W. (2012). *The Middle East in turmoil: Conflict, revolution, and change.* Santa Barbara, CA: Greenwood.

Harrison, N. (2006). *Complexity in world politics: Concepts and methods of a new paradigm.* Albany, NY: State University of New York Press.

Hayek, F. (1967). *Law, legislation, and liberty, vol. 2.* Chicago, IL: University of Chicago Press.

Heydemann, S. (2000). *War, institutions, and social change in the Middle East.* Berkeley, CA: University of California Press.

Heydemann, S., & Leenders, R. (2013). *Middle East authoritarianisms: Governance, contestation, and regime resilience in Syria and Iran.* Stanford, CA: Stanford University Press.

Johnson, S. (2002). *Emergence.* New York, NY: Touchstone.

Jones, S. (2012). *BRICs and beyond: Lessons on emerging markets.* West Sussex, UK: Wiley.

Joseph, S., & Slyomovics, S. (2000). *Women and power in the Middle East.* Philadelphia, PA: University of Pennsylvania Press.

Juarrero, A., & Rubino, C. (2008). *Emergence, complexity, and self-organization*. Goodyear, AZ: ISCE.

Kaplan, D., & Glass, L. (1997). *Understanding nonlinear dynamics*. New York, NY: Springer.

Kauffman, S. (1993). *The origin of order*. New York, NY: Oxford University Press.

Kendall, B., Schaffer, W., Tidd, C., & Olsen, L. (1997). The impact of chaos on biology:Promising directions for research. In C. Grebogi, & J. Yorke (Eds.), *The impact of chaos on science and society* (pp. 190–218). Tokyo, JP: United Nations University Press.

Kiel, D. (1999). The science of complexity and public policy. In G. Morcol, & L. Dennard (Eds.), *New sciences for public administration and policy: Connections and reflections* (pp. 63–80) Burke, VA: Chatelaine Press.

Krugman, P. (1996). *The self-organizing economy*. Oxford, UK: Blackwell.

Krugman, P., Obstfeld, M., & Melitz, M. (2011). *International economics*. Upper Saddle River, NJ: Prentice Hall.

Kuznetsov, Y. (2010). *Elements of applied bifurcation theory*. New York, NY: Springer.

Little, J. (1999). Governing the government. In G. Morcol, & L. Dennard (Eds.), New *sciences for public administration and policy: Connections and reflections* (pp. 151–176). Burke, VA: Chatelaine Press.

Long, D. E., Reich, B., & Gasiorowski, M. J. (2010). *The government and politics of the Middle East and North Africa*. Boulder, CO: Westview.

Lust, E. (2013). *The Middle East*. Thousand Oaks, CA: CQ Press.

Lynch, M. (2013). *The Arab uprising: The unfinished revolutions of the new Middle East*. New York, NY: Public Affairs.

Marx, K. (2012). *Das capital-capital: A critique of political economy, volume 1*. S. Moore, & E. Aveling (Trans.), Chicago, IL: Aristeus Books.

Marx, K., & Engels, F. (2011). *The communist manifesto*. Watertown, WI: Tribeca Books.

Maturana, H. R., & Varela, F. J. (1993). *Autopoiesis and cognition: The realization of the living*. New York, NY: Springer.

Matutinovic, I. (2006). Self-organization and design in capitalist economies. *Journal of Economic Issues, XL*(3), 575-601.

Miller, J., & Page, S. (2007). *Complex adaptive systems*. Princeton, NJ: Princeton University Press.

Moghadam, V., & Karshenas, M. (2006). *Social policy in the Middle East: Political, economics and gender dynamics*. Hampshire, UK: Palgrave Macmillan.

Morgan, G. (2006). *Images of organization*. Beverly Hills, CA: Sage.

Nicolis, G., & Prigogine, I. (1989). *Exploring complexity*. New York, NY: W.H. Freeman.

North, D. (1990). *Institutions, institutional change and economic performance*. Cambridge, UK: Cambridge University Press.

Nowak, M. (2006). *Evolutionary dynamics*. Cambridge, MA: Harvard University Press.

Olson, M. (1982). *The rise and decline of nations: Economic growth, stagflation, and social rigidities*. New Haven, CT: Yale University Press.

Ott, A. (2003). *The public sector in the global economy: From the driver's seat to the back seat*. Northampton, MA: Edward Elgar.

Overman, S., & Loraine, T. (1996). The new sciences of administration: Chaos and quantum theory. *Public Policy Review, 56*(5), 487–491.

Pierson, P. (2000). Increasing returns, path dependency, and the study of politics. *American Political Science Review, 94*(2), 251–267.

Poirot, C. (2001). Financial integration under conditions of chaotic hysteresis: The Russian financial crisis of 1998. *Journal of Post Keynesian Economics, 23*(3), 485–507.

Prigogine, I. (1996). *The end of certainty*. New York, NY: The Free Press.

Prigogine, I., & Stengers, I. (1984). *Order out of chaos*. New York, NY: Bantam.

Przeworski, A. (1986). *Capitalism and social democracy*. Cambridge, UK: Cambridge University Press.

Redmond, W. (2010). Rules and roles in the marketplace: Self-organization of the market. *Journal of Economic Issues, XLIV*(2), 337–344.

Reinhart, C., & Rogoff, K. (2011). *This time is different*. Princeton, NJ: Princeton University Press.

Ricardo, D. (2010). *On the principles of political economy, and taxation*. Highlands Ranch, CO: General Books.

Richardson, K., & Goldstein, J. (2007). *Classic complexity: from the abstract to the concrete*. Mansfield, MA: ISCE.

Ruelle, D. (1993). *Chance and chaos*. Princeton, NJ: Princeton University Press.

Sandri, S. (2009). *Reflectivity in economics: An experimental examination on the self-referentiality of economic theories*. Berlin, GE: Physica-Verlag Heidelberg.

Smith, A. (2010). *The wealth of nations*. Hollywood, FL: Simon & Brown.

Stiglitz, J. (2010). *Freefall: America, free markets, and the sinking of the world economy*. New York, NY: W. W. Norton.

Streit, M. (1993). Cognition, competition, and catallaxy: In memory of Friedrich August van Hayek. *Constitutional Political Economy, 4*(2), 223–262.

Taleb, N., & Blyth, M. (2011). The black swan of Cairo. *Foreign Affairs, 90*(3), 33–39.

Vesterby, V. (2008). *Origins of self-organization, emergence, and cause*. Goodyear, AZ: ISCE.

Wheatley, M. (2006). *Leadership and the new science*. San Francisco, CA: Berrett-Koehler.

Witt, U. (1997). Self-organization and economics—what is new? *Structural Change and Economic Dynamics, 8*(4), 489–507.

246

# ABOUT THE AUTHORS

**Mohammed M. Aman, PhD** is Professor of Information Studies at the University of Wisconsin-Milwaukee (UWM) and Editor-in-Chief of the peer-reviewed Wiley/PSO journal, *Digest of Middle East Studies (DOMES)*, and *Middle East Media and Book Reviews (MEMBR)*. He received his BA (with Hons) from Cairo University, Egypt, MS from Columbia University and his PhD from the University of Pittsburgh. He has held a number of academic leadership positions including Dean of the School of Information Studies at UWM (1979-2002); Interim Dean of the School of Education and Vice Chancellor for Partnership in Education (2000-2002); Dean of the School of Information Sciences at Long Island University (1976-79); Director and Professor, St. John's University, New York, Division of Information Sciences (1972-76); Information Officer, Arab League Mission to the United Nations, consultant to UNESCO, UNIDO, UNDP, Arab League, US State Department, and various Arab and African governments. He is the author of more than 200 articles and 15 books—among them: *The Gulf War in World Literature*; *Islamic Books*; *Information Systems and Services*; *Profiles of Academic Libraries*; and *Academic Library Management*. **Editor and Part 6, p.47.**

**Mary Jo Aman, MLIS** is Associate Editor of the peer reviewed Wiley/PSO journal, *Digest of Middle East Studies (DOMES)* and the *Middle East Media and Book Reviews (MEMBR)*. She received her BA from Fisk University and MLIS from Clark Atlanta University, Atlanta, GA. She held several positions in New York—among them Director of Library Promotion at the Viking Press; Consultant, Nassau County, N.Y Library System; Assistant Coordinator, Brooklyn Public Library; Member of the Board of International Board of Books for Young People (IBBY) and Editor of IBBY's *Newsletter*; and most recently Coordinator of Outreach, School of Continuing Education and Outreach; Director, Department of Technology, Division of Student Services; and Director, Education and Curriculum Library at the University of Wisconsin-Milwaukee. She lectured in Egypt and Kuwait and taught at St. John's University in New York, and Cardinal Stritch University in Fox Point, Wisconsin. Mrs Aman is the recipient of several awards including citations of merit from the Milwaukee Board of Supervisors and the Wisconsin State Senate, and the University of Wisconsin-Milwaukee's Spaights Award for Outstanding Contributions to UWM. **Editor.**

**L**amia Moubayed Bissat is Director of the Institut des Finances Basil Fuleihan. She holds the MSc degree in Agricultural Economics and Development from the American University in Beirut (AUB) and is candidate for the MBA degree from Ecole Superieure des Affaires (ESA). She was on the staff of the UNDP and the Economic and Social Commission for Western Asia. Ms. Bissat is a founding member of the GIFT-MENA Network Government Institutes for Training in MENA, supported by the World Bank and the French Government and INNOVMED Network of Innovation in Governance in the Mediterranean Region, supported by the UN Department of Economic and Social Affairs and other non-governmental organizations. **Part 7, p. 171.**

**Y**iyi Chen, PhD is one of the leading Biblical scholars in China, a pioneer in the field of Middle Eastern Peace Studies and leads the only Chinese think tank initiative to publish a Middle East Peace Index at Shanghai Jiao Tong University. Dr. Chen is the Editor-in-Chief of the *Journal of Sino-Western Communications* in the U.S. He has been a visiting professor in Graduate Theological Union (2008-2010) and the University of California at Berkeley (2006–2007). He also serves as a peer-review College Member of England's Arts and Humanities Research Council. Chen is the author of several books, among them, the Chinese college standard textbook *Introduction to the Hebrew Bible* (Peking University Press, 2011) and *Textual and Archaeological Background of the Hebrew Bible* (Kunlun Press, 2006). His Chinese translation of A. B. Yehoshua's Hebrew novel *Three Days and a Child* was awarded the annual prize by Israel's Institute for the Translation of Hebrew Literature in 1994. Dr. Chen heads several Chinese government- commissioned projects related to Jewish Studies, the Bible, Israel, and the Middle East. **Part 5, p. 31.**

**A**lexander Dawoody, PhD is Associate Professor of Administrative Studies at Maywood University, Pennsylvania, USA. He is the founding president of the Association for Middle Eastern Public Policy and Administration (AMEPPA), as well as the founder of two sections at the American Society for Public Administration (ASPA)— the first being the Section on Complexity and Network Studies (CSN), and the other being the Section on Effective and Sound Administration in the Middle East (SESAME), and Editor of special symposium on the Middle East for Issue 1 of volume 18, 2013 of *The Innovation Journal*. **Part 7, p. 157; 201.**

**I**brahim El-Ghoundour earned his master's degree in Economics and Public Administration from the Maxwell School of Citizenship and Public Affairs at Syracuse University. He recently co-authored and published *Measuring the Public Sector Wage Bill in 2011*, ASSADISA, Issue no.1, June 2011 (Arabic). He completed his undergraduate studies at the American University of Beirut where he graduated with a Bachelor's degree in Economics and a Minor in Political Studies. **Part 7, p. 171.**

**S**abine Hatem is an economist at the Institute of Finance Basil Fuleihan, a training and communication agency of the Ministry of Finance of Lebanon. She works in the field of development cooperation and capacity development in the area of public financial management for Lebanon and MENA countries. She is the Secretary General of the Network of Civil Service Training Schools and Institutes in the MENA region. Her current work involves the development of learning and knowledge partnerships and initiatives to foster South–South, Euro–Med and Arab cooperation, as well as the coordination bilateral and multilateral technical assistance programs and partnerships with local, regional and international organizations, and embassies and donors in support of the reform agenda of the MOF. She also evaluates a number of donor-funded projects aimed at building capacities in financial management in the public sector. **Part 7, p. 171.**

**T**ina J. Jayroe, MLIS, is research assistant to Professor Mohammed M. Aman, and fellow of the U.S. Institute of Museum and Library Services (IMLS) "Overcoming Barriers to Information Access" at the University of Wisconsin–Milwaukee. She has an MLIS in Information Science and Technology from the University of Denver, and a B.S. in Mass Communications from Emerson College. Ms. Jayroe is the Digital Libraries SIG Communications Officer and active member of the Association for Information Science and Technology. Her research interests and past publications address scholarly communications, information retrieval, and computer technology in libraries. **Part 6, p. 47.**

**P**eter Mameli, PhD is Associate Professor, Department of Public Management at John Jay College of Criminal Justice, City University of New York. He has served as the director of the Protection Management program, coordinator of the undergraduate Public Administration program, and Director of the Saturday Master of Public Administration program, at different times while at John Jay College. Dr. Mameli's current research interests include studying the impact of globalization processes on public administration, transnational crime and the oversight of public sector organizations. His recent projects have focused on such topics as government surveillance operations, national data protection authorities, international crime statistics and transnational human trafficking. Some of his articles have appeared in *Law & Policy, Critical Issues in Justice and Politics, International Public Management Journal, The Public Manager*, and, *Human Rights Review*. In 2011, Dr. Mameli and his co-authors published *Security and Privacy: Global Standards for Ethical Identity Management in Contemporary Liberal Democratic States*. His research focuses on the ethical dimensions of identity management technology—electronic surveillance, the mining of personal data, and profiling—in the context of transnational crime and global terrorism. The ethical challenge at the heart of this book is to establish an acceptable and sustainable equilibrium between two central moral values in contemporary liberal democracies, security and privacy. **Part 7, p. 119.**

**P**eter Marks, PhD is Assistant Professor, Public Administration at Erasmus University in Rotterdam, The Netherlands. **Part 7, p. 201.**

**J**osef Olmert, PhD is Adjunct Professor at the University of South Carolina. He is a former peace negotiator, political insider, author, as well as a seasoned public speaker. As Director of the Government Press Office and Advisor to then-Prime Minister Yitzhak Shamir during the first Gulf War and the International Peace Conference in Madrid, he secured press relations for Israel with the Soviet Union and China, and represented the Prime Minister in numerous conferences and appearances in the United States, Great Britain, Australia, China, Russia, Japan and South Africa, among others. His media experience has included penning a political column for Israel's largest circulation daily, *Yediot Aharonot*, as well as *The Jerusalem Post*, and numerous appearances on radio and TV programs at home and abroad. His forthcoming book is titled *Syria: The End of Stability without Legitimacy.* **Part 5, p. 5.**

**C**arl Rihan, MS, is Program Coordinator at the Institut des Finances Basil Fuleihan. He joined the Institute in 2009 and has served on the board of various training and capacity development programs organized with external partners and cooperation initiatives, particularly with the European Commission's Technical Assistance and Information Exchange Instrument (TAIEX). In 2010, he joined the board of publications and communication initiatives, including the journal of public finance and state modernization, *Assadissa*, which was launched by the Institute in 2011. He holds a Bachelor's degree and a Master's degree in Political Studies at the American University of Beirut. **Part 7, p. 171.**

**I**van Sascha Sheehan, PhD is Assistant Professor of Public and International Affairs at the University of Baltimore where he is Director of the Negotiation and Conflict Management graduate program and founding Co-Director of the Global Affairs and Human Security graduate program. His research focuses on the intersection of transnational terrorism, counterterrorism, and international conflict management. From 2007–2009, Sheehan served on the faculty of the University of Massachusetts, Boston in the John W. McCormack School of Policy Studies. He is the author of *When Terrorism and Counterterrorism Clash: The War on Terror and the Transformation of Terrorist Activity* (2007), and contributor to *The Washington Times, The Baltimore Sun, Haaretz, The Jerusalem Post*, and United Press International. He has spoken regarding U.S. counterterrorism efforts before diverse audiences in Europe, Harvard Law School, policymakers on Capitol Hill, and the National Press Club. Sheehan previously taught in the International Studies Department at Bentley College and at Tufts University. He continues to serve on the affiliate faculty at George Mason University's School for Conflict Analysis and Resolution and the M.A.I.S. program. **Part 6, p. 85.**

**S**tefanie Slaoui-Zirpins, MA, is a PhD candidate at the Institute of Political Science at Goethe University Frankfurt, Germany, and a Friedrich Ebert Foundation scholar. She lectured at the Goethe University Frankfurt as well as consultant for the European Commission. She has published on restructuring and transformations processes, local politics and state-society relations in Morocco and the MENA region. She has research interests in comparative politics, international political economy and public administration. **Part 7, p. 157.**


**D**ina Wafa, PhD is the Founding Director of the School of Global Affairs and Public Policy Executive Education unit at the American University in Cairo. Dr. Wafa has several publications in reputable journals, and her research interest focus on citizen voice, governance and education. She also serves as a project director of the accountability, culture and trust group for the annual international association of schools and institutes of administrative (IASIA) conferences in addition to serving on several scientific committees in international conferences and on the review committee of several journals. Wafa is also an active member of the Affiliated Network for Social Accountability in the Arab World. Throughout her career, Wafa has worked on fostering collaboration with international educational institutions, donor agencies and regional states working on governance issues. Her paper was previously published in The Innovation Journal: *The Public Sector Innovation Journal*, volume 18(1), 2013, article 17. **Part 6, p.73.**


**I**do Zelkovitz, PhD is Lecturer at the Department of Middle Eastern History & Department of Multidisciplinary Studies, University of Haifa, Israel, He is the author of *The Fatah Movement: Islam Nationalism and Armed Struggle Politics* (2012) [in Hebrew] and several papers and conference presentations at more than 20 international scholarly conferences in recent years regarding topics that range from Islamic struggles, to Palestinian political strife and movements, to student revolutions, to peaceful solutions. Zelkovitz is an expert on Palestinian society and politics and Middle East history lecturer and a research fellow at the University of Haifa's Ezri Center for Iran & Persian Gulf Studies. The title of his PhD thesis was "Studential Society, Culture and politics in The Palestinian National Movement 1952–2000." He is the recipient of the "KATEDRA" prize from the institute of Eretz Isreal and the Erasmus Mundus Post-Doctoral Research Fellowship at The Center of Methods in Social Sciences and the Institute of Sociology at the Georg-August-Universität Göttingen, Germany. Zelkovitz is also a member of the Board of Editors for *Ruah Mizrahit [East Wind]: Bulletin of the Israeli Oriental Society* and the Middle Eastern and Islamic Studies Association of Israel. **Part 5, p. 21.**